FACES

OF

UTAH

Faces of Utah: A Portrait

is a centennial gift to the people of Utah.

———— ————

It was made possible by

Mountain West Center for Regional Studies

·

Utah Humanities Council

·

George S. and Dolores Doré Eccles Foundation

·

Sorenson Industries

·

The Church of Jesus Christ of Latter-day Saints Foundation

·

Charles Redd Center for Western Studies

FACES

OF

UTAH

A Portrait

EDITED BY
SHANNON R. HOSKINS

GIBBS·SMITH
P
PUBLISHER

SALT LAKE CITY

This is a Peregrine Smith Book, published by
Gibbs Smith, Publisher
P.O. Box 667
Layton, Utah 84041

Design by Leesha Jones

FRONT COVER PHOTOGRAPHS, CLOCKWISE FROM UPPER RIGHT: submitted by Katie Rose; submitted by Leo Shepherd Jr.; submitted by Marian Bonar; submitted by Loretta Frei Adams; submitted by Jennifer Davault; submitted by Loretta Frei Adams.

Printed and bound in the United States of America

LIBRARY OF CONGRESS CATALOGING-IN-PUBLICATION DATA
Faces of Utah : a portrait / edited by Shannon R. Hoskins. —1st ed.
    p.   cm.
    "A Utah centennial project of the Mountain West Center at Utah State University and the Utah Humanities Council."
    "A Peregrine Smith book"—T.p. verso.
    ISBN 0-87905-766-1
    1. Utah. 2. Utah—Pictorial works. I. Hoskins, Shannon R., 1940- .
II. Utah State University. Mountain West Center. III. Utah Humanities Council.
F826.F34 1996
979.2—dc20   96-20877
                                                        CIP

Contents

ACKNOWLEDGMENTS

Many people and groups have joined together to make this centennial gift to Utah possible. From the inception of the idea to the final product of this book, hundreds of volunteer hours were needed. We would like to take this opportunity to thank people publicly for their assistance. We wish everyone could be listed individually, for without all of the willing hands and influential people involved, *Faces of Utah: A Portrait* would have remained just a good idea.

Norma Matheson and David B. Haight agreed to serve as chairs of the project and the Advisory Board. They provided experience, vision, guidance, and opened doors beyond our reach. The board—composed of James Mortimer, Lisa Eccles, Marilyn Nielson, Kim Burningham, Leonard Arrington, Fred Ball, Scott Bean, Rodney Brady, Fred Esplin, Cecilia Foxely, Scott Trundle, Jan Graham, Glenn Mecham, Jay Hudson, Hardy Redd, Jay Shelledy, Ray Uno, Diane Hatch Orr, Flora Ogan, F. Ross Peterson, and Charles Peterson—helped collectively with suggestions and in many special ways.

Two major institutions bore most of the responsibility of overseeing the project. Utah State University's Mountain West Center for Regional Studies and the Utah Humanities Council provided "Faces" directors Shannon R. Hoskins and Delmont Oswald and supportive staff. F. Ross Peterson, director of the MWCRS, provided a supportive atmosphere and relief from other responsibilities. Jenny Hone, Julie Anderson, and Natalie Rowe typed the majority of the manuscript with good humor and efficiency, and they deserve our special thank you.

Financial assistance was provided initially by the Utah Statehood Centennial Commission, and Weber and Salt Lake County Centennial Committees provided us with financial assistance for printing essay forms and advertising. FHP (Family Health Plan) and Union Pacific Rail Road donated funds to help with workshops for teachers and reading the overwhelming number of submissions.

Other organizations and companies provided us with in-kind services. Reagan Outdoor Advertising, John Evans Advertising, Smith's Food and Drug, *Standard Examiner, Deseret News, Salt Lake Tribune, St. George Times, Cedar Times,* Channel Two News, KSL Television, and KUED deserve recognition for getting the word to Utahns. The Utah Radio Broadcasters Association and Utah Press Association voted as organizations to support this centennial project and followed through with articles and news releases. The Utah State Library System and Smith's Food and Drug assisted with the collection and distribution of essays, reaching areas difficult to contact in other ways.

The public school system, from the State Office of Education to the individual teachers in the classroom, all eagerly contributed. Students from grades K through 12 wrote their essays and shared their thoughts. As a means of saying thank you, we have provided a listing of the participating schools in the Appendix.

Reading the hundred-thousand essays from which selections were made for this text were many groups of Utah State University students. Regretfully, there were too many to recognize individually. Some represented fraternities and sororities—including Chi Omega, Delta Sigma Phi, Alpha Chi Omega, Kappa Delta, Sigma Nu, Phi Kappa Alpha, Fiji-Phi Gamma Delta, Phi Alpha Theta, Delta Zeta, Kappa Tau/Lambda Delta Sigma, Alpha Nu, LDSSA—and others, themselves. Joe Soderborg, USU history student, spent many hours reading essays and chuckling as he found this one or that especially entertaining. Many dear friends and professionals volunteered to assist with the screening: Thomas Lyon, Billie Emert, Shirley Cazier, Thomas Alexander, Craig Fuller, Philip Notorianni, Jessie Embry, Jeff Johnson, Angela P. Ford, Nancy Moorman, Michael Johnson, Cynthia Buckingham, Thomas Allen, Kenneth Godfrey, Paige Lewis, and Sue Guenter-Schlesinger. BYU's Mormon History Student Association also spent an evening reading essays. We wish to thank them all.

The means of providing *Faces of Utah: A Portrait* to the public as a centennial gift were provided by the George S. and Dolores Doré Eccles Foundation, The Church of Jesus Christ of Latter-day Saints Foundation, Sorenson Industries, the Charles Redd Center for Western Studies, and the two public program agencies—The Mountain West Center for Regional Studies at Utah State University and the Utah Humanities Council. They sought to make *Faces of Utah* available to every school, library, and home in the state. To do so demanded the book be priced below cost. Their funds also made it possible to provide the color photographs and halftones that bring the faces of Utahns to life between the book covers.

Finally, without the thousands of individual Utahns who sat down and wrote about their private thoughts, concerns, roots and heritage, values, and their ties to the land, there would be no book and no archive. To those individuals who parted with photographs, drawings, books, calendars, schoolwork, genealogical sheets, and other special mementos: thank you—you have made this centennial book a gift to future generations of Utahns, a gift only you could give.

FACES OF UTAH:
A COMMEMORATIVE BOOK

January 4, 1996, is a special time in Utah history, for it marks the date of our one hundredth birthday as a state. After six arduous attempts as a territory to gain acceptance to the Union, President Grover Cleveland finally signed into law the bill that ended our long struggle and marked the beginning of Utah's history as the 45th state.

This watermark in time, the centennial of statehood, provides a vantage point to contemplate the past one hundred years and reflect upon the future of this great state. When I first heard about the "Faces of Utah's" request for essays on the topic "What it means to me to be a Utahn, how the land and culture have affected my life," I recognized that this was the perfect opportunity for Utahns to review their history and heritage and to identify those values they held most precious.

By 1896, Utah was a multiethnic society composed of Greeks, Italians, Native Americans, Scandinavians, Germans, Chinese, African Americans, and people from the British Isles. These migrants brought with them ideas about government. These ideas mingled with American colonial traditions of democracy to become the backbone of the new state. A century later, in 1996, new immigrants continue to add to Utah's population base, modifying the belief system and cultural patterns that provide the basis for community and state laws.

The essays in this book are personal. They state in private terms some of the concepts we hold most dear. Illustrative of the perceptions of general cultural and religious values, they can serve as a guide for representatives of state government who seek to serve. We must be sensitive to their expression and work to translate the seeds of those ideals into laws to govern us.

This remarkable treasure offers insights into our feelings and attitudes not found elsewhere. I am happy to participate in this centennial gift from the citizens of Utah to future generations.

Governor Michael O. Leavitt

PREFACE

Hearing the call to "bring the people of this great state together in a statewide celebration of the 'Spirit of Utah'," Utah State University's Mountain West Center and the Utah Humanities Council desired to contribute to the process of evaluation and celebration that is a part of historical events. They developed a joint project to focus on the centennial, to serve as a unifying element, and to further develop Utah's special sense of community. The project would honor the past, delight in the present, and leave something of value for future generations.

Several previous projects served as models for our work. Three stand out as particularly valuable guides: *May 17, 1988—One Day in an American Community,* directed by Carol Kammen; the WPA writers project of the 1930s, which is both familiar and of inestimable value to historians; and a third project, also a centennial celebration preserved by a perceptive teacher. In 1876, the state of Iowa asked teachers to send examples of children's schoolwork to the "Great Exposition." Lou Wilson preserved the work of her class, later reprinted in 1976 by the Smithsonian Institution. Her students had created individual "masterpieces" illustrative of their thoughts, ideas, and concerns, preserving a valuable portrait of their time and place.

The "Faces of Utah: A Portrait" builds on all of these. Every Utahn was invited to write an essay or personal narrative on "What it means to me to be a Utahn. How the culture and land have affected my life." The project was to involve each citizen in a thoughtful appraisal of his/her life in Utah and what it meant to live in this particular time and place. No constraints were made regarding age, gender, socioeconomic background, religion, occupation, nor ethnicity, for the portrait would be incomplete if any demographic segment of the statewide community was missing.

We sought to document attitudes, values, feelings, and personal experiences through visual images and the written word. The essays were the nucleus, but participation was not limited to the written word. We solicited photographs and original artwork. We wanted the archive produced to be invaluable to researchers for generations to come.

The question became one of implementation. How could we reach all citizens in Utah and get them to write down their thoughts? The methods used are important to the credibility of the document. They answer some questions and initiate others. Thus, a brief discussion of method follows.

The help, guidance, and support of a group of Utahns with statewide contacts were sought. These people formed an advisory board. Care was taken to include representatives of the media, especially newspapers and television. Historians, public servants, archivists, educators, government officials, and business people were also included. The Board was to play a vital role in taking the project to our citizens and asking for their participation and opening the doors to public awareness.

Two Honorary Chairs were selected, both known for their positions within the state and community and respected for their concern for the state. Norma W. Matheson, first lady of Utah for two terms, is recognized for her work with the elderly and on related health issues. David B. Haight, a key leader of The Church of Jesus Christ of Latter-day Saints known for his community service, also agreed to serve. Both served effectively, giving more time and personal energy than we had dreamed possible.

Financial resources and the imprimatur of the Utah Statehood Centennial Commission were of primary importance. The Commission, directed by Kim Burningham, provided some funding and official recognition as a centennial project. The county centennial committees of Weber County and Salt Lake County provided additional financial assistance. Grand County agreed to finance and distribute their county's essay forms.

From the business community came assistance to reach the public with forms and further financial assistance. Smith's Food and Drug agreed to transport forms to their stores along the Wasatch Front and to serve as a distribution point. The State Library System volunteered to distribute the forms through their local libraries and bookmobiles. Since each operates separately, each county library had to accept the responsibility of distributing the forms and serving as a collection point. Most willingly agreed, providing contact people within each library.

FHP (Family Health Plan) and Union Pacific Rail Road provided the much-needed financial aid without tedious stipulations. Their financial help was invaluable and a tangible example of their dedication to community service.

Superintendent Scott Bean, a member of the "Faces of Utah" Advisory Board, offered his support and assistance in reaching Utah's 469,000 schoolchildren. He saw the project as a unique teaching tool. The State Office of Education generously agreed to provide blank essay forms for each child and to provide access to Social Studies teachers through Nancy Mathews, Specialist, Curriculum Development and Law Related Education. Through her offices, a workshop was developed for 40 teachers in districts along the Wasatch Front and a second workshop for rural teachers through the Rural School Conference during the summer of 1994. Although the participation level varied by district, some such as Alpine School District boasted 90%–95% participation.

With participation of Utah's school students assured, we turned to other citizens of Utah. Two million people were invited to write an essay or personal narrative.

Our approach was to reach each individual through groups and gatherings: churches, clubs and organizations, seniors, minority groups, government groups and organizations, and county centennial committees. Senior Centers were contacted through the Area Aging Agencies (AAA). The AAA's twelve regional offices, each with regional offices responsible for the local senior centers within their geographic regions, enlisted participation of seniors. The state's churches were another important vehicle to reach individual Utahns. The Mountain West Center for Regional Studies sent letters to 3,600 ward bishops of The Church of Jesus Christ of Latter-day Saints. Church leaders of all other denominations listed in the telephone books were also sent personal letters requesting them to enlist their members in this effort to celebrate the Centennial.

The Charles Redd Center for Western Studies, at Brigham Young University, agreed to assist us in reaching the state's ethnic minorities. Rachel Nathan, a graduate student with diverse ethnic ties, was hired to reach the minority community concentrated along the Wasatch Front and to encourage them to become a part of the social history document this project would create. Groups she approached include Mexican Civic Center; Hispanic Congregation of the Madeleine; Calgary Baptist Church; LDS Lamanite, Asian, Spanish, Japanese, and Polynesian wards; Indian Council; Centro de la Familia; Governors, Polynesian, Asian, Hispanic, African American Advisory Councils and offices; NAACP of Ogden and Salt Lake City; Women's Historical Society; American Legions; African American Episcopalian COG; Paiute Indian Tribe of Utah; Skull Valley Goshute Tribe; Indian Walk-In Center; Ute Indian Tribe; Indian Health Recovery Center; State Office of Indian Education; Utah Coalition of La Raza; Filipino American Association of Utah; Tongan United Methodist Church, and many, many individuals.

An important aspect of presenting the "Faces of Utah" to the public was mass-media coverage, especially because no funds were available to purchase airtime on either radio or television. The Advisory Board was asked for assistance. With the encouragement of David B. Haight, Rodney Brady, and Don Gale, KSL Television agreed to produce and edit a Public Service Announcement. Leading citizens from the Advisory Board, including Norma Matheson, Senator Robert Bennett, Attorney General Jan Graham, Judge Ray Uno, Professor Ronald Coleman, and former Congresswoman Karen Shepherd, agreed to a guest appearance in the commercial. Channel 5 aired the 30-second spot many times over a two-month period and taped a five-minute interview also. In addition, Senator Orrin Hatch taped an interview in Washington, a tape edited by Channel 5, which generously printed seven copies for distribution to local television stations. Also, Diane Hatch Orr encouraged Susan Furniss and Phil Riesen of Channel 2 News to assist in the "Faces of Utah" coverage on Statehood Day, January 4, 1995. Governor Leavitt agreed to present his essay during the Statehood Day celebration. KUED Channel 7 used a five-minute spot strategically placed, invaluable because it was aired at least four separate times.

Radio and the print media played an important role in securing public attention. The Utah Radio Broadcasters, under the direction of Dale Zabriski, agreed to sponsor the

"Faces of Utah" as a centennial project. Norma Matheson cut a 30-second and a 60-second tape, and the Utah Radio Broadcasters Association duplicated the message and sent it to all the Utah stations. Announcers and broadcasters also provided airtime by interviewing the directors of the project, Delmont Oswald and Shannon Hoskins, and other spokespersons, and by mentioning "Faces" on their community news calendars.

The news media used two methods to reach the public: radio and television featured human-interest stories covering the concept and distribution process, and the daily newspapers *(Standard Examiner, Deseret News, Salt Lake Tribune, St. George Spectrum, Herald Journal, and Cedar City Spectrum)* included essay forms in their newspapers delivered to individual homes. More than 500,000 families were therefore reached in a timely and effective manner.

Outdoor advertising reinforced the messages the public was receiving from radio, television, and their newspapers. Reagan Outdoor Advertising and John Evans Company donated space, paper, and design production. Twenty Reagan signs were displayed January through March in 20 separate locations throughout the state.

To say that the implementation plan was successful is an understatement. For weeks mail poured into the offices of the Mountain West Center for Regional Studies on the Utah State University campus. The mail, measured in linear feet instead of number of articles, was regularly three to four feet high! Essays were delivered by hand, sent by parcel post, by university mail, certified mail, and special delivery. The essays came in individual envelopes, large manila envelopes containing 20 or 30 essays, in 14" x 36" boxes, in the original "Faces of Utah" mailing boxes and by school-district truckload. Respondents embellished their essays with portraits, photographs, framed oil paintings, video tapes, campaign literature, books, genealogy sheets, computer disks, and other documents—producing an exciting treasure. The estimate is that we received over half a million essays. As this book goes to press, essays are still being delivered.

The essays included in this volume are representative of the collection. Since Statehood Day 1995, more than 100,000 essays have been read. We have not been able to read everything submitted and still meet publication deadlines based on the 1996 Centennial year. We are certain that treasures lie buried in the piles of essays still to be reviewed, surely enough for another volume, but we did the best we could to select representative essays in the time available.

The editorial process was simple: keep each essay true to the author's own writing without editorial change. With this in mind, we published most essays as they crossed our desks. The few lengthy essays that required shortening were edited by eliminating entire paragraphs or sections, changes indicated by the traditional ellipsis (…).

Tone was of primary importance, since it allows the reader to assimilate the wide range of contributors' voices. To preserve the authors' tone, we avoided cutting sections and words that provided the flavor of the piece. The vast majority are printed entirely as they were submitted.

We did change what were obvious typographical errors. We saw no reason to embarrass individuals by printing misspellings. However, there was an exception to this policy. The work of children was left unaltered and appears in its original form. Again, we wanted to keep the voice of the essay undiluted.

We decided to eliminate the conventional trappings of scholarly works. For example, there are no footnotes. Originally we considered adding extensive informational footnotes to elucidate and clarify references to people, places, and events. This policy would have led to reference footnotes longer than the essay, and detracted from the author's distinctive voice. Also, you will find no bracketed *sic,* indicating an awareness of an error. It was an editorial decision.

These essays provide us with a glimpse into the hearts and minds of Utahns of all ages, religions, and ethnic backgrounds, and from every corner of the state. They will fill your heart with sympathy, rouse anger and resentment, make you smile. One of the readers found a profound sense of innocence in those he read. They are extraordinary portraits of ordinary lives, tales of their quiet decency and substantial achievements. They are Utahns' contribution to the Centennial of their state's admittance to the Union of States.

—Shannon R. Hoskins

Faces of Our Ancestral Past

The pioneers came to this arid Indian land of little water inexorably drawn by a new religion sprung from the rocky New England soil. Most of them stayed, fought bone-chilling winters, summer droughts, floods, and disease. They proselytized throughout the nation and abroad and sustained themselves with banners of their faith against the federal government. In their system of wards, stakes, church welfare and the community of their American, British, Scandinavian, and North European coreligionists, they found help and solace. They came to stay, to build their Zion. Generations later their progeny look back at them with pride and awe at their noble struggles.

They were not alone in their theocracy. The newly ploughed lands destroyed the food of the indigenous Native Americans—the seeds and small animals—and conflict erupted. Blacks, both free and slaves of Southern converts, had arrived with the pioneers and did the menial work then expected of their race. Almost immediately on settlement, a vanguard of Jewish merchants came, fleeing the pogroms and miseries of the European and Russian ghettos. Twenty years later Chinese laid rails for the transcontinental railroad, and a few remained to become cooks and laundrymen.

Then Utah's uncovered riches brought thousands of Balkan, Mediterranean, and Asian immigrants to dig coal, smelt ore, and lay rails. These new immigrants thought of themselves as sojourners. In their many languages they spoke of leaving impoverished, ancestral lands as necessary "to earn their bread." This encompassed age-old familial responsibilities placed on males: providing dowries for sisters and help for destitute parents. They would return, they told weeping mothers, they would return.

As they learned the ways of America and saved their wages, they brought over village brides, arranged through an exchange of photographs. Births followed, but still the sojourners believed they would go back to their native countries. Instead they lived, prospered beyond their expectations, and accumulated memories that were passed on from one generation to the next. When they died, they were buried by ethnic priests and rabbis in Utah graves. Today, their second, third, fourth, and a fledgling fifth generation call Utah home.

Other parts of the nation were green—water was plentiful; life was easier—yet, the pioneers and the newest of immigrants put down roots in this dry western state. They were not seduced by the luxuriant foliage of wasteful greenness elsewhere. The granite-tipped mountains, the sagebrush deserts, the red earth of Indian country suited their souls. Memories and family tied them to this land, this Utah they called home.

—Helen Papanikolas
Salt Lake City

Pauline Newman

Salt Lake County

Age 20th Century; **Birthplace** Price, Utah; **Occupation** Teacher; **Religion** Jewish; **Race/Ethnicity** Jewish

My parents, Sarah and Harry Gordon, long-time residents of Price, Utah should be writing this—as emigrees from Eastern Europe, they loved Utah—Carbon County—Price. My parents, no longer living, certainly deserve space in the *Faces of Utah Portrait*.

My parents came to Price shortly before World War I. They were literally pioneers in the coal country of Carbon County—young, inexperienced, the only Jewish family in the area.

They experienced the hardships of all pioneers in rural areas—no running water, indoor plumbing, sidewalks, or central heating. The nearest synagogue was 125 miles to the North in Salt Lake City. Food for Passover had to be sent from Denver.

Despite the obstacles, my parents settled into a most rewarding life in the environs of Carbon County. They established themselves in the business world. Their enterprise: *Price Hide and Junk* later became *Price Auto Wrecking Co.* My parents worked side-by-side, successfully combining business and home life. Our back yard was the business lot. Our kitchen served as office for "figuring" and writing checks to customers. Everyone was on a first name basis in the small community in which we lived, and business transactions always had a chatty sociability.

Four children were born to Harry and Sarah. The eldest, Lily, was born in Salt Lake City at the old St. Marks Hospital—Lily was a toddler when my parents moved to Price.

I was born in Price—(a home birth), Frieda and Robert (Bob) were born at the Price City Hospital. My parents were so proud of their children: Lily, an R.N.—graduate of the old Salt Lake General Hospital—Pauline, a teacher, graduate of the University of Utah. Frieda, a legal secretary, graduate of College of Eastern Utah, and Robert (Bob) a lawyer, graduate of the "U" law school, and vice-president of Utah Power and Light.

My parents were highly respected citizens of the community. My father, Harry, was given a commendation for his home front efforts and cooperation during World War II.

My mother, Sarah, was a long-time president of the *Woman's Club of Eastern Utah*. She was highly respected and dearly loved by the Carbon County Community.

My parents loved Utah. This verbal portrait is dedicated to them.

Submitted by Denis Nelson, Weber County.

Loretta Frei Adams
Washington County

Age N/A; **Birthplace** N/A; **Occupation** N/A; **Religion** N/A;
Race/Ethnicity N/A

Living in Utah is a feast of the senses. Smells, sights, feelings, sounds, and memories all contribute to a kaleidoscope of love for the people and for the beauty of the countryside. Living in Utah is an appreciation for my Swiss heritage. It is a common experience shared by all of us who grew up in Santa Clara, Utah. Utah is a place for the cleansing of the soul.

In Santa Clara we are like children from one big family. We know without shared words the Santa Clara experience which goes from one generation to the next. The whole town was our playground. We built secret hideouts on the red hill and dragged home rocks and black flint which we deposited in our parents' basements. We collected Christmas trees, asking for them weeks in advance before another "gang" could get them, and we built big Christmas tree bonfires on the hill and cooked gritty sand scrambled eggs and half raw potatoes. We searched for Indian arrowheads and pottery on the south hill. We caught polliwogs and frogs in the creek and sometimes cooked our supper on the rocky sand near the shallow water. Every small town in Utah has a swimming hole. Ours was the Boy's Pond, and we girls would sneak up on the boys to catch them swimming or go swimming ourselves if the boys weren't around. We had the vineyard where we played "jungle" and an underground house dug elaborately by the boys with willow reeds covering the ground for camouflage. Most of all I remember the smell of alfalfa and irrigation ditches during hot summer days. I remember sitting in irrigation ditches in my little white underwear, taking a reprieve from the hot fields and the stubble which hurt barefeet after the hay was cut. My small body would block the water in the ditch until it pushed me sliding along the moss covered slickness like a gentle waterslide. I have an image of big leafy trees with patches of sun floating on the cool water and the innocence of a free child in nature. Sometimes when, as Wordsworth said, "the world is too much with me," I long to sit in those irrigation ditches and once again feel the healing innocence of my soul or run, hair flying, a child trying to touch each crack that made up the squares of our town sidewalk. We played marbles "for keeps," made wooden guns that could shoot round circles of cut up inner tubes in play fights, went up the "hollar," cooked the melt when someone butchered a cow or a pig, braided the Maypole, and ran races on May Day.

Living in Utah is Red Rover, Kick the Can, and Town Bell. It's Christmas Eve programs, coloring Easter eggs, having Easter egg busts, and making Valentines in the old Swiss way. It's the towering blue of Pine Valley mountain, the brilliant scarlet of Ivin's mountain, the pink and white pyramid peaks of Snow's canyon, and the bright orange sand that surrounds us. Living in Utah is like living in technicolor instead of black and white. It is also the black lava rocks, the halfway wash lined with pink tamaracks, and "Uncle Ern's Res," which sometimes substituted for our swimming hole. Utah is cattlemen and cattle, invoking memories of long ago cattle drives when the cattle streamed over the red hill in late October and were driven into wooden barns to be fed during the winter. Utah is farmers and farms, the plowing, the ceremony of cracking open the first ripe watermelon, the sharp first taste of radishes and green onions, and the fuzziness of round ripe peaches. It is old handmade red adobe houses, mud-colored adobe granaries, and new rambling brick houses. It's like having fifteen sets of parents instead of one. Mainly it is a community of people. …

Jordan Parry

Davis County

Age 11; **Birthplace** N/A; **Occupation** N/A; **Religion** Mormon; **Race/Ethnicity** Native American

… I'm lucky because I have such a special heritage. My father is part Shoshone Indian (which means that I am too!), and his ancestors are famous for their outstanding contributions to the betterment of the tribe. He's proud of them and I am too. My great grandmother Timbimboo even bestowed an Indian name on me. It is Numaduenita. My mother's family history is neat too. Her ancestors came across the plains with other Latter Day Saint pioneers. They were a strong family. One of my mother's ancestors was Nick Wilson. When he was a small boy, he ran away because he was mad at his mother. Chief Washiki, of the Shoshone tribe found Nick and took him home with him. Washiki's wife had been very sad because they had just buried their small baby, so she was very happy when Nick came to live with them. He stayed with them for quite a while. This is special to me because my father is related to Chief Washiki and my mother is related to Nick Wilson. There is a book published about this story. It is called "The White Indian Boy."

I am glad that we live in Utah. It's a nice place without a lot of problems that some other states have.

Mandy Dawn Dixon

Salt Lake County

Age 16; **Birthplace** Murray, Utah; **Occupation** N/A; **Religion** Mormon; **Race/Ethnicity** White

I imagine the Pioneers didn't realize
As they trudged through the snow
Freezing and dying, that someday
It would be considered, The Greatest Snow on Earth.
Skiing the hills in Utah is like being
On the hills of the Alps.
The mountains they struggled over to climb,
Have became the best slopes ever known.
They might be even good enough to be
Accepted for the Olympics.
The streams they crossed became a
Fishermans heaven.
The lakes they bathed and baptized in
Are now a boaters paradise
Yes, the hardships of the pioneers
Are now Utah's settlers greatest
recreation!

Kay Nakashima

Salt Lake County

Age 75; **Birthplace** Ogden, Utah; **Occupation** Pharmacist, retired; **Religion** Presbyterian; **Race/Ethnicity** Japanese

Living in Utah means this is where I was born, this is where all my education took place, this is where all my immediate family are buried, this is where all my living immediate family live or are looking forward to retiring here to, and love all my friends and neighbors, business associates, and everything I own or use or enjoy, I owe to this wonderful state. I pay my taxes with gratitude for all it has done for me.

I played and grew up in Little Tokyo, a section of the city which used to be where the Salt Palace now is. I was given the opportunity to serve in the armed forces of this country, and although my eye sight prevented me from going over seas, many of my comrades did. I grew up as a Boy Scout and was given an opportunity to be a scoutmaster. All of my scouts became wonderful, high achieving citizens.

Living in Utah means this is where God wanted me to live. What a wonderful, beautiful, peaceful place. This is truly heaven on earth to me.

Eileen Stoker
Davis County

Age 39; **Birthplace** Ogden, Utah; **Occupation** Homemaker; **Religion** LDS; **Race/Ethnicity** Caucasian

On Memorial Day last year I was standing in the cemetery in Grouse Creek, Utah, a tiny farming community in northwest Box Elder County. It is not a beautiful place. The rocky soil is unyielding and had to be wet down to make it soft enough to dig places for the flowers to decorate the graves. My Grandma and Grandpa Lee are buried there.

As I thought of them, I was impressed with what they had made out of their lives and the legacy they have left to their posterity. They didn't have lots of worldly wealth nor did they have any college diplomas to decorate their walls, but they were people of integrity, thrift, hard work, and perseverance. They were survivors in an environment that was at times quite harsh and unforgiving.

Grouse Creek, even though not particularly scenic, is one of my favorite places in Utah. My memories of Grandma and Grandpa Lee and the values they stand for

make it so. And on that Memorial Day as I was surveying all the sagebrush and the dust I realized why Utah is so important to me.

Because of people like my Grandma and Grandpa Lee and because of places like Grouse Creek, Utah is indeed THE place to live. The pioneer spirit thrives even today because of those great people who gave us such a priceless heritage and also such great promise for the future.

Utah stands for faith, courage, obedience, endurance, and cooperation. Those early values exemplified in the lives of our pioneer ancestors are still in vogue and very much in need today.

I'm grateful we can raise our family in Utah, in an environment that seems to echo with the memories of our pioneer ancestors. In addition to the crops they planted and the cities they erected, they also planted enduring principles and values that can still be harvested even today by those of us left to carry on the legacy.

Utah: This is indeed the place! May it ever be so.

Jonathan Hopkins
Salt Lake County

Age 15; **Birthplace** New York City, New York; **Occupation** Student; **Religion** LDS; **Race/Ethnicity** Caucasian

Utah granite is something like grandfathers, especially great great great ones—solid, gray, massive, foundational, even luminous. I don't know if it is the whitening quartz, alkali feldspar, or the light gray plagioclase crystals in Little Cottonwood Canyon granite that convert the sun's light into the color "radiant gray," or if this color is simply formed by a connection between certain monumental granite structures with a particular great great great grandfather's gray eyes, chiseled visage, high stony cheeks, and carefully combed gray hair. Only a more enlightened "I" will ever know.

When I moved to Utah, I became, whether I liked it or not, a Utahn. I can't remember who was responsible. It was either Mom or Dad who was driving the car when we crossed the state line. At first I wasn't sure how long we were going to stay, but unlike any of our previous homes, we stayed in this one even though Mom seemed kind of … neutral about it. I wondered why, so I started to dig for more information.

Dad was born and raised in Los Angeles not far from Knott's Berry Farm, Disneyland, and the beach. Why on earth didn't we go *there* to live? I had overheard Dad talking to a potential employer from our last house, "My wife is from Utah, and three of my four brothers live there now." I remembered him telling Mom, "They need a surgeon in Tooele." That seemed closer to what I was sure the answer was. We never moved there, but even I knew why we didn't. Mom likes big cities. Pianists just do, she says. When we moved into our apartment on State Street, Dad pointed to the six-spired granite edifice two blocks away and said, "Kids, there's where your mother and I were married. One of your ancestors helped cut the granite for it from a quarry at the mouth of Little Cottonwood Canyon." With that, I stopped digging. I was certain I'd hit bedrock.

So, the real reason we'd come to Utah and stayed was the presence here of certain forms of granite, both animal—human actually—and mineral. Dad told us about both. The human form seemed more important to him. It began with the great great great granite grandfather I began to tell you about, Adam Hunter. He mined coal in Scotland all his life starting when he was only five. He married his cousin Elizabeth Patterson who also grew up mining coal in 1842. In 1848 some Utah farm boys dressed in dark suits came to their home in the little town of Devon, Clackmananshire, Scotland. They preached to him and baptized him and his wife in September of that year. In 1851 he made a big decision. He decided to leave Scotland and set out that year to cross the Atlantic Ocean, sail up the Mississippi from New Orleans to St. Louis, and there prepare to cross the Great Plains to Utah to build something like a utopia they called Zion.

In St. Louis he found work in a coal mine, and by 1852 he had saved up enough to send for his family. They barely escaped death from a small pox epidemic that broke out on board their ship in the mid-Atlantic, a riverboat steam engine that blew up just after letting them off in St. Louis, and the 1852 St. Louis cholera epidemic. Adam got cholera but didn't die because he prayed and begged God to spare him. He crossed the Great Plains with his wife and four children in a covered wagon pulled by a team of oxen he later donated as a gift to God for preserving him from cholera-induced dehydration and death, to pull stone blocks needed for a public-works project that was dear to him. His wife Elizabeth walked. She was pregnant and walking didn't hurt as much as riding in the wagon. Elizabeth gave birth to twins in that wagon at the mouth of Red Butte Canyon not far from the sandstone quarry. They built a home on Second South and Seventh East, and there they stayed until they both died. They scrounged for sego lily bulbs to help feed their large family that first winter and spring. Adam was a foreman in the Little Cottonwood Canyon granite quarry until he died at the age of 61 leaving his wife with six of their thirteen children unmarried to raise. She lived joyously with her family, which included 322 living descendants when she died at the age of 92.

Like the coarse-grained rock that makes up the largest part of every continent, Adam Hunter's legacy formed a kind of bedrock for me. His origins were igneous—a slowly and quietly cooled magma that became the kind of Utahn I would like to be.

"Papierschnitt." Submitted by Ada Redd Rigby, San Juan County.

Janet Roberts

Piute County

Age N/A; **Birthplace** N/A; **Occupation** N/A; **Religion** N/A; **Race/Ethnicity** N/A

Living in Utah means living in the old Dalton family home in Circleville, Utah. My great-uncle O.A. Dalton began construction of the house in 1896, the year that Utah became a state. His initials and the date of construction are carved in the wood trim on the west gable of the house. Before the house was finished, O.A. sold the house to his brother, M.C. Dalton. The house is a large, two story brick structure with walls made from three layers of homemade, red adobe brick. The woodwork was sent from Salt Lake City to M.C. Dalton via the railroad and had to be picked up in Marysvale by horse and wagon. The upstairs rooms were still being finished in 1901 when there was a strong earthquake and some of the walls were cracked.

My father was the youngest of M.C. Dalton's eight children and lived all of his life in the old house. My mother went to the hospital in Richfield to give birth to me and I was always upset because I wanted to be born "at home." Later I understood why she wanted to go to a hospital.

My childhood memories are mostly happy ones. I remember playing in the front hallway with my best friend, Dana. We would dress in my mother's old curtains and play "Here Comes The Bride" as we marched down the stairs. We would take turns playing the old pump organ and singing at the top of our voices. Another favorite place to play was the back porch where we dressed the kittens in doll clothes, made mud pies, and washed doll's clothes in my little toy clothes washer.

I liked mowing the lawn with the old push lawn mower. The lawn was so big that by the time I was finished, it was time to start over again. After a rainstorm I would pull on the branches of the many cottonwood trees surrounding the house and would pretend I was having a "shower." Every night during the summer I would sleep outside among my grandmother's shrub roses in an old iron bedstead.

Always there were the mountains surrounding my home to fascinate me. I never tired of looking at them. My most exciting days were when I got to go up in the mountains on a ride or for a picnic.

Before I was ready, I was out of high school and off to college. After college I got married, but we came "home" as often as we could. In 1973, while we were visiting, my father passed away in the same bedroom where his parents and two brothers also died. A year later my mother left the old house and Uncle Lawrence was left to live there alone. We would visit him every year and always felt a sense of homecoming.

Finally the old house was left empty for several years until the fall of 1990 when my husband Wallace and I were able to come home for good. …

Our greatest sense of accomplishment comes as we work on our old house and yard (see plate 3). We see many old houses falling down and we are happy to try and preserve ours. When we build a new picket fence just like the old one or put a new wood shingle roof on the house, we think of Grandpa. As we plant a lawn, trees, and flowers we think of Grandma who was a great gardener. The vegetable garden reminds us of Dad who loved to grow fresh tomatoes, cucumbers and ears of corn. The interior of the house reminds us of Mother who had such an eye for color and design. We hope to honor all those who have lived in and loved the old house by having the house and yard looking good for its 100th birthday in 1996.

All of this is what living in Utah means to me.

Janie Buchanan
Van Komen

Davis County

Age 43; **Birthplace** North Island, CA; **Occupation** Mother;
Religion LDS; **Race/Ethnicity** Caucasian

As I stand in awe of the magnificent majesty of the mountains, their greatness of size, their "large screen" display of whatever this season renders, and the constancy of their appearance, I am keenly aware that all of the mountains in this state look, to me now, exactly like they did when I was a child.

In my quiet moments of reverent reflection, I stand and wonder if my ancestors ever stood and wondered at those mountains and felt the same way that I do? Am I seeing the same visions of beauty they saw? Did the mountains look the same to them as they do to me?

When I turn away from the mountains and look at the valleys, I see growth and expansion everywhere, and with it comes the inherent problems that societal living brings to any people.

More than twenty two of my ancestors crossed the plains, settled farms and communities, built homes and businesses, raised families, and helped domesticate this great state. This gives me a sense of identity, a sense of unity, a sense of belonging, a sense of home.

I also feel a great sense of responsibility to carry on their heritage of work ethics, moral values, and devotion to God. I know the stories. I have heard from my youth of the sacrifices and hardships, the triumphs and tragedies that created this place as home for me and all others who have chosen to live here.

My husband was born in a foreign land and his family gave up wealth and prestige to bring their family to a place where people believed the same way they did, and where the people had the same moral values and standards they had.

Their appreciation for the sacrifices of my ancestors in some ways may even be greater than mine because they have known a different way of life and they have made a conscious choice to be here in Utah and to participate in and to share a heritage that sometimes I selfishly think belongs only to me.

This reality helps me to envision the great designs of my ancestors to provide a place that would be safe and welcome to all who would be willing to share uplifting moral values, work hard, and bow their heads in gratitude for their blessings.

From the top of the state in the north to the bottom of the state in the south, I can find relatives and friends working, breathing, living, and struggling with those same big questions of life that all of our grandparents struggled with. Their homes, conveniences, methods of travel, roads, politics, health practices, and living conditions have changed, the ways of the world have changed, but the questions of life and the mountains in Utah always stay the same.

Philip F. Notarianni

Salt Lake County

Age N/A; **Birthplace** N/A; **Occupation** N/A; **Religion** N/A;
Race/Ethnicity N/A

I am a second generation Italian-American, whose parents immigrated from the province of Cosenza, Calabria, Italy. Living in Utah means the fulfillment of a dream envisioned by those parents who came to Utah seeking opportunities not available in their homeland.

Filippo and Carmela Angotti Notarianni left Italy in 1920 and 1933 respectively, at a time when thousands of European, Asian, and Mexican immigrants formed a part of a massive migration to the United States and Utah. These immigrants harbored dreams for themselves, but primarily for their families. They stressed education and the need for children to learn English and accommodate themselves to the Utah social, political, and economic environment. Some found this accommodation easy, while others struggled in the attempt to balance two cultures. Prejudice and discrimination did not escape the Utah boundaries. Utah, after all, was a part of the United States, where ethnic and racial diversity hovered as central issues in everyday life.

Utahns are a culturally diverse people. In 1995, diversity is viewed as a strength and not a weakness. Children who were implored to learn the English language and "American ways," are now attempting to reidentify with their cultural and ethnic heritage. I married an Italian-American woman, Maria Teresa Maletta, whose family originated but a short distance from the little village of my parents' birth. Her parents, Carmine and Sestina Maletta, never visited Utah, but envisioned this state as one of opportunity, as had those immigrants from generations past.

Utah provides and provided many occasions for personal development. A noted writer of Italian-American history, Angelo M. Pellegrini, observed: "Many years later I was to realize that, to a child of nine years, emigration to America meant a new birth, to which a certain inevitable continuity with the past had given an added significance." Living in Utah has enabled many immigrants to combine the best of their cultural heritage with a state rich in opportunities.

Jo-Ann Wong Kilpatrick
Salt Lake County

Age 44; **Birthplace** Ogden, Utah; **Occupation** Paginator, Deseret News; **Religion** N/A; **Race/Ethnicity** Chinese-American

In 1951, my mother a second-generation Chinese-American was being treated for tuberculosis in the Ogden chest and lung clinic.

She was pregnant at the time and doctors said the baby helped push her lungs into a good position!

After I was born, my father a first-generation Chinese-American took me to Salt Lake City. He operated the China Village Restaurant on Main Street between Broadway and 400 South. He found a woman to care for me until my mother was released from the clinic. Several years later my father built a home two blocks north of the State Capitol building. Ours was the highest house on the road. I remember snowy nights when my father couldn't make it up the road because snow plows didn't clear there and so my father would turn around and go sleep at the restaurant. The field to Ensign Peak was my backyard and provided many good days of play.

Living in Utah meant that I had to spend two years in Layfayette Elementary school kindergarten because I didn't speak English. We'd carpool down the hill with some neighbors. I remember the walks home, straight up State Street with a daily excursion through the Capitol and up the road home.

My father and several other Chinese perpetuated cultural traditions by providing a community Chinese New Year banquet, Chinese movies at the Richie Theater, Chinese opera performances with singers from Hong Kong, community Lagoon days with Chinese food and Chinese language school. They also participated in the 24th of July parade with floats, a dragon or dances. They also built and dedicated a pavilion at the International Peace Gardens in Jordan Park.

Downtown has changed a lot for me. I remember Auerbach's, the Paris Company, J.C. Penny's, the Dollar Store and the Pembroke Company. The grand Centre, Utah, Uptown Theaters and Saturday matinees…Japanese town and the Newhouse Hotel, all gone.

Through the years I have enjoyed contributing to the annual Asian Festival. Other volunteer hours have gone to the Utah Federation for Youth, Inc., KRCL—Radio Board of Trustees, The Children's Museum, Utah Arts Council Multi-Disciplinary Grants committee, Intermountain Chamber Orchestra, the M. Lynn Bennion Elementary School PTA, Chinese for Community Action, The Asian Association of Utah, Boy Scouts of America and the Utah Asian American Advisory Council.

I loved spending time in Derks Field watching the Trappers. I follow the Jazz.

I love watching my son grow …

Donna I. Sato
Salt Lake County

Age 45; **Birthplace** Brigham City, Utah; **Occupation** Government Employee; **Religion** Buddhist; **Race/Ethnicity** Japanese

In the early 1900's, Hinojo and Nofu Sato came to America from their homeland of Japan via a long boat ride. They left behind three young children to seek fortune in the land of opportunity. They ended up in Box Elder County along with other Japanese immigrants. These Japanese immigrants endured cold winters, a strange language, and financial difficulties. They survived because of their strong work ethic, the strong bond of community with the other Japanese, and the sense of responsibility and tradition they taught their young children. World War II brought hardship, discrimination, and ignorance. These challenges strengthened their sense of self-worth. While the Japanese living in the West Coast were evacuated to Relocation Camps, these Utah Japanese families not only continued to provide a living for their families but helped other Japanese families move to Utah and a considerable number of their American-born offspring enlisted in the U.S. Army to help defend their adopted country.

Today, as part of our families and the Japanese American community, we still carry on the traditions introduced by our grandparents. Even though we are members of different religious congregations, we all share the wonderful traditions that link us to our heritage. We celebrate the Japanese new year, we use menus consisting of a variety of rice and Japanese dishes, and we relish Japanese delicacies. We still do many Japanese ritual ceremonies that probably no longer exist in the busy lives of Japanese in Japan. In September of 1994, I suffered a great loss—the death of my dad, Nobuichi Sato. Nob as he was most commonly called, was a pioneer onion farmer in Box Elder County. He also made sure all five of his children received educational opportunities which he and his siblings missed out on. He passed the same work ethic to us which his parents instilled in him. During his illness, I heard everyday heroic stories about my dad which I did not know. I heard about the fishing trips to the Logan River, moving a family from Price after a family's father had suffered an injury, and the help my dad gave to young onion farmers.

I am often asked how long I have been in this country. I definitely know my roots are here in Utah when I tell them my grandparents were the ones that ventured to this country and my dad was born and now buried in Box Elder County, UT. Living in Utah means carrying on those traditions, the sense of community, and strong work ethic passed on by my father and brought over by my grandparents on that boat ride many years ago.

"W. Grants Emporium, about 1895." Submitted by Joleen Grant Meredith, Salt Lake County.

Lori Anne Nelson Bolan
Cache County

Age 32; **Birthplace** Salt Lake City, Utah; **Occupation** Homemaker; **Religion** LDS; **Race/Ethnicity** White

I am a fifth generation Utahn. I am also a member of the Church of Jesus Christ of Latter Day Saints. My great great grandfather, Andrew Nelson Sr., (originally Anders Nielsen) emigrated from Denmark to Manti, Utah upon his conversion to the LDS church. His son, Andrew Nelson Jr. moved from Manti to Ferron, Utah and homesteaded the Nelson dairy farm. They spent their first summer in a covered wagon and their first winter in a dugout. The farmhouse my great grandfather built in 1895 is still standing. The alfalfa fields of Ferron are green and lush in contrast to the desert soil and red-rock plateaus that surround them.

My grandfather, James Rulon Nelson was born in May of 1901 in the bedroom he slept in all his adult life. He was the youngest of twelve children and had twelve children of his own. He ran a dairy farm and milked cows twice a day up until his eighties. Some of my uncles continue to work the land, though the milk house has been abandoned since my teenage years. My father, Monte Nicholas Nelson was born in Ferron. He married Janet

Arlene Samuelson and settled in Salt Lake City where I was born in 1963. He traded his farming overalls for a seventh grade math teacher's chalkboard and textbook.

My roots are in Utah—the land is very special to me. I lived as a girl in Salt Lake City and moved to Granger (now West Valley City) the beginning of my fifth grade year. The mountains of the Salt Lake Valley are among the most beautiful I have ever seen. Looking at them brings peace to my heart. … My favorite trees are the aspens whose bright circle leaves dance in the cool canyon breezes.

I moved to Logan in Cache Valley upon entering Utah State University in the fall of 1981. Except for summers home while still attending college, I have lived in Cache Valley ever since. My husband, Mike, and I met at USU in the 13th ward of the USU LDS singles stake. Our first date was in February 1986 and we were married September 6th of that same year. He is an immigrant to Utah from Casper, Wyoming. He and his best friend Brad Lewis, also of Casper, came to USU originally because they heard there was a good "male/female ratio." I guess they both found what they wanted because both ended up marrying girls from Utah and still live here in Cache Valley.

Cache Valley is a beautiful place, surrounded by mountains and filled with peaceful, clean towns and farmland. I love the country feeling here, even though it is growing quickly. I hope that the feel of open spaces will not be lost here as it has been in Salt Lake Valley. All the fields around my neighborhood when I was a girl have since filled in with houses. Logan Canyon is beautiful, (though it still doesn't compare to Big Cottonwood) and I look forward to many camping trips with my children. I am content to say that Cache Valley is my home. It is a place that I like being and where I would be happy staying.

Mike and I have been busy the past eight years carving out a life for ourselves and our children. We rented a very tiny and very old two bedroom house a year after we were married. We moved in with no children and moved out 5½ years later with three. We built a house in Smithfield six miles to the north. We now have four children—two girls and two boys—sixth generation Utahns. My husband is an assistant controller at an exercise equipment manufacturing company and I stay home with our children. …

I spend three days a week shuffling my second daughter Stephanie back and forth to pre-school while my first daughter Michelle is in kindergarten. I look forward to a rest next year because Jordan won't need to go to preschool for another year yet. But I know that soon I need to start the soccer practices and the dance and piano lessons, so there really won't be a lot of rest from the shuffling.

I think about how different my life is from my great grandmother's. Anna Lorentzen Nelson gave birth to her children in her bedroom. I hold my five month old son Cody and thank God that I had an epidural in a nice shiny hospital delivery room. I think of my grandmother Edna Dowdle Samuelson's story of washing our diapers in a bucket of water she had to fetch from a stream because the shack she and my grandfather were living in during part of their early married years had no running water. I throw my baby's disposable diapers into the trash and feel sorry for myself because I have to do all the changing. (My husband "doesn't do diapers.") My life is relatively easy.

But I find myself envying my grandmothers. Their lives were so much more involved in the land. I have often wished that I could have spent just a portion of my life living on the land which has been a part of my family for so many years. I loved visiting the farm in Ferron as a young girl, feeding grain to the cows as my uncles and grandpa milked them. I remember sitting on the porch of the old farm house and looking at one of my favorite views—the old "South Horn" mountain which now looks over Millsite reservoir in the canyon above Ferron.

… My step-grandmother, Ruth McConkie Nelson, always had the daily big dinner ready each day at noon. The menfolk needed their energy early in the day while they did their chores. I don't know how many hours she spent each day in the kitchen. She was also an elementary school librarian when her children were older. My grandmother Anna Louella Allermand Nelson died when my father was only five years old. Never having known her, I miss her just the same. I think of the association I have had with my Grandma Samuelson and wonder how things might have been. But then I would have never known Ruth. I love her, too. I wish I lived closer to my grandmothers so I could spend more time with them. Time marches on and they are getting older. My grandfathers are both gone now.

I also want to be more a part of the land. I try to compensate for our harried lifestyle by growing a flower garden. I plan on planting a vegetable garden this summer too, since I am not pregnant. Tilling, planting and weeding should be much easier. It feels good to dig up the weeds and watch the flowers and vegetables I've nurtured thrive. The same with my children. But it all comes back to the land. You cannot sow seeds when you have no soil. There can be no harvest without a place to plant. You cannot have a home without a spot of land. I feel that I am safely planted here.

Sometimes I feel like I'm floating from experience to experience just taking what comes instead of creating my own destiny. But now I think that I am ready to forge a path more of my own choosing. I haven't made a lot of difference to this place yet; but I am a child of Utah. I hope that someday, in some small way, I will make my mark here. Perhaps just raising another generation of Utahns who will love this land as I do will be enough.

Fay Ferguson Grover
Salt Lake County

Age 74; **Birthplace** Midvale, Utah; **Occupation** Elementary Teacher (retired); **Religion** L.D.S.; **Race/Ethnicity** White

Utah is the land of my heritage. It is the great great grandmother, newly immigrated to this strange desert land from her beloved England, growing food for herself and her children while her husband was serving as a missionary in Italy. It is the great great grandfather returning and being called to other service and dying on the plains at the hands of hostile Native Americans. It is my husband's great great grandfather, grandson of an officer in the American Revolution, bodyguard to Joseph Smith, who started with the first company of Pioneers and was left at the Platte River to ferry the wagons of others across and did not arrive in the valley until late in the fall. This heritage is a great grandfather, age sixteen, being left at Devil's Gate to guard the wagons of those who were rescued from the deep snows when they were unable to get to the valley. This heritage is a great grandmother, daughter of Irish immigrants, who certified as a teacher at age eighteen and taught school in her parent's home. It is a great grandfather who hauled stone by wagon from Cottonwood Canyon to build the Temple and another grandfather who hauled stone by rail to build the Capitol building. It is my grandmother who struggled to earn a living as a housekeeper after her young husband was killed in a horse and buggy accident on their second child's first birthday. This heritage is my husband standing on the steps of the Capitol building as a member of the Modern Mormon Battalion of the Marine Corps prior to service in the Pacific in World War II.

As a young woman I dreamed of traveling the world and knowing the people of other places. Utah has been the place where I could find the world right here. To the east of my home I can find the snows and mountains like the

Alps. To the west I find two bodies of water joined by the "River Jordan" as in the mid-east. I can travel to the south in the state and find the palms and figs of the tropics. The smell of salt in the air reminds me of the ocean. The sounds of the wind through the pines reminds us of the forests. The cry of the water fowls and the heat of the desert in summer remind us of other lands. In my neighborhood were people who had immigrated from Germany, Switzerland, Scotland, Mexico, and the Islands of the Pacific. I heard their songs and learned their customs. In the classroom where I taught were the children from Communist Czechoslovakia and China. There was the child from Iran and many who came from Indo-China—Laotians, Cambodians, Vietnamese, and Hmong. Added to these were Native Americans, African Americans, Hispanic, and Polynesian. Each brought a distinct pattern of life with them. There were children of poverty and of affluence, retarded and gifted, cherished and abused. We lived together in our own democratic society, each making the contribution they were willing to make and learning to appreciate each other.

I have been a wife and mother in Utah. I have treasured the school experience of my children. From the first days of Kindergarten to their graduation from the Universities. I have shared with pride their accomplishments in orchestras, glee clubs, A'Cappela, Tabernacle Choir, Utah Opera, gymnastics, Little League, Scouting, Roadshows and church activities. Together as a family we climbed the mountains of the Uintas, road vehicles in the sand dunes, and floated in the Great Salt Lake. We picked corn on a church farm, cleaned bricks at the old Riverside school to finance a new organ for our Stake Center. We filled sand bags to hold back the floods and cleaned the banks of the Jordan River. We have walked together in the beautiful marbled halls of the State Capitol and stood together in the animal sheds of the State Fair. We have worshipped together in the Temple built by our ancestors.

My husband's work took us into the fields of electronics and the industrial side of Utah. We saw the beginnings of the missile and computer industry and were also associated with radio and sound engineering. We saw an early heart monitor being developed in our own garage and the children and I were the test subjects. Being together with our family in the many activities we found in the state created a top quality of life for us.

For me now, Utah is a comfortable safe place to enjoy my retirement years. As I look to the east where my great great grandmother struggled for food, I see the home of my daughter where they live in comfort and prosperity. Likewise to the north where my husband's great great grandfather entered the valley, I see the home of my son who shares his ancestors pleasures in the outdoors and the active world of men in this state. To the west where our great great grandparents fought the grasshoppers to save their crops, I see the home of my second daughter. It is a home filled with learning, music, and laughter of a happy family. Utah is the best place to live for quality of life and the goodness of the people.

My concerns for the future are much the same today as they have been throughout our lives. Are we living in a mature enough community to provide opportunity for children to be properly educated and to live in a healthy environment? Perhaps our "love" for children is only on the surface not in our pocketbooks. Are we willing to do as our ancestors would have done when we find the homeless in our midst? Can we override political affiliation for the welfare of the people of our state? Literacy, health, good jobs, the arts and good recreation are the things I want for my grandchildren to enjoy during their lives. The panorama of events that I have witnessed in my three score years and ten plus three has made for an exciting life. I wish I might see the next three score and ten in this *Pretty Great State!*

Submitted by Megan Little, Cache County.

Milton Hoyt
Washington County

Age 56; **Birthplace** Orderville, Utah; **Occupation** Retired Professor; **Religion** Church of Jesus Christ of Latter-day Saints; **Race/Ethnicity** English/Welch

Living in Utah is living in a geographic wonderland with varied climatic zones and conditions. "On a clear day you can see forever"—unencumbered by man's devises. But, living in Utah encompasses far more than viewing its many splendored vistas. There is in Utah an heritage of a magnificent search. As with many of the settlers of the original colonies of the United States, a search for religious freedom—the right to worship "how, where, or what they may." Also, A dynamic need for independence from governmental control of the basic values—"life, liberty and the pursuit of happiness." These to be sustained in and through the concepts and principles of the United States Constitution and "The True Religion." God and Country was their covenant and creed.

My great grandparents were fully involved in the westward migration and colonization of the "outposts of Zion." They zealously responded to the call of their leader, Brigham Young, to settle permanent communities far from the center of their Zion. First, they settled in Nephi and Payson. The early years are characterized in the words of Samuel Claridge, "Well I put a crop in another year on *my own land* it being on the outside next to the prairie. The grasshoppers took that. I had a hard struggle the first four or five years. … Lived on a cornbread most of the year and I was only without bread three days."

"Our clothes now began to get very poor and when we could get blue drilling to make our pants and jumpers we were quite rich." A few years later he said: "I raised good crops and everything prospered with me. In 1863 and 4 I built me a new house and bought a larger lot and put out a fine orchard which done well." 1867, "everything went well with me I raised good crops, got me a good team and wagon, cows, and sheep, built me a good house, bought two lots, … had a nice orchard just coming to bearing." [1]

The Muddy Mission call came in September of 1868. Many of the successful settlers sold or gave away everything they had. Determined to make permanent settlements in the Moapa Valley they set forth. The northern portion of

---

[1] Samuel Claridge, *Pioneering the Outposts of Zion,* by S. George Ellsworth, Howe Brothers, Salt Lake City, 1987, pp. 65–57, 71.

Lake Mead now covers the soil they tamed and made productive. There, they lived in wagon boxes and adobe houses built from the mud of the Virgin or Muddy River.

... This time the move was to Long Valley, Utah where the small towns of Alton, Glendale, Orderville and Mt. Carmel are now located. On the foundation of invincible faith, courage and poverty they began to build anew. Orderville was settled by those individuals who wished to practice the "United Order." In this "order" they owned all things "in common" except their clothes and a shack for living quarters. All of my great grandparents were participants in this movement.

... Father was a firm believer in the Church which God established in this state. ... He could not tolerate lawmakers who, in the name of government, made intrusions into the lives of other citizens. He wrote many letters to governmental officials declaring that God established the Constitution for this country and men had no business going beyond the original articles therein. ...

... My birth was a few years prior to the depression which devastated many communities of the nation in the late 1920's and early 30's. At three months of age my home was a borrowed sheep wagon. I attended public school in hand-me-down patched overalls and shoes with cardboard soles. Yet no one told me that I was living in poverty nor that poverty was my lot for life. I did not feel impoverished. There was a spirit or feeling that with God's help everything would be alright ...

... I am not unique. Many generations from these small communities have with the same traditions and values followed this process to achieve success.

Now retired, I have returned to live in Utah to view those "scenes so dear to my childhood." To feel the atmosphere of religious values and liberty which abounds, in these small Southern Utah Communities. Living in Utah is much, much more than rocks, sagebrush, industry, tourism, environmentalism, people and cities. Yes! it is all

of these and more. But they are dwarfed by the overriding values embodied in rugged individualism as defined by those who gave everything to "make the desert blossom as the rose." As Irving Stone titles one of his books these were and are "Men to Match My Mountains"!

Their realism, buttressed by a firm faith in God and Constitutional Government was unconquerable. They succeeded where none could be expected to succeed. They made oases in the desert, and in the hearts of many individuals.

FACES FROM MEMORY

The following Faces of Utah not only reflect and name the landmark experiences which define human lives—warm memories of family, marriage, and home life, school, church, work, play, fortune and misfortune—but clarify the things which matter most to us as human beings, as Americans, as Utahns. And while these memories resound with the "Utah, We Love Thee" refrain likely to be stirred in natives of any state or nation, these essays take on native hues peculiar to Utah. For, folded into these Utah lives are profound memories engendered by the Utah land with its jagged skylines, hoodoo-studded canyonlands, mountain streams, cool canyons, and vast sagebrush flats. Utahns, then, are humanity with a twist.

Thirteen-year-old Erin Johnson, of Midway, puts it all into a matter-of-fact perspective: "Even though Utah is a desert, it's a neat place. ... I think we've settled in good here."

—Richard H. Cracroft
Provo, UT

Donette Fergus Southard
Cache County

Age 63; **Birthplace** Logan, UT; **Occupation** Home Maker;
Religion LDS; **Race/Ethnicity** Caucasian

Utah—To be more specific, Logan, Cache County, Utah. To be much more specific the time period of about 1932 to 1940—the greatest place and the greatest time to be a kid in Utah.

A time machine would be the best way to show you some of my memories. Since that invention has not yet materialized in real life, I'll attempt to tell you about a few of them.

As a child, I had no idea just how unique Logan was with a sewer system, a power plant in Logan Canyon, municipal water and golf course. Of course the Mormons had their Temple and Tabernacle and the Presbyterians, Episcopalians, Catholics and others had their meeting places as well. We also had two hospitals, the William Budge Memorial and the Cache Valley. My sister and I were born at home (real pioneers) but our brothers were born in the hospital. The Utah State Agricultural College was up on the hill and main street had three banks all on corners, (where banks seemed to be at that time) First National, First Security and Cache Valley. Since my Dad was a member of the Logan City Police Force during this period of time, I always felt well protected, although crime in Logan was practically non-existent. The only time we locked our doors was when we left for a few days and then only to keep the neighbor kids from running through the house. The locks didn't offer much protection anyway. They could be unlocked with a "skeleton key." Many people left their keys in their cars without a second thought.

Our home was on first west between 1st and 2nd north streets so it was fairly easy for Daddy to stop for lunch. We kids would keep busy, during this time, running to the "little corner" (the corner closest to our house—the "big corner" was in the other direction) to see if the "red light" was on. In the center of the intersection of 1st North and also 2nd North on a separate power line, was a red light globe. When it was turned on, it was the signal that a police officer was needed at the police office. … We often had native Americans (wrapped in their blankets) knock on our back door. In their hand would be a crumpled, rather dirty piece of paper with a request for food written on it. Not being very well off ourselves but wanting to help, they were usually given a bottle of "Indian Fruit." I didn't know for quite some time that the fruit was actually plums, not Indian Fruit.

There was a Japanese Laundry on first North just off Main street run by the Koyki family. They also lived in the building. The Logan Laundry and Dry Cleaners was about two blocks from our home. We were always able to hear the laundry whistle blow at 8:00 A.M., Noon, 1:00 P.M. and 5:00 P.M. If a child was lost, they would blow the whistle on and off for quite some time. I always wondered why. Also on first north street was the Cranney Garage, Blair Garage (with a drinking water fountain by the front door—it was a great day when I could get a drink of water without being held up). There was an empty lot between Cranney Garage and Blair's. I was told there was once a miniature golf course located there. It was just a scary place full of weeds and trees and off limits to us. Another off limits place was the public rest rooms under ground at 1st North and Main. Mack McKinney's Meat Market was on 1st North as was Newell Cahoon's Red and White Grocery (where you just might hear Emil Sjostrom yodelling as he worked). The Coca Cola Bottling Works was down the street west of the Red and White. You could watch coke being bottled before they covered the windows (guess they didn't want to be watched). Our neighbor Mr. Roundy worked there.

Logan's three large grocery stores were all on the west side of Main street between 1st and 2nd North (Dinner

Horn, American Food and Safeway). Monson's Market was by the Capital Theatre and every neighborhood had a market for "convenience shopping."

If you had a reason to go to town early in the morning you'd probably see many of the store owners washing windows and washing off the sidewalk in front of their store preparing for the day's business. You'd more than likely be "waited on" by this same store owner.

Logan had one of the nicest dance halls in Utah, the Dansante (operated by Alma Lundahl). It was on 1st west between center and 1st south streets. I don't know when it was built, but it did hang on thru the 40's so I had the privilege of dancing there. It was a great place to see people who had been away on missions, school, the military or what ever and were home again.

Just walking down Logan's main street was a great place to see people you knew. It was especially fun on Saturday, when folks from the surrounding towns would come to Logan "all dressed up" to shop.

The town I grew up in has changed a lot in 60 years. However, Utah *was* and still *is* the greatest place to live.

Effie Euzina Glover

Salt Lake County

Age 87; **Birthplace** East Jordan, now East Midvale; **Occupation** N/A; **Religion** L.D.S.; **Race/Ethnicity** N/A

My name is Effie Euzina Johnson Glover. I am 86 years old. I was born 16 Nov. 1908 and have lived in Utah all my life.

I think Utah has a lot of beautiful places to see and the scenery is beautiful and I have seen many changes, for instant the cement roads were made on State Street when I was young. Some of the first cars bought.

We used to have street cars that ran from Midvale to Salt Lake and areas around.

We rode in a covered wagon to go to school and in a bobsleigh when there was a lot of snow, this was fun. Charles Sharp was the teamster and was kind to us. When Mr. Sharp quit driving my grandfather took us to school with horse and buggy. Then we got student tickets to ride the street car and we walked home which was quite a long way.

My father passed away in 1917 so my sister and I helped our mother with the work on our 3½ acres of ground. The plowing and heavy work was done by my fathers older brother when we would shuck the grain (wheat), pile the hay and help haul the hay to be stacked for winter use. There was sugar beets to be thinned, weeded, topped and put in the wagon to be hauled to the beet dump.

We helped pick up potatoes and put in sacks to be put in the potato cellar.

It was nice to watch the threshers when the wheat was threshed and sacked which was used for flour for us to make bread and other things and bran for the pigs to eat and wheat for the chickens.

Mother taught us to clean house, we had a black stove that had to have blackening put on, then when dry we had to shine it with a brush until it shined.

We had a pretty range that had a water heater in the one side so we always had warm water in the winter when we used the stove for heat, also had a heating oven on top to keep things warm to eat.

We had coal oil lamps for lights, then in a few years we got electricity had a cord in center of the ceiling with a globe in and that was our light, we were really glad to have it.

We had a dog that we took to mutual with us tied it to a tree on the Bishops lawn until Mutual was over then he would walk home with us. My sister and I felt a lot more brave to walk home in the dark when we had our dog. Oh yes we had a well and it had good water to drink. We had a cupboard with 4 shelves covered with burlap and lined it with white material, this is where we kept our milk and cream cool by having a large pan of cold water on top with 4 long pieces of heavy material, so the material would soak up the water and wet the burlap, this was very nice to have.

I like Utah and I am glad I live here and that our grandparents settled here. They were among the first ones to come to Utah and I am thankful they stayed in Utah too.

I married Leo James Glover and we had 8 children 3 boys and 5 girls and we all love Utah.

Leo passed away 18 May 1960 age 57 year I married Oral D Despain 1 Feb 1972. Oral passed away 14 Oct 1972.

Richard Holton Cracroft
Utah County

Age 59; **Birthplace** Salt Lake City, Utah; **Occupation** Professor of English; **Religion** Latter-day Saint; **Race/Ethnicity** Caucasian

Born at 1068 Norris Place in Salt Lake City, just up the alley from Victory Park and tennis courts, in the Eleventh Ward (10th East, between 1st and 2nd South), I grew up *Mormon, Salt Lake,* and *Utahn,* and, intensely so in those exciting World War II years, *American.*

There were vacant lots in those days, from 1942–1945, wonderful adventure lands laden with sunflowers, whose heads I mercilessly cut off with a captured Japanese sword, as I patrolled the neighborhood with my red wagon, collecting tin cans and newspapers for the war effort, stopping enroute to the collection corner or to buy a loaf of bread (money tied in a handkerchief) at Dovell's little store on 2nd South ("Hi Dick, how's tricks," he'd call) to climb into the swings at Victory Park, where, emulating a P-38 pilot, I rock-bombed the sandpile-created Japanese fleet below, and relived, a thousand times, the Japanese attack on Pearl Harbor. Those were exciting years to an eight-nine-ten-year-old with one brother serving as a captain in the U.S. Marine Corps on islands with exotic and strange names like Bougainville, Guadalcanal, Guam, and Iwo Jima; and another brother a lieutenant in the U.S. Army infantry, training for the invasion of Japan.

It was thrilling to watch Dad don his Civil Defense helmet and go from door to door checking the blackout status of each home; thrilling to experience a total blackout and watch the searchlights penetrate the heavens looking for rumored Japanese bombers; thrilling to huddle with fellow pupils in the cement walkway tunnel under South Temple at Wasatch School as we awaited the all-clear sirens; thrilling to hustle home and have Mother sign my air-raid-drill sheet certifying that it took me twelve minutes to jog-walk-run directly from school to Norris Place; thrilling to watch as neighbors, ward members, and then our family replaced the two or three blue stars in the window, signifying the number of sons and daughters at war, with (awe) silver stars (for those wounded in action) and (awe and grief) gold stars (for those fallen or missing in action). How well I recall the terror in the court when a messenger would drive up, alight from his olive-drab vehicle, and deliver a telegram beginning, "The President of the United States regrets to inform you. …"; how well I recall the terror of that morning when he arrived at our home to inform us, in the stead of President Roosevelt, that my Marine brother had been wounded in action; how well I recall the tears, the fear and the family prayers, the waiting and worrying; and then the joy and pride, months later, at watching that Marine major limping (oh how I envied that limp), cane in hand, up the front walk; and the fervor with which I sang "From the Halls of Montezuma to the Shores of Tripoli," and, with my Daisy training rifle in hand, moved snappily through the manual of arms under command of my military-minded but accountant-equipped

"Antelope Island—6." Photograph by Anna Campbell Bliss, Salt Lake County.

Plate 1

"Utah State Capitol Building." Submitted by Judith Ann Blain, Salt Lake County.

"Delicate Perfection: Snow and Ice Crystal in City Creek Canyon." Submitted by Anne Ewers, Salt Lake County.

"Old Farm Machinery." Hand-colored photo by Robert T. Beckstead, Weber County.

Plate 2

"Old House—New Root." Submitted by Janet Roberts, Piute County.

Above: "Cattails in autumn." Submitted by Shannon R. Hoskins, Weber County.

Left: "Dramatic Mystery: Balancing Rock in Canyonlands." Submitted by Anne C. Ewers, Salt Lake County.

Plate 3

"April 1985—Southern Utah." Submitted by Beverly W. Johnson, Weber County.

"Vermillion Cliffs." An original watercolor submitted by Skip Atkinson, Salt Lake County.

"Boulder Mountain in the Fall." Submitted by Tonia Van Dyke, Wayne County.

Plate 4

"Antelope Island—1." Photograph by Anna Campbell Bliss, Salt Lake County.

"Part of my father's farm: hay stubble, old fences, Snow's Canyon in background." Submitted by Loretta Frei Adams, Washington County.

Submitted by Jennie A. Gosling, Tooele County.

Plate 5

"March 1993—Honeyville Pond." Submitted by Marinda Miller, Box Elder County.

Bottom Left: "Four Seasons: Summer skies of azure blue / over school graduates / in formal gowns, roses in bloom." Painting by Adrian Van Suchtelen, Cache County.

Below: "The Sentinel, Zion." Watercolor and ink by Valerie Cohen, Iron County.

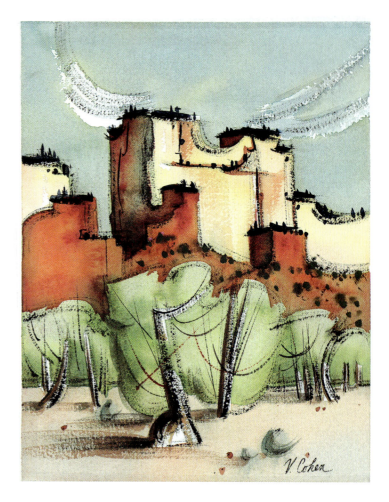

Plate 6

"Winter at Liberty Park, Salt Lake City." Submitted by Catherine Harline, Salt Lake County.

Submitted by Lisa Hansen, Washington County.

Submitted by Lisa Hansen, Washington County.

Plate 7

"Capitol Reef." Submitted by Tonia Van Dyke, Wayne County.

"Looking towards Torrey Knoll, near Torrey, Utah." Submitted by Tonia Van Dyke, Wayne County.

"Autumn at Liberty Park, Salt Lake City." Submitted by Catherine Harline, Salt Lake County.

Plate 8

father. And how exciting it was to be dismissed from school and dance in the streets and rock the street cars on South Temple on V-E Day, an event followed, at last, by our awe-struck wonder at the unleashing of the atomic bomb, and the subsequent in-street rejoicing—even in staid Salt Lake City—on V-J Day.

It was a thrilling time for this young Mormon-Utahn to become aware of the world, and everything seemed a bit anti-climactic when it was all over, and we could put away the "C" gas coupons (which Dad had used occasionally to take us on "rides" to Orem, where we would drive around the P.O.W. camps and look at the Germans and Austrians and Italians interned there—young men who looked disturbingly like our own young men and not at all like the monsters we had expected to see) and food-stamps and plastic mills and plastic dog-tags (ordered with Kix cereal boxtops)— and cease wearing tennis shoes made of compressed cardboard which came apart in the first earnest puddle, and take down the blackout curtains and close the air-raid shelters and let the lights blaze long into the night as we read in books made once more of quality paper and patronized shops which had long been "Closed for the Duration." Yes it was over—that ominous but exciting era—may it never return.

And suddenly it was 1947, and the celebration of the Centennial of the arrival of the Mormon Pioneers. Every school child participated in the event. We took the "Know Utah" nightly quizzes in the *Deseret News,* learned to sing (but not enjoy) "Utah, We Love Thee," memorized the names of every county and county-seat, learned the history of the Utah "Days of '47" pioneers, the names of the individuals on the sparkling new "This is the Place Monument," and gave (and listened to each week of this year) youth talks in church on Mormon pioneers (my talk was on Bavarian Mormon Georg Konrad Nagel). And Miss Crow, our marvelous music teacher at Douglass Elementary (and member of the Tabernacle Choir, to boot), taught us pioneer songs and, without hesitation or fear of the A.C.L.U., "Come, Come Ye Saints." I thrilled to the heritage of growing up in a high desert country which had been tamed by men and women whose faith and vision had unified and driven them to remarkable feats. And I thrilled to my father's impassioned speeches as he took me on tours through the State Capitol Building and Temple Square and Fort Douglas, and to the graves of Brigham Young and Heber C. Kimball and Wilford Woodruff and Orson Pratt, and made the City Cemetery come alive with real people, from Orrin Porter Rockwell to Joseph F. Smith. And I learned to reverence Brigham Young and a host of other men and women, great souls who seemed made "to match these mountains" (and still do). I got goose-bumps when I heard the Choir (Tabernacle, of course: is there any other?) sing "Let the Mountains Shout for Joy … and the Valleys sing … and be glad before the Lord." And I still do.

For it was all mixed in my mind with the religion of the people of Utah—Mormonism, with the aftermath of that event in the Sacred Grove in upstate New York, as depicted in that Ramsey painting which dominated the front of the Eleventh Ward Chapel (a part of it still hangs in the new Eleventh Ward on First South), which stood on 10th east—I wouldn't learn until I was thirteen that "Theast" wasn't another name for "Street" in Salt Lake; we would ask, "What Theast do you live on"—and get an answer). It all imparted to me a sense that this People of Utah was a chosen people who had been tried in adversity and persecution and found peace and prosperity and stability in the reaches of a desert—"freedom's last abode"— which no one else had wanted. They had put down deep roots and shot grids out to Kolob and established a Zion where people could worship as they pleased—and it pleased the vast majority of us to worship, without apology, as Latter-day Saints, to enjoy our Peoplehood, our unity, our uncommon common faith. It was from that valley, rimmed like a giant "C" with mountains, that I would go forth, in

1956, at the age of twenty, to teach the precepts of that faith to the people of Austria and Switzerland, and be an emissary of distant Utah in the tops of the mountains, a place which Isaiah had prophesied would one day be an ensign to the nations. And I would repeat the act, in 1986, going from Utah as a Mission President and Utah emissary to German Switzerland. Where I have been in this world—and I've seen much of it—it has always been as a Utahn, in the back of whose head echoed the Utah song of the Meadowlark, "Utah is a pretty-little-place." It is.

So I grew up in the Salt Lake Valley, imbued with this Mormonness, for which my four grandparents—John and Sarah Ann Holton White and George and Clara Louisa Williams Cracroft—had left England, and imbued with my native Utah provinciality, as one who always thought of Utah not as a dry and dreary desert but as perfect place to live, "high on the mountain top." It was, after all, to those mountains and their delicious canyons that the Cracroft/White families fled, regularly, of a summer's evening. Mother would "cook a roast," with all the trimmings, pack it up, and Dad would load it all in the Chrysler or Dodge and we would hie for Kolob—usually Mill Creek or Big Cottonwood Canyon—and a picnic table by the stream, which I would use to cool the submersed watermelons and, after dinner, to float ships made of watermelon rinds, propelled by elastic-driven paddles and toothpick-masted sails. It was to these same mountain canyons that my friends and I would hie, searching the old water cave up Dry Canyon above Federal Heights and the mausoleum, or sneaking over the mountain and down into forbidden Red Butte Canyon, where we would camp overnight, subsisting on slaughtered porcupine (which we enthusiastically and falsely pronounced "delicious"), on C-Rations or other military canned goods bought for nine cents a can from surplus stores on State Street. At the end of long mountain hikes to Pinecrest, above Mountain Dell Reservoir, or overnight campouts in Parley's we would swim in dammed-up streams on the Fort Douglas Reservation (about where the University Park Hotel stands today), or in forbidden Mt. Olivet reservoir, or in Parley's Creek (below Hogle Zoo). Somehow, skinny-dipping, a term unheard of then, made it all more delicious (until I jumped in atop a broken Coke bottle and spent the summer of '50 on crutches). And I haven't even begun to recall the scout trips into the Uintahs—to Mirror, Spirit, or Moon Lakes, or the bird-watching excursions into the marshes and bayous of the Great Salt Lake or far up City Creek Canyon.

In the winter we fled the smoky inversions of the valley for the glorious blue skies above Brighton or Alta, skiing on $2.50 day passes—Alta was always more expensive—and a quarter for a bowl of chili, or overnighting at Kenneth Smith's cabin (Ken was in the ecclesiastical possession) next to the T-Bar run (today's Majestic) at Brighton; and in the summer hiking to Silver Lake. The canyons around Salt Lake City framed my youth—and still beckon to me with their offer of "wondrous cool/Thou woodland quiet/Thee a thousand times I greet/Far away from rush and riot/Ah, thy soothing sounds are sweet"—words we sang in *a capella* at East High, under the batons of Miss Lisle Bradford and Miss Lorraine Bowman, who taught generations of Utahns to sing "our mountain home so dear."

So, working my (half-aware) way from Wasatch School (Mrs. Una Smirthwaite, Miss Sessions, Miss Gesselman, Miss Starr); to Douglas (Miss Crow, Mrs. Jensen); to (now awakening a bit) Roosevelt Jr High (Miss Zimmerman, Mr. Robinson, Mrs. Kramer, Mr. Merrill, Mr. Tanner, Mr. Smith, Mr. Kartchner, Miss Rappaport); to (wide-awake) rich days at East high, and real imagined football glories (coached by Tally Stevens and Don Jespersen) and singing (with Miss Bradford, Miss Bowman), to tasting learning (from the likes of Miss Shannon, Mr. Zarr, Miss Van Pelt, Mr. Bennett, Miss Gorlinski, Mr.

Glendon Iverson, Dr. Fred Arbogast, Miss Tregeagle, and Mr. Gilbert); to discovery at the University of Utah (with explorers such as Dr. Durham, Dr. Folland, Dr. Chapman, Dr. Don D. Walker, Dr. Clapp, Dr. Adamson, Dr. Snow, Dr. Slager, Dr. Webb, Dr. Sturges, Dr. Miller, and a dozen others)—through these various Utahns I unfolded, awakened to awareness and adulthood and appreciation—each contributed enhancing brush-strokes to my composite portrait of growing up Utahn—a portrait which has been refined and polished by my teaching career of more than three decades at Brigham Young University, itself a noble institution entwined, since 1876, in the history of Utah, and, forever, in my soul.

All of these men and women and institutions are joined in my Utah composite by my unabashedly pro-Utah mother, Grace Darling White and my rabidly Utahn and estimable father, Ralph, my bright and articulate brothers Laurance W. and R. Paul, and their wives, Kathryn Davis and Kathryn Storrs, and my wonderful sister and her husband, Helen Grace Cracroft White and John L. White, and my unforgettable maiden aunts-*cum*-mothers, Cicely J. White and Florence G. White, both of whom served as secretaries to some of Utah's great men—all of these became essential parts of my Utah of "that child that went forth every day"—all of them have contributed to the mosaic that made growing up in Utah very special to me.

It was special. And it was special in similar yet very different ways for my favorite Utahn, favorite wife, and best friend, Janice Marie Alger Cracroft (born 1937), whose Sunnyside-Price-Carbon County upbringing, with its cosmopolitan composition of race and religion, makes her particular Utah like mine in many respects, but with a unique ethnic cast that has enriched her vision with some tones and shades muted in mine.

But it all spells U T A H. "Far in the glorious West/ Framed on the mountain crest/In robes of statehood dressed/Utah we love thee." It still isn't glorious poetry,

but as I write this I look from my window here in Prove to Mt. Timpanogos, and the snow shining on its summits and western slopes in the late afternoon sun, framed against a rich blue sky, and I realize that, after all, my feelings for this special place that is Utah are ineffable. "Utah, we love thee" will have to do. For now.

I dedicate this essay to our children, natives of Utah Valley: sons Richard Alger Cracroft and Jeffrey Ralph Cracroft, and our late and sorely-missed daughter, Jennifer Cracroft Lewis (1968–1994).

"Mike Andersen," submitted by Julie Andersen, Cache County.

Annette Larsen Proulx
Salt Lake County

Age 43; **Birthplace** Salt Lake City; **Occupation** Secretary/ Homemaker; **Religion** LDS; **Race/Ethnicity** White

I still remember believing that a hot summer day would never end, and that the cobalt blue sky that reached from Monticello to Tremonton, and back again, was created just for my friends and me. We would stop in delight when we heard a meadowlark call, "Utah is a pretty little place." We knew that, and we appreciated the fact that the much travelled birds knew it, too. We kids would run joyfully through the field next to my house and chase the garden snakes that slithered from the muddy irrigation ditch to the west. We never knew from year to year which cash crop would be grown in the field; but our favorites were wheat and alfalfa. The wheat was great, because the field smelled so good after a sudden summer shower; but we equally loved the alfalfa because it was so much fun to chase the thousands of tiny white butterflies that always hovered over the delicate purple flowers. I remember feeling like Maurice Abravanal as I attempted to conduct the symphony which was created by the bullfrogs and katydids that serenaded us from the creek which bordered the field. There was no doubt about it. Utah, in 1960, was the best place in the world for an eight-year old child to grow up. I was one of the lucky ones.

Dad and Mom built their first and only home in the growing town of Midvale as part of the movement to settle away from the "big" city of Salt Lake. My earliest memories include the very sleepy little city that we called "Down-town." By 1960, Midvale had already long since reached its peak, and the down town area on Main Street was starting to get very sleepy. That had not always been the case, however. Long before my time, Midvale was the bustling junction of the south end of the county. It connected Salt Lake City with the agriculture lands to the south, with the mining concerns to the west, and the poultry farms to the east. Midvale was known for its fine stores, entertainment, and good job market. Like I said, however, that was before my time.

As a child, I remember going to what was left of "downtown" with my parents to make purchases at one of the two 5 and 10 cent stores, and to buy school clothes at J.C. Penneys. That was before the first shopping malls were built, or before the freeway blocked off 6th Avenue, which connected State Street to the east, to downtown Main Street. In those days, before the advent of the modern new Arctic Circle, a real treat was a chocolate malt at Vincent's Drug.

I grew up believing that when God created the world, he saved Utah for last because he wanted Utah to be the showplace for the rest of the world. I would guess that by the time that I was 12, I had seen the entire state. Aside from our yearly vacations, every autumn, during the school break of UEA, we would load up our car and head to a different scenic point of Utah. I hiked under Delicate Arch, and stood on a ledge at Dead Horse Point, and imagined that I could fly. I hiked to the top of Doughnut falls, and felt the spray of Big Cottonwood Creek wash over my body. I remember positioning myself, so that I could be in four states at the same time, and had my picture taken with an old Indian on the Ute reservation.

I learned to ski on "the greatest snow on earth," and thrilled as we tubed on the Weber River, or hiked to Lake Mary in the Wasatch Mountains. I remember walking through the ghost town of Standardville, in Carbon County, and singing to the ghosts, from the town's gazebo, that was practically all that was left of the once bustling mining town.

In 1960 Utah was still pretty much unknown to the rest of the world. Park City was a run down, mass of empty buildings, not a posh ski resort, beckoning people from all over the world. Highways 89 and 91 were the main thoroughfares through the State, and the towns on their routes flourished with farming, agriculture and various enterprises. My little town of Midvale, and my state as a whole were about to see significant changes. The freeway, bypassing many of the little towns to the south, eventually cut them off from tourist and travel trade. The old town of Midvale became practically non existent as large shopping centers and fast food establishments grew away from the old run-down city.

And my field … My field soon gave way to a large new meeting house for the Church of Jesus Christ of Latter-day Saints. Change is good, but it is so hard to watch. The tall spire, soon blocked my view of Mt. Majestic, and the smell of fresh mown alfalfa, or wet wheat was replaced by the noxious odor of cars in the church parking lot.

But change, as I said is good. Our little southern Utah towns are again awakening, as "out-of-staters" from all over the country have heard about the wonders of Utah, and have chosen to make it their home. My "old run-down" city of Midvale has also found new growth, as it is being refurbished and remodeled with an Old Town motif.

I miss the quaint old Utah that I grew up with, but I truly love the Utah that I enjoy now. Entrepreneurs, careful not to detract from the charm that Utah has always held, offer its beauties to the world. During the next few years, people from all over the world may have the opportunity to know and love Utah also, as we look toward the prospect of hosting the 2002 Olympics, and past that, towards the future of our State. Knowing the people of Utah, I know that we are up to the challenge.

Elaine Heaton Hoyt
Kane County

Age 67; **Birthplace** Kanab, Kane County, Utah; **Occupation** Retired Housewife; **Religion** Church of Jesus Christ of Latter-day Saints; **Race/Ethnicity** White

Because I was born and raised here!! It has been a pretty good 66½ years!

I was born of goodly parents. May 30, 1928. They were George Earl and Jennie Palmer Heaton. My mother was in Kanab, Kane Co., at a midwife's home.

Then we went home to a small hamlet in the mountains of Long Valley, Alton—nestled under the Pink Cliffs—over the hill west of Bryce Canyon.

As a child and teen we lived the summer in a place called "Rush" a beautiful meadow just below "the Pinks."

I remember my father loading the children, on "Ol'" Dick, the horse—walking and leading him and his precious load up on East Fork to fish. A willow, a string, and hoop worm served as equipment—they nearly alway had a fish meal in the evening—and saw many interesting things—

We milked cows by hand. We took milk to town, every other day—then the U.S. Mail delivered it to Panguitch to the Cheese factory.

Dad piped water from a spring to a cool house—He fixed a place to immerse 10 gal. cans into the water, and they were made stationery by the handles, in a frame. It was icy-cold. We could even set jello on a shelf above the water. The water ran in and out. That's where we got our drinking water and carried water to heat.

We lived in a small lumber cabin, and a wood floor and frame with a canvas tent stretched over.

There was a huge rock just east of the cabin—many is the time I climbed up to read a book, or survey the beautiful scene—Quaken aspen, meadow, and hills. The cave (sand) to the south and up the canyon always made a good play house—screened by maple trees. It was an easy place to leave our mark too.

Well I remember the "Ol' Cook Stove" a warming oven on top—the fire box oven and resevoir to fill and heat water in.

Many is the morning I remember waking to the smell of quaken aspen smoke.

———

When I went to the Elementary-room-school in Alton, we had 4 grades in each.

At recess in the winter (some winters we walked over the fences to school) we could make it up the road—to what we called "the twin pines," the road west between— and sleigh ride into the school yard before the bell rang.

In the fall of 1940, I boarded the first school bus to go to Orderville to Valley High. I was a mighty 7th grader.

In the eighth-grade I went to Kanab and lived with my Aunt. It was there in the old high school building we sat in the gym, and listened to President Roosevelt announce that we had entered World War II!!

Then in ninth grade back to Valley. Our school spirit was great—though a small school—we had good teachers—and did well in sports—Still do!!

I graduated High School in May 1946. That fall I married Dilworth Hoyt.

"Dill" worked in the coal mine, in the timber and with sheep—and was a good trapper on the side. This was when trapping was in Vogue.

We added 3 children to the 2 that he brought into our family when we married—All 5 graduated from Valley High School. One has moved and raised his family in Merced, Calif. One went to help my Sister in Nampa, ID. Met a soldier—so they went to Philadelphia, PA and have raised their children there.

We had—5 that turned to 10 children with spouses, 25 that turned to 36 Grand Children and spouses, so far

16 Great Grandchildren, Bless them all!!
We Love them! …

———

Our home burned in Alton on January 31, 1974. We found just how many friends you do have at a time like this. The whole County rallied to help us. We are thankful for our [friends] in Glendale.

Dill passed away May 2, 1990—after living the most part of his life in Utah! He was in the Pacific during part of World War II.

My family and neighbor friends are still taking care of me.

One thing is that it is fairly hard to find employment down here and now Kaibab is closing. …

Marlene Durham Pinkney
Salt Lake County

Age 63; **Birthplace** Delta, UT (Entire Lifetime in SLC); **Occupation** Writer, Interior Design; **Religion** N/A; **Race/Ethnicity** White

A Light-hearted Remembrance of Downtown Salt Lake City

ITEM: Architects Study Latest Move in Unlocking Downtown's future…the block (57) should be a unique centerpiece of a revitalized downtown that will attract people to the city." *The Salt Lake Tribune,* 4/10/88

"You can forget all your troubles, forget all your cares, just go DOWNTOWN-N-N," sang Petula Clark some twenty years ago. Will another siren song lure us again "downtown," or is the heart of the city altered and forsaken beyond recall? Main Street is now quiet, State Street is largely given to boarded windows and panhandlers.

Native Salt Lakers, growing up in the 'Forties and

'Fifties, remember other sights, sounds and even SMELLS of the city. There is a sense of deja-vu, brought on by a certain essence, transporting us instantly to another time, another place. An aroma can still waft us back to the days when we loved to go downtown.

MOLASSES was the mouth-watering emanation from the confectionery next to the Rialto Theatre near Third South on Main. I often stood outside its window, nine-years-old and goggle-eyed at the flailing steel arms of the taffy machine, endlessly weaving up ropes of warm candy.

"ARPEGE" fragrance evokes the two black-haired, elaborately coiffeured sisters who reigned for many years over the Auerbach's department store cosmetics counter. For teenage shoppers in ponytails and Tangee "universal orange" lipstick, these women were the epitome of exotic beauty. They are still mind-images, conjured by a hint of imported perfume in the air.

ETHER and MENTHOL combined in a medicinal pungency pervading the Boston Building at Exchange Place and Main, where many of the City's medical practitioners were officed. Countless young patients breathed gut-wrenching whiffs of dread as they trudged past the pharmacy counter to waiting elevators which carried them upstairs, to their doom, TO THE DENTIST!

BUTTERED POPCORN can create an aura plunging us back to a Saturday morning when fifteen cents would admit one child to "THE POPEYE CLUB," a five-hour film extravaganza dear to the hearts of most city kids. From the packed main floor of Main Streets' Utah Theatre, we bulged into the balcony's highest reaches, cheering as Bugs Bunny and Elmer Fudd overpowered cartoon Hitlers and Tojos. Cheering again as Buck Rogers, space-bound in his tin-can rocketship, overpowered Emperor Ming. And cheering yet louder as John Wayne and John Payne overpowered Erich von Stroheim, the perennial celluloid Nazi.

In culmination of the day's entertainment, a spotlight would blaze through the darkness, and Charlie Pinkus,

combination theater manager, ticket-taker, bouncer and emcee, appeared on the proscenium. After furiously cranking a drum filled with ticket stubs, he would finally extract the lucky ducat to be declared "winnah" of the week's coveted Schwinn one-speed bicycle.

CIGAR SMOKE, reeking to the sidewalk, announced the "Mint Cafe" on Second South near Richards Street. No women or children in *this* macho sanctum, where our dads and their downtown office cronies met for a Wednesday lunch of hot pastrami (and, it was rumored, to place a bet on a Joe Louis fight or the Brooklyn Dodgers' game). …

Architects and planners may develop and rebuild endlessly, seeking to thus "Unlock Downtown's Future," but there will always be a redolence of the city's past they cannot restore; it is locked within the memories of those who walked the bustling streets and peopled the vanished places that were "downtown."

Perry A. Peterson
Salt Lake County

Age 61; **Birthplace** Centerfield, Utah; **Occupation** Physician/Surgeon; **Religion** LDS; **Race/Ethnicity** Caucasian

It was not a pretty apple. It was a rock hard, small, red Jonathan apple with dents and brown smudges in the skin that were evidence of a life of struggle, and kept it from being chosen from the pile by fussy grocery shoppers. But the sight of it and the first flavorful bite gave my senses a powerful nudge: a flashback to age twelve and a late summer night in the little town of Centerfield, Utah in the 1940's.

Don't confuse Centerfield with Centerville. The latter we considered a big city town where people live rich, have lush, backyard vegetable gardens, and drive fancy cars. By contrast, Centerfield was 100 farm families trying to scratch out a living working poor alkaline soil with short-rationed irrigation water. It was once called Skintown, then Hardscrabble. Our postmistress, Afalone Jensen, said so. And she should know having placed in the post office boxes over the years any number of letters and mailings, purple stamped: "Missent to Centerville."

We had box 215. Into that box came all the stuff I sent for in an active probe into the world beyond our town. First there was a monthly subscription to Disney Comics—we called them "funny books"—later it expanded to jokes and magic tricks from Johnson, Smith & Co., then supplies for my chemistry set from Porter Chemical Co. in Portertown, Md., and real books from the Adventure Book Club somewhere back East. Each time something bigger than a letter came, Afalone would put a little slip of yellow paper in the box with the excitingly simple word "parcel" written on it, and we had to present this at the main window for pickup. She would always comment, "my that's a nice big package" or something like that, and it made the whole experience quite special.

Our postmistress wasn't the only one with the name Jensen. This was a Danish, Mormon town. My neighbors were people like Ole Larsen, Chris Peter Jensen, Soren Peter Sorensen, Alfred Westlund, Alexus Jensen, Amanda Fjeldsted, Thaddeus Hansen, and Andersen, Petersen, Olsen, Lund, Madsen, Christensen, and on and on. They're all gone now, but their children and the kids of those children are still around. Many of them still in Centerfield.

I was born in this town and grew up here. There wasn't a day when I didn't look up, at least once, at the mountains to the East where Old Mt. Baldy and Musinea peak marked their indelible outline on the horizon and on my mind. (For apparent reasons, Musinea was referred to by the locals as "Mary's Nipple.") The dusty fields and occasional old house in the forefront of this view were also part of the daily vista. That was where grandma Christensen lived. I would stop at her house on the way home from grade school for bread and honey, and a glass of homemade barley beer she'd bring up from the cellar.

Grandma was born here in this town too, in the same old house up on the farm where my mother was born. Her grandfather converted to Mormonism in Denmark in 1853, and came here in one of the first groups of handcart pioneers. He fought Indians in Ephraim, and the Blackhawk war in Sevier, and had helped establish the town of Sterling before moving to Centerfield at the young age 85 to retire and start homesteading a farm. He lived to within weeks of 100, and so did my Grandma—all in the same town. Talk about roots; that means six generations of us lived in the same home town. Most of *my* generation were encouraged to leave for college and better jobs. At high school graduation we got gifts of luggage, and were expected to use them. I did.

That little apple sure brought back memories: My paternal Grandma lived in-between Centerfield and Gunnison in a little frame house with a barn and orchard in back. The area was called Hamilton and the old Mormon Hamilton Ward house was across the street, where an occasional car passed, on highway 89. That summer night some boys and I were playing bicycle tag with the whole town as our playing field. We had been on our bikes coming home from the early show at the Star Theater in Gunnison—fourteen and under: 10 cent—and stopped in Grandma's yard to eat apples in the dark. There was an old Jonathan apple tree there that had the hardest, tartest, best tasting apples ever. I'm sure some pioneer had planted it, but she outlived it. When they stopped irrigating the lots in town most of the backyard trees died.

I'm still living in Utah. I feel comfortable with these mountains and barren valleys, some of which are now filled with cities. I've never regretted being a part of the "big city" of Salt Lake, but the wonderful memory of growing up "out in the sticks" will always be a priceless legacy. In spite of periods of adventure, living for a while in Europe, the

Far East, Canada, and in the tropics, I always came back to my home state. I guess what draws me is the small town pioneer heritage and those hard, struggling, little Jonathan apples.

Amelia A. Bennion
Salt Lake County

Age 76; **Birthplace** Bennington, Bear Lake, Idaho; **Occupation** Retired; **Religion** Latter Day Saints, **Race/Ethnicity** Caucasian (English and Scandinavian)

Living in Utah means nostalgia of a happy childhood. The sketch attached represents just one of those many precious years:

"WHO PLANTED THE WATER CRESS?"

"Put on your jacket, and if you like, we'll go for a little walk up the canyon," my mother announced one spring morning.

I ran to fetch a sweater; my enthusiasm matched any other ten-year-old, eager to abandon chores for fun outdoors. As we went along together, I wondered how my mother knew I had spring fever. Did she have it, too?

We paused here and there to admire bits of green sprouting up along the country road—shared that unexplainable magic of being young. I danced two steps ahead, and it was as though my mother had abandoned all *her* cares, for we walked almost a mile up East Mill Creek Canyon to a small cove. The stream of mountain water was dangerous during spring runoff, so we found a safe spot along the creek bank, while my mother renewed her strength. Unlike my father and brothers, who always carried fishing poles, we just sat together, listened to sounds of the rushing water, and gazed up at the surrounding mountains. Not a care in the world!

"I brought a little bucket, in case we find some water cress," Mama said. She searched along the edge of the stream where water splashed over larger rocks, forming a shallow pool with a sandy creek bottom—a growing place covered with moss.

"Here's some cress," Mama shouted above the roar. "Hold onto me and I'll pick a bunch." Excited over our first find, we soon had a good supply.

"Manna from Heaven!" Mama declared. (I'm certain she told me about picking water cress with her mother and how pioneer great grandmothers travelling across the plains sought greens at fresh springs to supplement their meager diets—how grateful they were for the canyon streams surrounding the valley.)

At home the cress was washed, salted, and put between slices of bread—mama's freshly-baked bread, spread with margarine she had artificially colored yellow to substitute for butter. Reluctant at first to sample the green "weed," I soon discovered taste for such a treat.

Today, whenever I see cultured water cress in the market, I think of our canyon walk; I remember how carefree my mother was recalling her own childhood that day, when, actually, these were devastating times for parents all over the nation in *1930*. Because I was a child, I was spared the hardships—allowed to take for granted my needs. I didn't ask who had planted the water cress, nor how it came to be along the creek bed, for the beauty of growing up in Utah meant learning about Pioneers and, yes, taking for granted a heritage of "manna" from Heaven.

Submitted by Megan Little, Cache County.

Eldon Leon Miller

Carbon County

Age 65; **Birthplace** Sandy, Utah; **Occupation** Retired School Teacher; **Religion** L.D.S.; **Race/Ethnicity** Caucasian

REFLECTIONS OF A COAL CAMP KID

I have lived from the extremes of Alpine on the north to Cedar City on the south. I have spent over 30 years in a two-season area of California and a little over a year in green Pennsylvania, Japan, China, and Korea was my residence while in the army. But my fondest memories are of Utah. Southeastern Utah to be exact. My youth was spent living in nine of Carbon County's communities and one of Emery County—Clawson, my favorite. But my reflections are to dwell on one of the six coal camps that I lived in during the years of 1938 to 1941. To begin with let me say that my father was a frustrated farmer. He had worked in the coal mines since he was 14 years old. His ambition was to make a living at farming and so when the mines slowed down in the summer we would find ourselves in Emery County, except for two years in Alpine. I never spent a full school year in any one school and one year I was in three different schools. I'd start the school year, usually in Ferron Elementary and then Pa would get a job in one of the nearby coal mines and we would move there until the following spring or early summer and away to the farm we'd go. I loved Clawson, and I loved Spring Canyon, and I loved Hiawatha, but that town came later. Spring Canyon is the subject of my reflections.

Utah's coal camps were unique in many ways but one of the most obvious was the town site layout. Most of the camps were settled as close to the mine as practical. The coal seams were on a horizontal plane and so the mines had openings like a tunnel into the side of the mountains. The mountains of Carbon County are rather steep and so the campsites were set up in as convenient an area as possible. Many towns would be divided up into miniature communities since the areas large enough to build houses on were small and so it was not uncommon to find four, five, or even more sections of the coal camp scattered along the more accessible areas of a canyon side. The larger area would usually be designated "town." The community buildings such as the post office, company store, church(es), community amusement center, boarding house, and the most popular building, the confectionery, was located.

Most of the other sections contained homes only. These sections of the camp were called by names such as Greek Town, Jap Town, or Tent Town, Around the Bend, Tennis Court, String Town, Tram Town. The names are rather obvious. Each section had their own click that they were loyal to. The boys tended to run in gangs and they had much competition, usually friendly ball games, etc. Sometimes one boy would form a grudge with a boy from another section of town and then the competition might not be so friendly for a time. I remember being picked on by a few of the "Tent Town Tigers" when I first moved to Spring Canyon. I was a new comer and I lived Around the Bend, Later on I moved to Tent Town and I became a leader of that "gang."

Price is the County Seat and the largest city. Helper, the next largest city was the railroad center. The kids from the camps were considered not as tough as the Helper boys, and the Price boys were the toughest of all, at least in our minds. Whenever we would thumb a ride to Helper it was the wise thing to let the Helper kids that approached you know that you were from Price. If your bluff worked they were friendly otherwise you'd find yourself being bullied something fierce.

I remember an incident that happened on one such occasion. An older boy and I had had some luck in gathering up some beer bottles that we could collect the deposit on. We decided to take them to Helper and to go to the matinee at one of the two theaters. We thumbed a ride to the upper end of Helper and as we were walking down to the Rainbow Inn to cash in our bottles we were met by four or five Helperites. They guessed what we had in our sacks and proceeded to try and convince us that they could get more money out of the bottles than we could, if we would let them do such a kindness for us. We thought we'd forego their "kind" offer and to our surprise they let us go. After we got our money we thought we had better get back home just in case. Sure enough our friends appeared again and offered to help us spend the money. As the discussions progressed they became a little more insistent and so we decided that it might be time to hurry on our way and so we took off running. This decision erased all doubt from their minds that they could get our money by guile. They chased us for a couple hundred yards and we dashed into Fabrizio's store the last refuge in town. Mrs. Fabrizio, a small featured lady noticed our anxiety and when we told her our story, she stormed through the front door and with a few choice words had the Helper boys away from there in a hurry. We thanked her and hurried on up the canyon road to the safety of our little coal camp. Fruit in the coal camps was always at a premium. Those few fruit trees in or around the camps were hardly ever allowed to fully ripen. It seemed that we all felt if we didn't get there first we wouldn't get any and so as soon as the least color change would occur, off and down it would go.

But there were times when the best fruit in the world would appear on the scene. It was not often that a stranger in town was taken much notice of. There were times though when an out of town person would show up that all the kids would try to be the first to win his favor. The fruit peddler. Now some peddlers wouldn't let us kids within twenty yards of his vehicle. They had had experiences with some of us before. No peddler would, by choice, come into the camps alone. It would take at least one person to take a sample of the fruit from house to house and another man to stay with the truck. If a peddler was alone and had no one to watch the truck for him, he would then be forced to "hire" some of the kids to do his soliciting. If the boys did especially well and the peddler had a good day there was always the possibility of a nickel or two in addition to the promised fruit for payment. In those days a penny was rather difficult to come by and so most boys would vie for the job and then run their, already ragged tennis shoes off to please the vendor. Actually, as I recall, it was rather fun to peddle fruit. It kinda made you feel grown up and you really took notice of the younger kids look at you with not a little envy.

The owners were known as "The Company." The company occasionally furnished the goodies for special events, such as Christmas and Labor Day. One Labor Day the activities culminated with a watermelon bust.

The company had brought in a truck load of Green River watermelons. These are the sweetest melons available to mankind. We boys had been ogling them all afternoon. The "Bust" was held just after dark on a flat area on the side of the canyon near town. A couple of the boys were a little more greedy than the rest of us and had worked up enough nerve to help them selves to two of the melons. Not having any way to hide them they had rolled them down the side of the hill. Out of sight of the big bon fire we'd assembled around. The word had been passed around to a few of the "in" boys and so we decided we had better not eat a whole lot at the bust since there were two big melons awaiting us just out of sight of the bon fire. Imagine our disappointment when we couldn't find them later in the dark. The next morning we hurried to the site with much anticipation. There to our dismay we found what was left of them at the bottom of a ledge, Apparently they had picked up enough momentum to carry them over. Crime just doesn't pay!

The coal camps were fine educational facilities. I felt I was a member of one big family. I may not have realized it fully at the time, but ethnic and cultural associations were a tremendous asset to me. We were all just people with common weaknesses and strengths. There were those that were super ball players. I envied them. There were those that seemed to have special personalities. I wanted to be like them. There were those that had some weaknesses. I was like them too. My memories are a monument to those many wonderful people who lived, loved, worked, and played as a community made up of the ethnic strains that have made America such a unique and great country. That has made Carbon County a unique and great county.

That is what living in Utah means to me. Utah, I love thee!

Raymond S. Uno
Salt Lake County

Age 65; Birthplace Ogden, Utah; Occupation Retired District Court Judge; Religion N/A; Race/Ethnicity Japanese

Living in Utah means to me opportunity. Opportunity for a first class education, challenging employment, healthy family life, cultural enrichment, unlimited recreational activities, and much more.

Although born in Ogden, Utah (in a Yellow Cab whose driver is my namesake), my family moved to El

Monte, California around 1936. This move was the beginning of a series of unforgettable life shaping experiences.

The first was being enrolled in a segregated public school in El Monte, California called Lexington. It consisted of about five hundred or more Hispanics and twenty five or so Asians. Then, several years later, the wrenching episode of the entire family being uprooted from our home and sent to the Pomona Assembly Center, Pomona, California because of the attack on Pearl Harbor and the declaration of war against Japan. From there, we were forcibly removed by troop train to Heart Mountain, Wyoming, one of America's infamous concentration camps. Next, catastrophic tragedy struck. It was one of the most traumatic events of my life, the sudden and premature death of my father less than a year after we were incarcerated.

There was irony in my father's death. He served in the U.S. Expeditionary Forces in France, was a naturalized American citizen, an active member of the American Legion, a member of the El Monte and Wyoming draft boards and assisted in administration of the interned Japanese. The American Legion was one of the most powerful voices crying out for the removal of the Japanese from the West Coast. Yet, the American Legionaries from Cody and Powell as well as from Heart Mountain joined in giving my father a military funeral. Under these peculiar circumstances, it was probably the only one of its kind during the war.

My father's death marked the last time our family lived together as a family unit. Our family relocated back to Ogden, Utah in 1945. My mother and sister lived together at Esther Hall a Methodist Women's dormitory in Ogden, Utah where my mother was lucky to get a job as a cook and housekeeper. My brother and I lived together at a family friend's house behind 25th Street in Electric Alley. He was later inducted into the service and left for overseas to Japan.

At age fifteen, living alone with an aged couple, was the introduction to my streetwise education. I went to work at a cannery in Roy, got a job as a gandy dancer on an extra gang for the Union Pacific Railroad working out of Palisades, Nevada for the summer of 1946. Then went from Central Junior High to Ogden High School. The summer of 1947, I worked again for the U.P. Railroad on a Section out of Ogden at the age of sixteen.

I graduated from Ogden High in 1948. During my two years at Ogden High, my football and wrestling coach, Cluff Snow, helped turn my life around. He made me learn discipline and competitiveness. This helped me for the rest of my life. After graduation, I volunteered for the Army and thanks to the excellent education I received at Ogden High School, I was able to graduate from the Military Intelligence Language School. Thereafter I was sent to Japan and worked in Military Intelligence and Counter Intelligence and was given an involuntary extension during the Korean War. I was discharged in 1952.

My unexpectedly fruitful educational opportunities in Utah started after my discharge. I enrolled at Weber Junior College with my G.I. Bill in 1952. I transferred to the University of Utah in 1953 but got my Associate Degree from Weber College in 1954 and my Political Science degree from the U in 1955. I enrolled in Law School thereafter and graduated in 1958. Continued on with school and got my secondary teaching certificate and went to work for the State Welfare Department as a caseworker. I received a stipend to go to the Graduate School of Social Work and received my Masters in Social Work in 1963.

Thereafter started my opportunities for challenging employment. After my graduation in 1963, I was committed to repay my stipend to the State of Utah, so I got employment as a Referee of the Juvenile Court. From there I became a Deputy Salt Lake County Attorney, Assistant Utah Attorney General and subsequently went into private practice for about seven years.

In 1976, I was appointed a Salt Lake City Court Judge. From there, by statute, I became a Utah State Circuit Court Judge in 1978. In 1984, I ran for and was elected a 3rd District Court Judge and retired in 1990 and became a Senior Judge. At the present time, I am called to hear cases upon Court Administrator's request.

In many of my various educational and employment endeavors, I was among the first or the first Asian or Minority. It was a real challenge to break the race barrier with no or very few role models. These various experiences were intertwined with my love for politics. In 1968, I was asked by the Democratic Party to run against W. Hughes Brockbank in Senate District 1 for the state senate because they could not field a candidate since Hughes was considered unbeatable in a traditional Republican area. Out of over 20,000 votes, I lost by around 300 votes, a definite moral victory. Thereafter, I enjoyed serving on many county and state committees and positions for the Democratic Party.

In addition, community service had many open doors. Because of the tumultuous times and the civil rights movement, I became enmeshed in many movements. I had the opportunity, pleasure and arduous task of serving on many committees, boards, and working with loads of civic, service and other community organizations as well as federal, state, county, city and other local agencies.

Somehow, sandwiched in between, was my family life. Rearing of five sons, sending them through school, helping them in their various activities and employment, was fulfilling and scary. In addition, I had the rare chance to be the home for my mother for whom I am now a caregiver. Living at my home, she has had the joy, challenge and hardwork of being a grandmother to five boys. She came from a well-to-do family in Japan, graduated from the Japan's Women's University in Tokyo, was school teacher in Japan and taught Japanese part-time in the United States. These experiences and her lifetime of working hard and keeping active has blessed her with a long life. She will be 101 on March 1, 1995. She may go on for a few more years. I have been fortunate to have her with me for over thirty five years. She still has a few good years left (see plate 22).

To keep me as young as possible and healthy, too, recreational activities have always been available. Football, baseball, boxing, judo, basketball, chess, bridge, ping-pong, swimming, tennis, skiing, dancing, going to Wendover and Las Vegas have helped keep my body and mind in shape. A lot of travel over the years has opened my horizons to other places and other times.

The exposure to all things has meant meeting a lot of wonderful people and making great friends. There are so many other intangibles that escape my mind, but are there.

Yes, Utah has meant opportunity. And, believe me, I have taken advantage of as many as my mind, body, and soul have allowed. And, as long as I live, I intend on accepting the opportunities and challenges that living in Utah has provided. Thank you Utah, I love you.

"Utah State University Campus." Submitted by Dave Neiswender, Cache County.

Noble Langton Chambers

Cache County

Age 90; **Birthplace** Smithfield, Utah; **Occupation** Retired;
Religion LDS; **Race/Ethnicity** White

To me, living in Utah means to be living in the best place in the world to realize the American dream. … This

is demonstrated in many areas of our community life. I will mention just one area and relate it to Cache Valley (which is most familiar to me); … I refer to the great number of volunteer programs serving the needs of the valley. I will briefly give the story of just one.

In the summer of 1948, L. Boyd Hatch was visiting the home of his grandmother. The owner of the home operated a nursing home. He found the home to be very sub-standard and immediately went to work to do something about it. He solicited the help of his brother, Adrian Hatch, his brother-in-law, Attorney Asa Bullen and O. Guy Cardon. They soon selected twelve other community-spirited individuals to help. Within weeks, a non-profit corporation known as Sunshine Terrace Foundation was created.

In October of that year, the Foundation took over the operation of the Nibley Home which was then a nursing home operated by Cache County. There were fifteen residents at that time. In 1953, after the Budge Memorial Hospital abandoned its nurses training program, which was adjacent to the hospital, the Foundation took over the facility as the new Sunshine Terrace Nursing Home with a capacity of 80 residents.

In 1966 after the construction of a new 125 bed facility, the nursing home was moved to its present location at 225 North 200 West in Logan. Two years later another 20 beds were added. Then in 1982 plans were made to add two new wings thereby adding another 47 beds. These wings were completed in 1983, and almost immediately the extra beds were filled.

Early in 1983 the board made the decision to finish the basement floor for a day care center. This was finished early in 1984, and the Sunshine Terrace Day Care Center opened for service with a capacity of 50 clients.

Each time the board made a decision to move or to add wings, that decision was influenced by a waiting list for admission to the Terrace. Most of the time, the extra beds were filled immediately.

It has been a privilege for me to have been involved in the operation of this facility from its inception. I marvel at the dedication of the many individuals who have served as directors; for their time and means given over a period of 46 years. The community has also been very supportive. The Terrace employs 250 individuals (some of them are part-time), and two years ago ranked 258th in the state of Utah for the number of individuals employed. This year's budget is over 5 million dollars. Volunteers give approximately 4000 hours of their time each month to the Terrace.

Sunshine Terrace Nursing Home and the Day Care Center enjoy the enviable position of being ranked at the top of the industry. Each of them have received national recognition. The Terrace is a shining example of what can happen when a need is recognized and people go to work to so something about it.

The contribution of Sunshine Terrace, along with all the other volunteer programs operating in Cache Valley, certainly enhance the quality of life in our communities and create an atmosphere conducive to the realization of dreams.

.

Davis Bitton
Salt Lake County

Age 65; **Birthplace** Blackfoot, Idaho; **Occupation** Professor of History; **Religion** LDS; **Race/Ethnicity** Caucasian

The pavement was hot on the soles of my tennis shoes. That's what I was wearing while walking down the middle of Salt Lake City's Main Street. It was July. The sun was bright. I was thirsty. And I hadn't seen anything yet. Continuing right down the middle of the street, I walked long blocks, turned east, continued for many more blocks, and, exhausted, finally sat down on a dry hillside to rest.

Seventeen years old, I was marching in the centennial parade of 1947 with a troop of Explorer Scouts. Crowds of people cheered and applauded from the sideline. Early in our march, a ripple of applause greeted a motorcycle that sputtered and passed us. In its sidecar was none other than a waving, white-goateed George Albert Smith, president of the LDS Church.

As a beginning freshmen in 1948, Utah to me was Brigham Young University. I wore a beanie, learned to sing "Rise and Shout, The Cougars Are Out," and cheered a football team that fought bravely but almost always ended up the door mat of the conference. The 5,000 students included many ex-GI's. Incidentally, I also received excellent instruction, not only in my religion but also in subjects like geology and bacteriology, medieval history, astronomy and music.

Nearly a half century has passed. Utah's history has absorbed much of my time. Its schools have taught my children, its mountains have provided hiking and skiing and summer camps. At the University of Utah, I have taught cohort after cohort of wonderful students, Utahns by birth or adoption.

For three years, my wife, JoAn, and I served as volunteer guides on Temple Square, where we introduced hundreds, perhaps thousands, of tourists to handcarts, seagulls, and the Tabernacle organ and directed their attention to the state's capitol.

Utah, we love thee.

Douglas D. Alder
Washington County

Age 63; **Birthplace** Salt Lake City, Utah; **Occupation** College Professor; **Religion** LDS; **Race/Ethnicity** Caucasian

Why wasn't I born in Casablanca, or Prague, or

Odessa, or Manchester? This I wondered as I visited each of those places. History birthed me instead into Utah; my progenitors chose America from England, and Utah from Wisconsin. They were emigrants—some as early as 1847, others as late as 1900. They lived in dugouts and tents until they could better their condition.

My fourth generation father and second generation mother had wandered to Chicago where they met and married but they returned home to Utah just in time to experience the 1929 Depression. They bought a condemned pioneer home for $900. My earliest memories recall a house remodeled through their effort. I loved every corner. As a child I explored the attic to find the square nails which held the beams together; the cellar was made of stone and seemed eery. It was my assignment every night to fill the stoker with coal and remove the klinkers from the furnace. That I did, keeping a wary eye for spiders crawling on the floor joists overhead.

I was a city boy—born and bred in the capital. Oiled streets with curbs and gutters were the sign of civilization for me; I was sure that relatives living in Spanish Fork were still pioneers, not only because of the gravel roads but because they milked cows, pumped water with a hand pump and used an outdoor cranny. Instead of tipping over outhouses for fun like our country counterparts, we city boys built doodlebugs, made dugouts in vacant lots (complete with battery-run lighting systems), competed at marbles, sent away for Jack Armstrong rewards, listened to the "Green Hornet" and "The Lone Ranger," built cities with bottle caps, rode bicycles clear to Sandy, and delivered newspapers. When we chose sides to play football on the ward lawn, Vaughan Featherstone picked me even though I was a liability. He could make up for that all by himself. We all longed to buy a car and knew every make and model but Bob Williams was the only one who had one.

Growing up, I thought the capital city was the center of the universe. The trolley bus passed in front of my house and took me to the hub of downtown life. There I found the swimming pool at the Deseret Gym and the hot dog stand in the basement of ZCMI. Sometimes Dad took me to lunch at the Grabeteria, where we stood at the side counter with our foot on the shoe rail and read the newspapers tacked to the wall while eating Morrison's meat pies. Later, as a delivery boy downtown, I rode with elevator operators to offices in the Continental and Walker Banks, the Boston, Newhouse, Judge, Utah Oil, Tribune, McIntire and Medical Arts Building. For extra special treats Dad and I lunched at the Lion House where Brigham Young seemed to be just in the next room.

On other days I would slip into the elegant Hotel Utah lobby to gaze at the chandelier, listen to the pianist, and watch matronly ladies sip tea and eat cakes. On other days I attended the Tabernacle's noon concert to hear Frank Asper or Alexander Schreiner command the great organ. I was transfixed.

Even as city boys, we roamed the land. The Wigwam Scout camp drew us to Millcreek Canyon where we cooked chili in a pot for two days and it still was not done. Our bodies turned blue swimming in the cold waters of the camp's pool. We preferred the stream side, where we could swing on a rope tied to a branch of a great cottonwood tree. We hiked up Parley's canyon, into the abandoned railroad tunnel at Kimball's Junction, and explored the dilapidated buildings of the Park City ghost town. As teens we night hiked Timpanogas from the back side up "the glacier," to experience dawn from the summit. Twenty of us conquered the Uintas; we skinny dipped in a lake three times a day and climbed over huge boulders deposited by the long-dead glacier whose escarpment made the lake. Winter was our time for skiing at Brighton and then Alta—first with a rope tow and then with the luxury of a chair lift.

Schooling in the capital city was an advantage, from Arvella Brown's library hours at Hawthorne School to a real live artist, Mary Kimball Johnson at Irving Junior

High, to being in the school play at Roosevelt, to encountering J. Hazel Whitcomb in B-10 at East High. She intended her history classes as preparation for Princeton. I compromised and continued at the U. of U. where Emil Lucki, G. Homer Durham, Sterling McMurrin, Leland Cree, Henry Eyring and especially Lowell Bennion were giants. After years of graduate study in the "big time," even in Europe, these scholars still inspire me.

To my surprise, later career development years out of state turned me back to Utah, but not because the mainstream was disappointing. Quite contrary. Simply, the best opportunity, the best offer, was in Utah. So we returned, this time to the "provinces." My second quarter century was in Utah's alpine north, Cache Valley and Bear Lake. As my bride and I drove through Sardine Canyon into Cache Valley, we felt a filtering effect—smog peeled off, crowding left behind, noise forsaken. The full circle of mountains there presented a refreshed lifestyle. We could envision a fur traders rendezvous back in 1826; certainly we knew the winter crispness they felt when caching furs near Hyrum…

Logan Canyon treated us the same—another four-season wonderland: rich bronzes in the fall leaves below and bright reds near the summit. It was even more filtering. The hour drive to Bear Lake left us disconnected even more from urbanity as stone cliffs passed, then oak groves, then aspen, followed by pine and finally rock outcroppings at 8500 feet. The panorama of the lake from the overlook was simply spiritual, its silence stretching over three states with tiny specks of "civilization" dotting the level spots among the foothills. The lake crossed the Idaho-Utah boundary quite innocently, not knowing that the fictional line had any meaning.

High up on the Sweetwater hill we sat on our family-built cabin deck, listening for chipmunks or deer. The silence was sometimes broken by a semi-trailer shifting down, five miles away, or a jetliner 35,000 feet above. We studied the flight of the hawks, their glides, dives and attacks. Occasional visits from sage hens, squirrels, weasel, rabbits, porcupine, deer and elk made it clear that we were merely guests on their turf. Mice, birds, wasps defied our attempts at control. The moonless sky of August nights brought hundreds of falling stars; we counted them lying on our backs, gazing into our universe's depth, hardly remembering that cities existed.

An unexpected job change switched our family to St. George. We started over in defining Utah. This was red sand, volcanic boulders, sandstone mesas, towering white cliffs, sheer gorges—all screaming, nothing subtle. This was a landscape that commanded everything else. Communities were dwarfed by its peaks, its heat, its aridity, its sunlit blue skies day after day. Water became king. Tiny streamlets sustained pockets of green, oases that had known the Anasazi and the Paiute. We sensed our fragility and short tenure as we pondered the petroglyphs that stopped abruptly at 1300 A.D. without explanation.

Now in my third quarter century, I never tire of the beauty of weather as it caresses me daily; I stroll in its warmth, choosing to walk instead of drive, arising very early to feel the cool crispness of summer mornings while running around the stadium track, before the heat takes over by noon to command until midnight. My wife and I feel smug watching the evening TV news in the winter as Dixie's temperatures advertise our delight.

Yes, landscapes from alpine to desert and lakes to mesas are an irresistible presence in our life because we lived in Utah. The culture, however, has influenced us more. Friendship has never ceased to enrich the bonds with those we trust; they are many, not few. Our common commitments, shared values, from north to south, have made our moves simple. Utah is all one homeland. Though the scenery and land are revered, the sense of community is paramount. This is a place where people have always served, from building roads together in the 1860s to sandbagging State Street with Mayor Ted Wilson during the flood of 1983. So while the setting is ever stimulating, the real message of Utah is people, wholesome people who cooperate even though individual enterprise and creativity are also important, people who wave you on at stop signs, people who believe civility is worthwhile and picking up litter is a good idea. Sure we gripe too; sure there is some cynicism, but we get over it. It does not consume us.

I know that my good fortune of being the sixth generation in Utah means I have harvested what others planted. I realize that Utah is immensely benefitted by being part of the American Union. We Utahns must remind ourselves that our bounty is not only of our making. We are favored people, a somewhat enlightened people. We have an exciting future tumbling in on us; that's why I intended to complete my last quarter century right here in this, my home state—the beauty, the community, and the change that is Utah.

Gene Fullmer
Salt Lake County

Age 64; **Birthplace** Bingham, UT; **Occupation** Retired Rancher (Mink and Horses); **Religion** LDS inactive; **Race/Ethnicity** White

Utah has always been my home. I would not want to be anywhere else. My boxing career began here with the Golden Gloves as an Amateur, then with Marv Jensen as a pro. After winning the World Middle-Weight title in Jan. 1957 in N.Y., I returned home to Utah and was welcomed by over 40,000 people in Salt Lake City (see plate 27). A thrill I will never forget. My Utah fans were wonderful. I was married to Dolores Holt for 28 years until she died of a massive heart attack Jan. 1983. We had 4 children that we will always be proud of: Kaye, Delaun, Bart and Marianne. From them there are 8 grandchildren. Karen has 2. In Aug

1983 I was introduced to Karen Davey in St. George. We dated by phone until we were married May 19, 1984. Utah has been my life. I raised Mink for years and had several other businesses that have enabled me to retire early to enjoy my horses, pigs, and grandkids. Life doesn't get any better than this. I've loved the mountains, deserts, and valleys all my life. I live on the land I grew up on. Karen and I look forward to many more wonderful years together here in Utah.

Lucy Chamberlain Parr
Salt Lake County

Age 75; **Birthplace** Kanab, Kane Co., UT; **Occupation** Homemaker/Writer; **Religion** Latter-day Saint; **Race/Ethnicity** Caucasian

Living in Utah means that I have the privilege of continuing to build on the great heritage that my Mormon Pioneer ancestors bestowed upon their descendants. My great-grandparents, Israel Hoyt and Clarissa Amanda Miller, their parents, and other family members, were in the Jedediah M. Grant wagon train. They arrived in Salt Lake Valley in October, 1847.

They had a part in settling the Salt Lake Valley. Then were called to settle Salt Creek (Nephi) while Indians were a great danger. They were sent on to the Muddy Mission in Southern Nevada, then to Long Valley in Kane County. Here they helped establish Mr. Carmel and the Orderville United Order, the most successful of all the Latter-day United Orders.

My Esplin, Chamberlain, and Carroll ancestors had similar experiences; also helping to found Tooele, Provo, and Heber City. All came together through the Orderville United Order. So I have strong ties with much of the State of Utah, from its earliest history.

On July 24, 1924, my twin sister (Lillian) and I were born at our Grandmother Chamberlain's home in Kanab, Kane County. This home now is "the Heritage House."

Living in Utah means a joyous childhood, in spite of few material advantages. It is growing up in Orderville, where we associated with elderly United Order Pioneers, fascinated by their stories of love and sharing. It means shared pride and love that still exists among the descendants of these Pioneers after many generations.

It means close ties with all of the Kanab Stake communities, including Fredonia, Moccasin, and the Paiute Indian Reservation, in northern Arizona.

There are strong memories of living in Orderville during the nine school months, and at our Clear Creek ranch in the summer. It is the first day of school, with a new dress, a new teacher, and sadness that we would go to the ranch only a few times before mid-May.

Living in Utah means summer picnics in the east part of Zion National Park, just two miles from our ranch. It is memories of the construction of the "Zion-Mt. Carmel Highway," including the famous tunnel. Our father "worked on the road," providing his own team of horses, and came home with a huge check for one-hundred dollars.

It means growing up with constant hard work, with the knowledge that, for a family to survive during the Great Depression, even small children must accept a share of responsibility. But it also included breath-taking sunsets, the sweet scent of night-blooming primroses, the pungent odor of sagebrush and rabbit brush. And parents who were never too busy to take time to teach their children appreciation for the wonders of a loving Heavenly Father's creations.

It means growing up safe, encircled by the love of relatives, many levels of relationship. Almost every house was a "safe house." It means having seven Grandmas, all of whom loved us.

I learned gentleness from a strong father. I learned courage from an invalid mother, who believed that complaining didn't make pains disappear, but did make everyone else miserable. My tiny elderly grandmother taught us by example that a sense of humor can make troubles and hurts easier to bear.

A special United-Order grandfather helped to teach us that hard work is honorable. Until he was eighty-five years old, he rode his horse to the field north of town, putting in long days of work. Then, for two more years, he condescended to ride on the wagon with a grandson, and continued farm work. During the Depression, he offered work to some strong boys in town, in exchange for farm produce. They laughed at him. It was far easier to have Franklin Roosevelt's welfare truck deliver boxes of commodities to the door. *They* had whole boxes of oranges. *We* had one or two a piece on Christmas Day. It was here that I learned respect for those who work to the limit of their ability. And here that I developed a strong dislike for the Welfare Ethic that is so prevalent now.

Living in Utah also meant never quite enough water in the high-desert country, except when cloudbursts hit. We could pick up the sound and smell long before the big floods reached the part of creek that passed our garden. It was frightening as we watched huge boulders being washed downstairs, constantly deepening and changing the creek channel.

After Hoyt's house burned to the ground, bottled fruit popping like shots, almost the whole town cooperated to get the family settled into a vacant store building before dark. Food, clothing, bedding, tools, utensils were contributed. An early lesson in neighborliness that remains a part of my life.

Along with the sadness and struggles, there was laughter and fun. Locally produced plays and programs. Dances where all ages danced together. There was games and foot-races, horse-races, and story-telling around campfires.

It includes neighbor kids, sometimes four to a sled, sleigh-riding down the slope at the end of our street. The excitement of guiding the sled across the center of the wooden bridge so we didn't go off into the creek. Or pulling sleds all the way to the school hill, then evading bigger boys who attempted to "bulldog" us so we would go into the wash.

It is walking two blocks on a winter night to watch the big boys "burn the V" on the hillside behind the school buildings. Then walking home in the cold, as millions of stars almost touched the cliffs north of town.

It means being a small child in a town of around five-hundred residents; being far less skeptical of the Santa Claus fable than were children who lived in cities. (Kanab, at around fifteen-hundred, was our "city.") Even on our skimpiest Christmases, our mother would look around her family and say, "My, have you ever seen so many presents? A lot of people in the world will have nothing today." Suddenly we were rich. Rich enough to share with the large Paiute family that often came from the Moccasin Reservation. Camping above town, they came to selected homes to ask for "Kismus gifts."

Because we raised most of our food, the Depression was not as terrifying for us as it was for people in the cities. We didn't know that we were *poor,* just that we didn't have some things we would have liked. Most others in Kane County were in the same situation. There was no shame in wearing mended or obviously outgrown clothing. But it was quite another thing to be shabby or dirty in public. We had a father who wouldn't accept "Relief," but cared for his nine children and shared with others. My parents never turned a hungry person away, though Mother did keep separate "tramp dishes." These were thoroughly washed and "disinfected" in the hot sunshine for use by the next one in need. Plastic wrap and plastic bags, and other plastic and foam containers that we take for granted, had not yet been invented. Few were able to afford wax paper for general use. Clean white cloth served as sandwich wrap, and even that was scarce.

Through the years, my father gave away tons of prize watermelons, and other produce, making us feel wealthy.

Living at the ranch meant frequent summer parties— usually "corn roasts" or "melon busts"—with other ranch families within a few miles of us. It was a rare treat to have meat roasted over sagebrush or cedar-tree and pinon-pine coals—occasionally it was "government mutton" (venison).

Most summer Sundays, we went fifteen miles to Orderville for church meetings. It was a long day, starting with pre-dawn farm chores and ending with after-dark chores. At first we traveled by wagon, a choice memory of the horses' hoofs going plop-plop, clomp-clomp on the road. After the highway went through (right across the upper part of our ranch), Dad bought a second hand car. The trip took far less time, though we were much more cramped in the little car. And the journey lost the magic of starlight, crickets, and horses' hoofs.

Living in Southern Utah meant *watching out for* snakes and black-widow spiders. *Watching for* polliwogs and toads, horned toads, lizards, and bright-colored moths and cicadas before they changed to the duller adult coloring.

There were endless hours spent herding cows. Or helping to bottle, dry, or preserve the food we raised. We carried water from the spring on the hillside, and carried food to the spring tunnel to keep it cool.

We helped to haul hay—even little girls could "tromp" the hay as Dad and the boys pitched it onto the wagon. Ah—the misery of hay leaves creeping under shirts and overalls.

We fashioned an "Adam and Eve" apron from raspberry leaves, pinned together with pine needles, for our little sister. It was finished just as a car stopped out front. We ran to hide, but the pine needles prevented Ann Carroll from moving. Tourists, stopping to fill their car radiator from water in the ditch, whooped in laughter.

We searched for Indian arrowheads and bits of pottery on our knoll and Uncle Henry's. We felt a kinship for those ancient people who had camped there many generations before. We stared at the rare small plane—perhaps "Alf" Brooksby from Fredonia—that dipped and circled low to excite small children playing below.

Living in Utah means a myriad of other small memories—a combination of trivia and important situations, all a part of our lives: It is moving into our wonderful new home, with "indoor plumbing" and electricity. I was twelve years old when Orderville got its first electric plant, powered by wood and coal, and operated a minimal number of hours each day. We soon joined GarKane Power Company for full-time power.

Living in Utah meant Kane County's staunch loyalty to the Republican Party—even now. It is an election day when my grandfather was entering the polling place when met by a slovenly, careless citizen. She gloated, "You can bet *I* voted for that Franklin Roosevelt." Grandpa looked her over slowly, then answered, "I'm sure he would be right *proud* of that," and continued on his way inside to cast his straight Republican vote.

The Japanese attack on Pearl Harbor had an immediate impact on our lives. Some of the boys in our class had passed their eighteenth birthday and would soon be subject to the draft. We went to school several Saturdays to allow them to graduate with us before they went "in Service." Wartime was difficult for all of us, with word of deaths and injuries bringing grief to our "safe" valley. Boys whom we had known and loved since earliest memory were not coming home. The World had reached in and changed us.

In 1944, I accepted a job in Hollywood, California. Here I met my husband, Robert Emmet Parr, a native of Salt Lake City with early Pioneer heritage. Leaving Utah was one of the most difficult choices I've had to make. I never lost my love for Utah, and my desire to return.

While in Southern California, a relative asked me what the word "home" meant to me. My answer was: "First, it means wherever I live with my husband. Second, it means Orderville, Utah. And then it means Salt Lake City." After twenty-three years in Salt Lake City, I find that my loyalty to Northern Utah is about equal to my love of Kane County …

Kenneth H. Lambson
Washington County

Age 67; **Birthplace** Union, Utah; **Occupation** Retired (Design Engineer); **Religion** LDS; **Race/Ethnicity** Caucasian (British Isles)

Sitting here in St. George, age 67, searching for the right words to start, I choose "Dyed in-the-wool." Wherever I have worked (most of my adult life in other states) people always knew I was from Utah. …

In the army, most men would eventually talk about home. They were proud to be from New York City, or Philly, or L.A. Being Utahn seemed better to me. For one thing, most Utahns were straight shooters—in life as well as at the rifle range. In 1947 I took leave to be home for that centennial.

In 1953, married-with-children, I accepted an opportunity with Boeing in far away Seattle. Two years college had little weight. My greatest asset was the *"Utah work ethic."* My motivation was *"Family."*

My conscious memories as a child coincide with the great depression. Father had lost his job at the smelter; following that he trucked coal from Carbon county (Price, Utah) to Salt Lake valley, but his truck met a train one night in Price canyon. The truck rolled down a deep slope, during which the cab was partially collapsed. The truck burning with father trapped inside. He was able somehow to force a door open and escape. (The physical strain caused him much pain, which he never talked about). Then he lost the farm land which was mortgaged. Bankruptcy! That used to be a matter of shame.

The best hope for my pioneer ancestors was to acquire some sagebrush land for which irrigation water could be obtained. They would have to build some kind of shelter; clear away the brush; till and grade the soil. Also, there was necessity for a canal to bring water to the land. A dam would be required for diverting water from some creek. Having done all this, they could seed the ground. But there were drought years when the newly sprouted plants would wither and die. Also, the occasional plague of crickets which devoured the crops. If a bumper crop year, the market price might be less than the growing costs. Also, there was little money in circulation.

Unlike a tractor, horses must be fed all year. With no crop of hay, and lacking money to buy it, there was a no-win situation. For many, it would come down to loading what you could into the wagon(s) and driving away. All that work and privation gone with the dusty wind …

I don't use the words "Utah Work Ethic" loosely. By age 4, I had chores. There were eggs to be found; cucumbers to pick; peas to shell; whatever. Too soon I would inherit heavier duties. A worry to me, being the youngest boy. Cleaning the barn, the pigpen, the chicken coop. Killing a chicken or rabbit. Sawing the hay from the haystack, and otherwise feeding the animals. Milking our Jersey cow, weaning the calf by wetting my hand with warm milk—then leading the calf's mouth into a partial bucket of milk.

About age 8, I was chasing "Mutt," a clever horse who loved fresh peas, out of the garden. He whirled; I whirled; he kicked; I flew. Landing some 15–20 feet distant, desperate for air, I just laid there watching him savor those wonderful fresh peas. A brother came by and carried me to the house. I was breathing. No problem. No doctor. (In '39 an older brother took the horses to Wellington, Ut. He tried to farm, but he was drafted to the Army.)

We could work for the neighboring farmers. That meant thinning, later topping sugar beets. Picking up potatoes. Pitching/hauling hay. Also wheat. Most of this work meant that we would get some hay, or potatoes, or wheat.

Age 12, the paper route became a source of cash for me. I had become an independent contractor. I bought the papers, delivered them, collected from the customers, paid all my own expenses such as: rubber bands, bicycle tires and tubes, canvas bags in which to carry the papers. Neither rain, snow, ice, or zero temperatures would stay my rounds. The paper cost me 39 cents per month, and I could collect 78 cents per month. My route was more than 10 miles long, and my "net" was about 18 dollars. 2½ years was enough.

Age 13, I weeded, and dug holes for a local nursery. $1.00/day.

Age 14, I worked as a carhop for an A&W style drive-in. 15 cents/hour.

Age 15, Worked at the cannery in Murray. Lost the ends of 3 fingers. The pay was perhaps 50 cents/hr. I don't remember that so well.

Age 16, Pressed clothes at Camp Kearns. All summer. Most Fridays and Saturdays thru the school year. 5 cents per garment.

Age 17, Worked the summer at ordnance depot on Redwood Road. 57 cents/hr. During school year worked evenings as busboy at Hotel Utah. Paid about 55 cents/hr, got dinner free, waitresses shared tips.

Age 18, Read electric meters in/near SLC. $117.50/month. Enlisted in U.S. Army.

Age 20, In college. Worked weekends at Kennecott Copper open pit mine. Worked on track gang, mostly new track at the mine bottom.

Age 21, Worked in Murray smelter operating 2 types of "roaster." One kind exposed me to sulfur fumes; the other to arsenic. 2 months. Worked briefly as laborer in the 4 mile tunnel to Lark mine.

Age 22, Worked in the "Lark" silver mine, about a mile below surface.

There were many times that I dug trenches, or helped put in pipe lines, starting at age 13, ending age 25. Worked for older brothers. My family always paid at least "scale" for honest labor.

My "career" began at Boeing. But I moved around quite a bit, always on my volition. A wonderful life. My latent talent for mechanical design broke through so I had many interesting assignments. Also, I was quite determined to do superior work on every task.

There may have been some hostile envy of my choice assignments. I did finally learn that senior staff would ask to have "that guy Lambson" do their design; and sometimes a job would be on 'hold' till I was available.

As a dyed-in-the-wool Utahn, I always felt I should represent the good, even noble, character of my beloved home state. The heritage, or legacy, of being Utahn is a force that doesn't let go.

I could talk about the fantastic scenery, the wonderful snow, the great people of Utah birth, and much more; but "The force" goes deeper and further than can be expressed by this soul.

Marlene Cooley Gorton
Salt Lake County

Age 63; **Birthplace** Grace, Idaho; **Occupation** Secretary/Bookkeeper/housewife/Mom; **Religion** L.D.S.; **Race/Ethnicity** N/A

My name was Marlene Cooley and I was 8 years old when my parents and my little brother moved to Salt Lake City, Utah in 1940. My father went to work for the Remington Arms Plant. We lived with my mothers aunt on 13th East and 2nd South in a 2 room attic apartment. We used to sit out in front of the house and watch the Trolley go by. We waved at the conductor and he rang the Trolley bell at us. That was really fun and made us laugh. We loved it here in Salt Lake, the weather was wonderful from the harsh weather we had in Idaho. My parents were soon able to buy a small home on 5th North between 1st and 2nd West. I attended Washington Elementary School, and Horace Mann Jr. High School. In the fall of 1945 when I was 13 years old, the school asked for volunteers to go to Bountiful to pick fruit on a Saturday. They would pay us for each crate we picked. It was the end of September and there was a bumper crop and they needed pickers to get the fruit off the trees. After we picked all day we were waiting for our ride back home and some of us found a large concrete bowl with water in it. Now that I reflect back on this day I realize it was probably a type of reservoir built to catch the run-off from the mountains just east of the fruit trees. Probably to protect the properties down below it. Well, being kids we were hot and tired and thirsty, some of us decided to wade in this water. I do remember it being very dirty but it felt so good as we waded through it and splashed in it. I do remember bugs and all kinds of stuff floating in it also a green scum, but it didn't seem to keep us out of it. I don't think I drank any of it but we did splash and have a water fight. The ride came and we went home.

About a week later, I got very sick with symptoms of the flu. I couldn't seem to shake it off. I would feel better for a day, then go to school and come home sick. Finally after about 10 days of fever, vomiting and being very sick and getting very weak my Mother called our family doctor, Dr. Floyd Cannon. He came to the house and checked me, I remember him checking my reflexes with a little rubber hammer, then he called an ambulance and they took me to the Salt Lake General Hospital on 21st South and State Street. I think they took me to the top floor and I went through many examinations including a Spinal Tap, which I remember very well. After a few hours they diagnosed me with Infantile Paralysis or Spinalmenengitis and moved me into the Isolation Ward. I was there 2 days when they diagnosed me with Infantile Paralysis, more commonly known as Polio. At that time there were many cases of this disease in the State of Utah, in fact so many that they had to open up a wing in a building North of the main hospital for all the Polio patients. After I spent about two weeks in isolation, I was moved into a room, at first a large room where there were 13 of us. I remember our beds were so close the nurse could barely squeeze between each bed to take care of her patient. By then I realized that I was paralyzed. I could barely move my left arm and had no use of the right arm. I couldn't lift my head as my neck was afflicted. I remember I could just barely move my legs but I was thankful that I could at least move them. The routine of my days, as I remember, was being washed in the early morning to get ready for breakfast. I had to be fed by a nurse as I couldn't sit up and I couldn't use my arms for anything. After breakfast we started the hot packs. This was very essential for our recovery but we really hated them. We had them 3 times a day. In the morning, in the early afternoon and late afternoon. They had round machines, they put these wool packs into them and when they took them out they were so hot the nurses couldn't hardly handle them and had to lift them out with sticks of wood. There were 2 kinds of packs. The Prone pack was long pieces of wool that went from your neck to your toes. I don't remember the name of the other ones but they were cut in individual pieces to fit each special part of your body. One went around my shoulder then a plastic was wrapped around the pack to hold the heat in then it was covered with another material and pinned to hold it in place. One pack went over the forearm and one over the hand. One large one for the

back and one for the chest and then a special cut one fit over the thigh area, one for the leg and one around the foot. It was quite a process and alot of work for the nurses. The prone packs stayed on for 30 minutes each time and the other packs stayed on for 1 hour. I remember as they cooled, they got extremely itchy and I couldn't scratch because I couldn't move.

Twice a day we received physical therapy. Mine was usually in the mornings around 11:00 and in the afternoon after the day of hot packs usually after 3:30 or 4:00. Then it was supper time and lights out and to bed at 9:00. I don't remember the name of my physical therapist but she was very nice and really worked hard for me. I have a picture of her in my album. After a short period of time we were moved into a room with just 7 girls, the room was small but we had more room and that made it nicer for everyone. I had a lot of nurses, some very nice and some pretty bad ones. It seems like a Dr. from the main hospital came to visit us about once a week, but there was always interns coming down to look at us and check us and see what our different problems were.

They tried to provide entertainment for us, to help us pass the time. Once in awhile a movie star would come to see us. I remember Shirley Temple came one time and I have her autograph. This was wonderful because she was my favorite movie star.

The food was absolutely horrible. I didn't like to eat any way, so I really had a bad time. All the girls in my room came up with the idea that after surgery up in the main hospital, they took the bones from surgery and threw them all in the pot with 1 potato and 1 carrot and boiled it all day and that was our dinner that night. We had soup alot and it was really bad. Some difference from the way hospitals are today, people just don't realize how good they have it nowadays but they still do more complaining than we did. We suffered together and by ourselves and laughed and snickered at the idea that we all knew what they were feeding us. This is what helped all of us through a very bad time in our lives.

Slowly, I improved and was helped into a wheelchair for 30 minutes each day. This was so wonderful to be able to get out of bed even for just a short time. After about 3 or 4 months I progressed very well, but they were very strict with us. They warned us to never get out of bed and to never go against their rules. I could feel my legs getting stronger but they wouldn't let me walk on them. I felt like I had to and that if I didn't I would never walk again, so one night after lights were out I told the girls I was going to slide out and stand beside my bed, they warned me not to, but my mind was made up. I slid off the bed and had no idea how far it was to the floor. My legs held me for about one minute then buckled beneath me and there I was on the floor and couldn't get back up on the bed. The girls rang for the nurse and we told her I fell out of bed. She put me back in bed, and warned me sternly and turned out the light. I lay there looking at the ceiling with the most wonderful feeling, I had just experienced the most fantastic accomplishment since getting this dreaded disease. And I knew that I was going to do it again no matter what. A few nights later I told the girls I was going to do it again, and I did and I mastered getting back on the bed by laying down and swinging my legs up, as my right arm was completely paralyzed and my left arm was so weak that they couldn't help me anyway. It took me a few tries to do it but I made it and each time it became easier for me. Soon every night I was running errands for all the girls in the room, taking something from one girl to another from bed to bed. That makes me remember the night I made it all across the room to the other side, I had to lay on her bed to get strength enough to get back across the room to my own bed. It was great, and today I truly feel that if I hadn't done that, I could possibly be paralyzed in my legs and in a wheelchair today. Then one day, a girl told on me. That afternoon I had the head nurse, 3 other nurses, 2 interns and the Dr.

from the main hospital all surrounded my bed and shook their fingers at me warning me that I was not ever to get out of bed myself. They didn't know that by then I was a real pro at it, stronger than ever and I was never going to let them take that away from me. I kept improving and the physical therapy became less painful for me. Finally after seven long months, in May 1946 I was able to leave the hospital with my parents. It was truly the happiest day of my life.

My parents didn't have much money, they barely made a living and because of the March of Dimes, they never had to pay one dime for all the care that I had received. What a wonderful program. It literally saves peoples lives. I know it sure did save my family. My mother was instructed as to what exercise I was to do every day and what she had to do to help me. I saw a Dr. a few times after my release from the hospital.

I remember there were parties put on for the crippled children, I don't know whether it was private or put on by the March of Dimes. We had dinners and programs all the time that were invited to. It was a wonderful program for all of us. It helped us to socially learn how to adjust to our circumstances. When I was 16 there was a Valentines Day party for all of us and they chose a Queen for the party which was a girl friend of mine that had been in my Polio ward and I was chosen as her 1st Attendant. We wore formals and had our pictures taken and that was a very uplifting experience for me. It helped me realize that I was still a person and I was special even though my life had been changed drastically.

The polio had left me with a completely paralyzed right arm and my left arm had about 50% use in it. The polio had destroyed the triceps muscle and I have never been able to reach over my head for anything. My back was weak but the muscles were all good and my legs were considered near normal. I really have felt very fortunate that I was as good as I was for what I had been through. I went back to Horace Mann Junior High School. That adjustment back into the mainstream is another story, it was very difficult but I made it. Then I attended West High School. I loved West High School. I had wonderful teachers and counselor and I did well. About once a month I was visited by a counselor from the Rehabilitation Program. What a wonderful program this was funded by the State of Utah.

I have given this program alot of credit for what I did with the rest of my life. This program helped me get an education. They helped me enroll in the University of Utah. All of my education was paid for by the Rehabilitation Program. Things were much different in those days, I had to carry many large books to class from building to building and if I was late getting to the building and there was no one going through the doors I couldn't open the doors with my arm full of books, I became extremely stressful and discouraged and I talked to my counselor about this problem. After one quarter, he decided that I might do better in the Salt Lake Vocational School as my aptitude test showed I had alot of interest in the business field. At this time I transferred to the Vocational School in the Business course. I had a wonderful instructor and I did very well. You might say I took to it like a duck takes to water. I loved every phase of it and grabbed all the knowledge that I could. I made accomplishments and a letter of recommendation from the Women's Legislative council was presented to me and the article appeared in the *Salt Lake Tribune.* These articles are copied on the last page of my story.

I was signed up to go back to school in the Fall but I spent one month in Idaho visiting my grandparents and I met a wonderful man and in October 1951 at the age of 19, I was married. But the education I had received did not go to waste. I have worked as a Secretary and a Bookkeeper and have done well with the knowledge and education that I received through these programs in the State of Utah. We had two fine sons that we raised and educated and they are productive and upstanding citizens with families of their own.

In 1978 I developed Post-Polio Syndrome. At first I didn't know what was happening to me. My body became very weak and my left arm showed great signs of weakness which was a terrifying and stressful thought to me. I became so weak and tired that I couldn't finish out a day at work and was forced to resign.

I came to the University of Utah Hospital and was diagnosed with Post-Polio Syndrome and not really promised anything only that it was progressive and something I would have to live with. I learned to live with my handicap and was successful at work and in my personal life and it was very difficult for me to accept the fact that this dreaded disease had come back to wreak havoc on my body once again. The cold weather is my worst enemy, so when my husband retired from the U.S. Postal Service we moved to West Jordan, Utah where the winters are much kinder to me. It is wonderful to be back in Utah again, I feel as though I have come home.

Once again I am being helped by living in Utah, I have attended a program sponsored by Easter Seals about Post-Polio Syndrome. This has really helped me understand what this disease is and what to expect and how to cope with it.

I truly appreciate the State of Utah, the people are so caring about the handicapped, the programs that are implemented and the funding that is given to these programs to help handicapped people become contributing citizens to society. These programs have helped me to be an independent and contributing person to the community and to my fellowman.

Thank you Utah for being there for me when I needed a helping hand.

M. Christine Cottrell

Emery County

Age 40; **Birthplace** Glendale, WV; **Occupation** Homemaker; **Religion** LDS; **Race/Ethnicity** Caucasian

We, like the pioneers, came from the East. My husband brought me as a bride to a small town in Utah. But his job took him away from us often and we moved around a little.

We moved up a canyon near a monument dedicated to some pioneers who had been massacred there by Indians a hundred and thirty years before. There was a book written about the one woman in the party and how she struggled to save her child from the murderers.

I thought of that woman often as I worked on our small farm up that lonely canyon. Things hadn't changed so much in a century—it was still wild, still beautiful. I often thought I could write a sequel to that book.

My two small children and I spent a year on that farm by ourselves. I raised a garden and carefully preserved it; I tended our animals and gathered eggs; I papered and painted our little house till it was bright and cheerful; I planted a new lawn and lots of flowers.

I also killed rattlesnakes by our barn and hauled water for three weeks from the creek and from town, seven miles away, when our water lines broke that winter. I shoveled tons of snow and reclaimed more lawn from weed patches (so there would be less hiding places for snakes).

We watched a mother deer with three fawns graze almost every evening through the summer in a meadow across from our living room windows. I had never heard of a doe having three fawns before, but there they were. Then in the winter bald eagles came to the same meadow. A herd of elk traveled the mountain trails surrounding our house.

We had men stop by our home when they tracked mountain lions up our creek bottom and tagged them.

Then more men came when I didn't know it—until opening morning of deer season—it sounded like a war going on around our house.

I had friends who thought I should leave that farm and move into town with the children till my husband came home but I didn't want to leave. We were safe, we were learning and growing. We were happy.

The freedom I felt there was wonderful. We did things we had never had an opportunity to do before. We could make mistakes and try again. I developed many skills and talents there and overcame a lot of fears.

Comparing our lives to the pioneers was a constant, daily thing. We may have had more conveniences but our situations were similar in many ways.

The experience I had there will be with me forever. They all added up to make me a better person.

———

There were pleasant times and hard times, scary times and peaceful times but eventually those times came to an end. My husband's job was taking us back to the East. We drove our little caravan through Salt Lake City past the July 24th Celebration one night as the fireworks lit up the sky. Excitement swelled within my breast. It had been seven years since I had lived in the East. Oh, what things I had to share with my family. Things I had learned in Utah.

It was pleasant back East. I've always tried to make the most out of my life wherever I am. But it wasn't the same as Utah. The greatest difference I saw was we didn't have as much freedom. The type of freedom to see children playing happily in a school yard. I very seldom saw that where we lived in the East. There wasn't much freedom or opportunity to make certain choices, to make mistakes and try again. Everything seemed so guarded, so regimented.

We are back now. We've come back to that same small town we started out in so many years ago. Did time stand still? The same people are here who took us into their hearts then. The sky is just as beautiful. We're right across the street from the school and I watch our children play on the playground every day. They are learning so many new things.

As I look out my window and watch them play I remember life on that little farm and how I grew. I hope my children will have the opportunities I had to grow and learn, make mistakes and try again.

They may not choose to live on an isolated farm but wherever they choose to live, I feel we've brought them back to a land of opportunity.

Just as the pioneers came so long ago seeking opportunity and freedom and eventually built up this wonderful state, so our family came and we hope to give something of ourselves.

All the good we've learned in life we hope to reinvest. We hope we've taught our children well and that they will continue to learn good things that they, too, will reinvest. I feel they will because when I think of Utah I think of opportunity and freedom and peace.

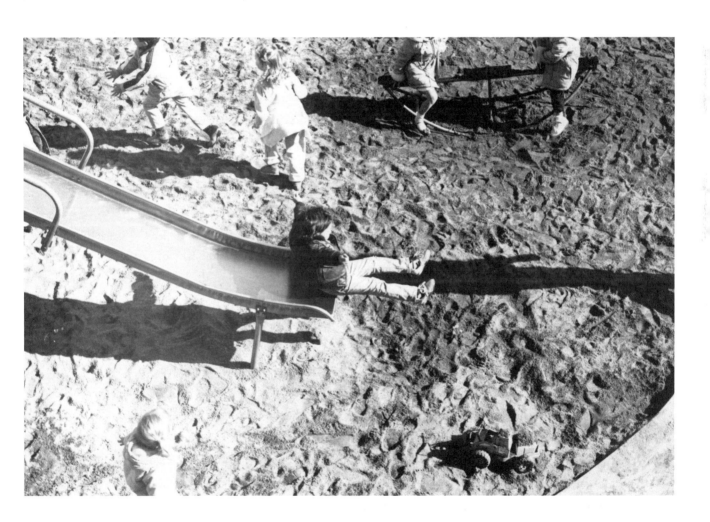

Submitted by Megan Little, Cache County.

Wendy Ann Silver

Salt Lake County

Age 53; **Birthplace** Sutton Coldfield, England; **Occupation** Librarian/Interviewer; **Religion** L.D.S.; **Race/Ethnicity** White (English)

I arrived in Utah as an English immigrant about a quarter of a century ago, after a three-year interlude in northern California.

Most immigrants imagine they will find greater prosperity in the new world than they were accustomed to in the old. My experience was exactly the opposite of this expectation but, paradoxically, this state of affairs had a positive effect on my life as it spurred me to learn more and exert myself more strenuously. I became more aware of the opportunities that did come my way, and grew more able to take advantage of them. Years of poverty also taught me greater appreciation for the good things of life that I did enjoy.

We moved to Provo for four years so that my husband could attend Brigham Young University. After his graduation we moved to Orem and rented a house which proved to be exactly the right place at the right time. About six months later we were able to buy an old pioneer home a couple of blocks away for a very good price when a pending sale fell through at the last minute, right before the owners had arranged to move to Georgia.

The house was in bad shape when I first looked at it. The wiring and plumbing were in dire need of attention, the kitchen demanded major renovation, and the garden was a mess. But the moment I stepped into the house I sensed its potential, in spite of the grey wallpaper on the wall of the front room.

The thick walls provided excellent insulation both winter and summer, and the garden consisted of a full acre of land with water rights and more than twenty mature fruit trees, two or three of each variety. The home was the poorest-looking house in a good, though sparsely populated, neighborhood.

Since that time the gravel road has been paved, a beautiful new church house has been built across the street, and many new and expensive homes have been built around the property. During the seventeen years I lived in that home, the house itself was enlarged and improved and the land carefully nurtured and preserved.

I resisted the belligerent tactics of certain developers as they began to build houses all around me, and was relieved as the garden finally became landlocked.

My experience in Utah has brought me very close to the land. My love of gardening began when I was a child in England. I established a small rock garden and admired the handiwork of my stepfather and a professional gardener, whose efforts transformed an acre and a half of land into a beautiful and productive garden.

I remember that we had a grapevine in one greenhouse, and that tall and wonderfully odiferous tomato plants filled a second small greenhouse. In our orchard there were chickens and a real gypsy caravan brought in by my grandfather for summer sleepovers.

It became a tradition to attend the annual Chelsea Flower Show in London, where my stepfather would make a point of seeking out the latest varieties in dahlias. Every year our herbaceous border encroached a little more onto the front lawn as he made room for his latest finds.

My Utah garden laid the foundation of the health my six children and I have enjoyed over the years. It was mostly an organic garden, enriched by truckloads of aged horse manure and innumerable sacks of leaves.

Each fall I became quite a bag lady, stuffing my small station wagon with sacks and leaves conveniently set out on sidewalks, ready for the taking. I timed my trips to be a few blocks ahead of the garbage truck, and covered my garden with a veritable patchwork quilt of multi-colored leaves.

So the land grew more productive and more beautiful as the years went by. I planted more trees, including different kinds of nut trees and apples grown from seeds I once smuggled out of England. I dared believe that, by dint of hard work, I might eventually eliminate every weed from the garden, at least for a short time. The different blossoms made the garden a beautiful sight each spring, and every harvest became more abundant than the last.

I enjoyed the bounty of fresh fruits and vegetables but I was always most concerned with building up the intrinsic health of the land itself. I felt that it was a great privilege to be able to call this little spot in Utah my own. I had a sense of stewardship as I took care of it to the best of my ability.

I envisaged a small ecosystem and introduced chickens and goats after building two pens and small barns. I was able to take advantage of the opportunity to tear down a barn and remove all the materials without charge as long as the site was left clean. I hired some out-of-work miners from Job Service for a few days and worked alongside them, pulling nails and overseeing the job. There was plenty of good lumber with which to build the two animal shelters.

My plan was to rotate the animals from year to year, to plant a garden in the unoccupied pen after the livestock had spent the previous year fertilizing the ground and eating all the weeds and bugs. My corn grew nine feet tall where the chickens had enjoyed sunning themselves and taking dust baths.

Ten years spent as a single mother, without benefits of any child support, helped me learn how to become an excellent manager of both time and resources. I often juggled three or four part time jobs, while finding time to garden and put away food for the winter. Actually I had little time to do much else than work during the summer and early fall.

I was fortunate that money from my grandfather's estate had enabled me to pay off the house in full. Otherwise life might have been very different.

As time went by my oldest daughter suggested that I go back to school in order to secure more regular employment. I had taken classes in religion and genealogy at BYU when I first came to Utah. I also had an honors degree in Russian language and literature from the University of London.

My daughter and a couple neighbors paved the way for me to be accepted as a graduate student at the School of Library and Information Sciences at BYU, just in time to graduate before the school's closure in 1993.

I have thoroughly enjoyed the classes I have taken at BYU over the years, including classes on a variety of topics at the annual Education Week, which I attended some years. Such educational experiences constituted a very unique part of my life in Utah.

I believe that years of poverty encouraged a certain adventurous spirit in me as I used my ingenuity to survive and embarked on different endeavors. I have sold health products door-to-door and worked as an enumerator for the Census Bureau. Over the years I gained a reputation as an interviewer which has enabled me to travel all over the United States. I never imagined such opportunities would be mine when I started my first job after my divorce doing political surveys over the telephone from an old building in downtown Provo.

Utah has been a good place in which to work as a librarian. Libraries are flourishing in this state, the circulation of books and other materials increases every year, and I find libraries to be treasure troves of useful information and entertainment. To me, working in a library is somewhat like being in a candy store and not having to worry about calories.

Finally, living in Utah has meant so much in terms of family associations in general and children in particular. Where I came from the two-child family is the norm. If I had stayed in England I would certainly not have had six children.

I find I appreciate my children more as I grow older. They are still a source of wonder and amazement to me. In spite of our differences, my ex-husband and I were a good match from a genetic standpoint, and we were fortunate in having three boys and three girls.

I had never had much to do with babies growing up, and had never considered myself to be a particularly maternal person. I certainly made plenty of mistakes and the divorce obviously took its toll on our children, but the experience of raising children has meant more to me than anything else.

And Utah has been a good place in which to raise children for the most part. Dedicated teachers have enabled my children to receive a good education, and even made it possible for my middle daughter to be accepted by the Massachusetts Institute of Technology and receive scholarship money amounting to twenty thousand dollars a year to study biomedical engineering. She graduated in three years and has gone on to pursue an education in medicine.

Worthy goals and values have been taught in both church and school in Utah, and have helped my children become who they are today.

My life has taken many unexpected twists and turns since I left England thirty years ago. Things have not turned out the way I expected they would. But life has been a very rich and interesting experience, and over half my life has been spent in Utah.

At the time of my divorce I was asked if I planned to go home now that I no longer lived with my husband. I told the person, who seemed to be making certain assumptions, that I was already home, because my home was here in Utah.

I like liveing in Utah because my family lives here, My friends live here, because not one state in the world is better, Utah has beautiful trees and mountains, Utah is where I live, Utah is my state, I like Utah!

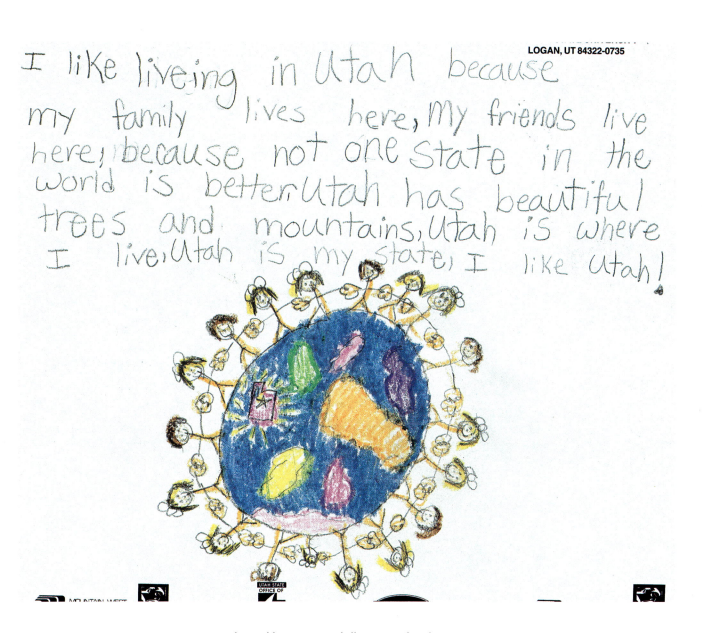

Submitted by Lauren Michelle Hunt, Salt Lake County.

Plate 9

"Peekaboo in Goblin Valley." Submitted by Katie Rose, Salt Lake County.

"1976—John Tilby, WBBA, Butler League." Submitted by Wilma Tilby, Salt Lake County.

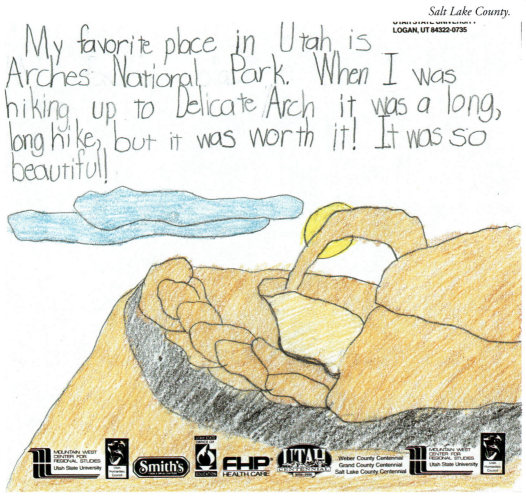

My favorite place in Utah is Arches National Park. When I was hiking up to Delicate Arch it was a long, long hike, but it was worth it! It was so beautiful!

Submitted by Erica Jones, Salt Lake County.

Plate 10

Submitted by Shalece Elynne Christiansen, Salt Lake County.

"Summer 1994—Bolger Reservoir: Donald (14), Melanie and Edmund (7)." Submitted by Vaughn E. Silcox, Salt Lake County.

Plate 11

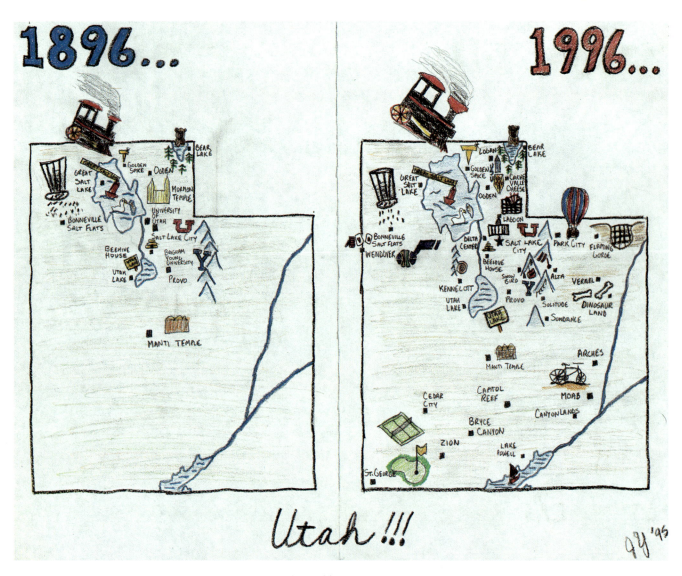

Submitted by Justin Yumas.

Plate 12

Submitted by Daniel Jepperson, Salt Lake County.

I like living in Utah becouse of the President Clinton.

Submitted by Kim Koeven, Utah County.

Plate 13

"Tyler F. and Christopher J. Madsen at Cascade Springs (1994)." Photo by Peter W. Madsen, Salt Lake County.

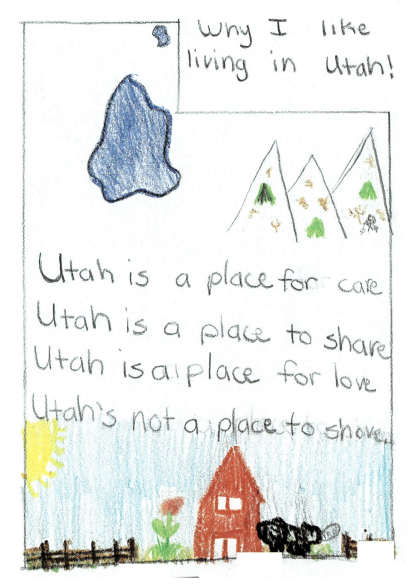

Why I like living in Utah!

Utah is a place for care
Utah is a place to share
Utah is a place for love
Utah's not a place to shove.

Submitted by Megan J. Hall, Weber County.

Plate 14

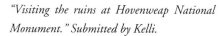

I like living in Utah because of my grandma and her flowers.

Submitted by Malea Stanger, Utah County.

Left: "A Cowboy from Kaysville." Submitted by Eric Ripple, Davis County.

Plate 15

"Sego lilies on the hillside in Tridell, Utah." Submitted by Lorna R. McKee, Uintah County.

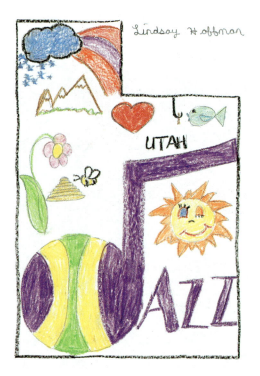

Above: Submitted by Lindsay Carroll Hoffman, Carbon County.

Right: Submitted by Guadalupe Rodriguez, Salt Lake County.

Plate 16

The Voices of Our Children

The unfettered spontaneity of children's voices bursts from the pages of these essays and poems. Not yet confined by the adult requirements of proper spelling, sentence structure, and caution, these young writers tickle us to laughter, stir our souls to compassion, shake our conceptions of reality, and invite us to reconsider ourselves and the place we live. In painting their word-pictures, they have not felt obliged to stay in the lines, forcing us to look afresh at the unnecessary boundaries we draw around ourselves, our spirits, our cultures. They remind us of the magic we experience when our imagination spills over preset margins.

The warmth of family and friends and splendor of our scenic environment are reoccurring themes throughout most of the essays—often with reminders of our responsibility to our natural and social words. Whether these young people are listing what they like best about living in Utah or simply telling us what a normal day is like for them—taking both the good and the bad in stride—they impart an earthly wisdom.

—Linda Newell

Viana Karla
Salt Lake County

Age N/A; **Birthplace** N/A; **Occupation** N/A; **Religion** N/A; **Race/Ethnicity** N/A

a mi me gusta todo soley porque hay mucha seguridad lo uni co que no me gusto fe que los ninos son muy rebeldes y asen lo que quieren en Mexico esta mejor la situasion delaedo casion pero lo que me gusto mas fuero las montanas y como neva todo eso es nuevo para mi por que en mejico no neva y hay montanas pero muy pocas.

Translation by Angela P. Ford

I like all of Salt Lake because it is very safe. The only thing I don't like is that the children are very rebellious and they do anything they like [to do]. In Mexico the situation is much better concerning that [the children]. But what I really like is the mountains and how it snow [here]. All this is very new to me because it doesn't snow in Mexico. There are mountains [in Mexico] but very few.

Angie Rizzuto
Davis County

Age 13; **Birthplace** Cheyenne, WY; **Occupation** Student; **Religion** N/A; **Race/Ethnicity** N/A

Picture yourself in the emergency room of your local hospital. Doctors and nurses screaming and yelling, people all around you. You don't know what is happening to you. The reason you are in the hospital is that you need a heart transplant. What a scary thought. This is what happened to my mother. In September of 1990 we moved here to Utah for medical care.

In the last four years, we have many reasons to enjoy Utah. From the pretty deserts, like Moab, to the majestic mountains, like the Wasatch Range. The different types of terrains makes Utah very unusual. Then when you throw in the different types of climates and it is even better.

But one important reason is the people. The state is geared to the family with allot of things for the family to do. This makes it a fun place to grow up. We have made many

---

good friends and neighbors here. So you can see that Utah means allot to me.

Toby Sorensen
Kane County

Age 12; **Birthplace** Kanab, Utah; **Occupation** Student; **Religion** LDS; **Race/Ethnicity** White

I love living in Utah. There are so many things in Utah that I like. There are mountains, animals and parks. I've got a mountain not very far away. I go on it in the summer, somtimes in the winter. This picture shows a big rock we call it the V. V stands for Valley. Every year Valley paints the year they graduate in on the rocks. I will graduate in the year 2002.

About 20 miles there's a 5,200 acre ranch. A little ranch not too big. There are green field's and no pollution. Just a nice little ranch.

At home in my back yard I keep my very own horse. I feed it every day and water it. I'm tring to get it broken. I put a saddle on her sometimes.

Ten miles from home there is a park and we call it "The Sand Dunes." My famaly goes there sometimes for Easter. Not too away there are Indian writings that I visit. Close by is where our town used to keep our water in a rock.

One time my friend Thomas and I were hiking by the "V." We got stuck on a ledge and I had boots on. Thomas helped me out and we got home safely.

On January 29, 1995 the Valley Elementary school got one foot of water in the basement. My dad DarLynn and I got our water truck and pumped water out of the basement. It took me one hour to get the water out. There were around 8,000 gallons of water in it. This is a list of the names of the people who get it out: Ray Spencer, Earl Sorensen, Gerry Hoht, Gerald Spenser, DarLynn Sorensen and Toby Earl Sorensen.

I lik at ther are deer

Submitted by Mark Rowley.

Megan Hall
Weber County

Age 10; **Birthplace** McKay Dee Hospital; **Occupation** Student; **Religion** Mormon; **Race/Ethnicity** White

WHY I LIKE LIVING IN UTAH!
Utah is a place for care
Utah is a place to share
Utah is a place for love
Utah's not a place to shove.

Wesley Russell Stapley
Salt Lake County

Age 10; **Birthplace** Pochatello; **Occupation** Student; **Religion** Chirch of Jesus Christ of Latter Day Saints; **Race/Ethnicity** Caucasian

Living in Utah means equality for boys and girls.
Living in Utah means friendship and understanding hearts.
Living in Utah means great mountains like the Wasatch Mtn. and the Rockies.
It means love and knowing that you are safe.
It doesn't have very many tornados.

It's a special state because it has the only Salt Lake in the world.

It has something that's hard to find on earth, love.

If you want love, you have to give it.

Utah was great when I was alive, and I hope it still is.

Stuart Harman
Utah County

Age 10; **Birthplace** Salt Lake City, Utah; **Occupation** 4th Grade Student; **Religion** LDS/Morman; **Race/Ethnicity** White

One time a Utah Jazz player named Tyrone Corbin came and gave our team tips on how to play basketball better, he said "I'm short" and I said, "I'm short too."

At Christmas time my family goes up to my Aunt Carries, she lives in the mountains. We go sleding, and open presents.

In Utah I caught my first fish, my cousin was throwing rocks into the water too.

Once when my family and I went upto my grandpa and grandma's cabin, We saw a doe and a 2 point. I got a few good pictures of them together and by themselves.

Thats what Utah means to me!

Tynan Jakins
Davis County

Age 13; **Birthplace** Durban Natal; **Occupation** Student; **Religion** N/A; **Race/Ethnicity** Caucasian

Utah is very beautiful. The scenery is majestic because of all the wildlife and the plants. I love looking at the mountains because they change every season.

The people are much nicer than they are in other parts of the U.S. and in other parts of the world. I love all the different kinds of animals we see because we live in the mountains. Especially the deer, we get to see alot of those.

The school system here is a lot better than The South African one. I am very happy about the fact that we don't have to wear uniforms. Here we have nice teachers that understand. We have more choices about what subjects we are going to pick.

When you go to the store, the people that work there say hello and are polite to you and I like that alot.

In this essay I have explained to you why I like living in Utah and I really do enjoy it here. It is a lot better than some of the places that I have lived in.

David Jones
Utah County

Age 17; **Birthplace** Payson, UT; **Occupation** Student; **Religion** L.D.S.; **Race/Ethnicity** Caucasian

Living in Utah means a lot to me. There are many reasons why I like living here, and there are even some things that I dislike about our state. But after weighing them out, there is really no place that I would rather live. Here are some of those reasons.

I like the isolation that we have in Utah. I lived in Eureka, Utah for about four years. I really enjoyed having access to the outdoors there. I could easily go on hikes, go camping, or go out and shoot guns without being bothered or bothering anyone. Most of the state of Utah is this way. Aside from three counties, Weber, Salt Lake, and Utah, the population density is very low. This makes Utah an ideal place to live, or to visit, because one can get away from the hassles of everyday life.

Northern Utah is a mountainous area. This make it a great place for hiking, hunting, and especially skiing. In the southern part of the state, it is a desert climate. It is a good place to visit, for it has many National parks. I really like the variation of geography in Utah. I like the climate also, but I would like shorter, warmer winters.

I like the fact that, presently, Utahns aren't as involved with gangs and violence as in other states. It is not as big of a problem here as it is in California or New York, but I fear for the future with the gang problem arising.

One of the things that I don't like about Utah, is the heavy religious base. I'm all for people being involved in the church, and I have no discrimination toward those people; but I don't like how others, like myself, are often condemned for their choices not to be as involved. It is a great accomplishment, I believe, to be involved in their religion, but I was not brought up that way. I was baptized L.D.S., and I agree with religion, but I am not heavily involved. Sometimes I wish that I was raised different, but I wasn't.

I also think that Utah should legalize some forms of gambling. I think that it would help the economy of Utah. A lot of Utahn's go to Wyoming, Idaho, or Nevada to gamble or play the lottery. I think that all of that money going to other states would help Utah and it's people, if it was going into our economy. It might even bring up the tourist rate of Utah.

In my opinion, I have listed some of the positive and negative aspects of living in Utah. Even though there are a lot of things that I don't agree with about our state, I enjoy living here and I don't know that I'll ever leave. I think it is a great place to live. or a good place for tourist to come and visit.

Drew Miller
Salt Lake County
Age 17; **Birthplace** Sacramento, CA; **Occupation** Education (student); **Religion** Mormon; **Race/Ethnicity** White

I like Utah because it is a very simple state to draw. Utah looks like a rectangle with a square missing from one corner. All the lines are straight and intersect at perpendicular bisecting angles. The North-South lines are basically parallel, and even if you don't draw it perfectly, nobody will ever notice. Nobody cares if you screw up and put the square missing in the wrong corner—everyone still knows it is still Utah! I used to draw it wrong everytime, but everyone just thought I was creative and was doing it in abstract. Utah looks good if you draw it in any artistic medium—I personally have tried colored pencil, crayon, marker, oils, watercolor, and paint-by-number. I liked my colored pencil piece the best because I shaded it really good. My mom got mad with me when I used oils because I spilled blue all over our couch. Utah looks good if you color each line a different color. It scares me to think of living in Texas, Florida, or Idaho with all those squiggly lines. Utah's cool.

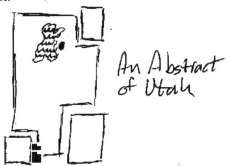

An Abstract of Utah

Vivien Wade
Davis County
Age 14; **Birthplace** Fairfax, Va; **Occupation** Student; **Religion** LDS; **Race/Ethnicity** Hispanic-American

UTAH IS THE PLACE FOR ME,
TO RUN AND JUMP, TO SING AND PLAY,
GO TO THE CANYONS OR SEE A PLAY
GO TO THE OPERA AND TO THE BALLET
AND AFTER THAT SEE THE JAZZ PLAY.
IT'S ONE-TO-NOTHING AT FRANKLIN QUEST FIELD,
THE BUZZ ARE AHEAD AND, YES, THIS IS REAL.

THIS HAPPENS IN UTAH ANY ORDINARY DAY
FOR KIDS TO PLAY SPORTS LIKE SOCCER TODAY.
I KNOW WHAT YOUR SAYING AND
    WANT TO KNOW MORE,
SO STAY IN YOUR SEATS AND
    HOLD ONTO YOUR HAT
CAUSE YOU SURE WON'T HAVE TIME
    FOR A LONG WINTERS NAP.
WHILE PEOPLE ARE SKIING AND SKATING TODAY
OTHERS ARE SHOPPING AND ARE WATCHING
    BALLETS.YOU MAY BE AT HOME AND
    WATCHING T.V.
BUT I'D RATHER BE HIKING AND BIKING FOR FREE!
YOU MAY LOVE THE OCEAN BUT
    OUR LAKE IS THE BEST,
IT'S CALMER AND SAFER AND SALTIER I GUESS!
THE PEOPLE ARE FRIENDLY AND HELPFUL AND FUN
YOU'LL NEVER BE BORED
    WHEN YOU PLAY WITH UTAHNS.
THERE'S NO NEED TO WORRY
    ABOUT COLOR OR RACE,
NO NEED TO HAVE BODY GUARDS
    CRAMMIN' YOUR FACE,
NEVER A GUN POINTED STRAIT AT YOUR FACE,
WITH FRIENDLY POLICEMEN
    MAKING UTAH THE SAFEST PLACE.
SOME PEOPLE THINK UTAH IS ALL L.D.S
BUT WITH A WALK AROUND TOWN YOU'LL
PROVE THOSE PEOPLE WRONG.
WITH CANYONS, MOUNTAINS, SKIERS, AND LAKES,
SPORTS TEAMS, AND SHOPPING MALLS
    ALL OVER THE PLACE,
THERE'S SKATERS AND SAND DUNES
    IN THE HOTTER PARTS
YES SKIERS, AND SLEDDERS UP NORTH
    WHERE IT'S COLD.
I HOPE I'VE CONVINCED YOU
    THAT UTAH'S THE BEST;
THE PAST ONE HUNDRED YEARS
    HAVE MANY STORIES TO TELL
BUT JUST TO SAVE TIME!
I THINK UTAH SWELL.

Andrew Beach
Salt Lake County

Age 8; **Birthplace** N/A; **Occupation** N/A; **Relgion** N/A; **Race/Ethnicity** N/A

My name is Andrew Bucklin Beach. My hobbys are palentology and science. My favret animals are Tigers, Lions, Coyotes, hippos, monkeys, elephants, and eagles, dont forget the chtas! and thats just half of my list I live in Springvile Utah. I go to Grant elimentry and I like Utah cuse you are born free.

Tyler Knoles
Davis County

Age 14; **Birthplace** Bountiful, Utah; **Occupation** Student; **Religion** Mormon; **Race/Ethnicity** Cacasions

I love living in Utah! The four seasons give us variety in our lifestyle. The beautiful scenery is always changing. The mountains, lakes, deserts, and streams provide endless recreational opportunities.

Winter is my favorite season because I love winter sports. Utah has the greatest snow on earth and I can get to any ski resort in less than an hour. My favorite resort is Snowbird because of its good snow and challenging chutes. There is always a new adventure every time I hit the slopes.

After being dormant, everything in Utah comes alive in the spring. I like this time of year because I can mountain bike and hike in the mountains near my home with my golden retriever. When everything starts to turn green again, there is always excitement in the air.

Then comes summer … a more laid-back time of year. This is my second favorite season because I can always be outside swimming, or in the mountains rock climbing.

I like to hike in about a couple of miles into Mueller Canyon with my friends and go camping. I am always amazed at how easy it is to get away from the hustle and bustle of city life.

Last but not least is Fall. I like the fall because that is a time where you can enjoy the beauties of the desert in Southern Utah. I like to ride my bike on the slick rock trails near Moab and enjoy the natural environment of the red rock country. I also enjoy rabbit hunting with my dad and brother in the fall.

I'm glad that my ancestors came across the plains to Utah and that my parents chose to stay here. … That's what living in Utah means to me.

Carolyn Zeibig
Salt Lake County

Age 15; **Birthplace** Cottonwood Hospital; **Occupation** School; **Religion** Mormon; **Race/Ethnicity** Caucasion

What does living in Utah mean to me? When I think about our state, I think about all the hiking that I do in the summer. I remember riding a Seadoo over a beautiful lake and loving the scenery. I felt happy to be alive at that moment. I think about the admirable man that lent me a quarter to help me pay for a pair of shoes because I was short .16 cents. I love to just turn my head east and see the splendid Wasatch Mountains everyday as I walk to seminary. I feel so lucky to live here.

I also am delighted in our seasons. Some states have almost the same season year-round. Having four seasons really gives you something to look forward to. Sledding in the winter, sunshine, flowers, and rain in the spring, swimming in the summer and leaves in the fall. I particularly like the winter and summer. Winter, because I love to sled and have snowball fights. Summer, because I like to

swim and ride our Seadoo. This winter I am planning on learning to snow ski. I am really looking forward to it. So in conclusion, I'd just like to say Utah is a great state!

Eric Jones
Weber County

Age 13; **Birthplace** Ogden; **Occupation** None; **Religion** Mormon; **Race/Ethnicity** Caucasian

Living in Utah means many things to me. By living here I have a chance to ski, hunt, fish, boat, learn and live a happy life. It means a chance to meet new people who help me with whatever I choose. Living here means that I am able to live in a clean environment with safe neighborhoods. I can play any kind of sport I want, all year round. It seems that we get chances that many other people don't get. We have farms to grow our food on and farms where cattle and other livestock are raised for food. We aren't poverty stricken or poor. We have a strong and wise government that makes good choices to keep us safe.

I am glad I live in Utah where other states respect us. We have a great professional basketball team and some other minor league teams who do well. I know this is a great state and under control or else we wouldn't be a candidate for the place to host the Olympics.

I have proof that Utah runs a good educational program because my school and many others have been nationally recognized as Centennial Schools who are drug free. Out of all the states I have traveled to including California, Nevada, Idaho, Wyoming and Colorado, our state is the best. Our state is better because I have seen people in these other states act like they were more important or richer than we are. But in Utah, the majority of the people seem to treat you as an equal.

Christine Alana Smith

Washington County

Age 15; **Birthplace** Whitten, California; **Occupation** Student;
Religion N/A; **Race/Ethnicity** Caucasian

In truth, Utah doesn't "mean" anything to me. We moved here to get away from all of the gangs, violence and, mainly, earthquakes. This state is so much better than California. The scenery out here way exceeds that of California. The view of Pine Mountain with snow on it is breathtaking. It is more than beautiful, it is gorgeous. Such beauty I have never before beheld. The statement "What Utah means to me," might infer to what I think of Utah. Utah is, to my family, a sort of salvation, if you will. In Utah we have succeeded in qualifying for a loan, despite our previous credit difficulties, and have purchased a home. It is near the Red Cliffs Mall. There are some real nice people here, too. They are so friendly and the families are huge. Also, the prices are very low, and tax. In California it is around 7 to 8 percent. Here it is only about 7 percent. Cool, huh?

Brady Pope

During this essay I would like to express my feelings in regards to bicycle routes, smoking, and the influence gangs have concerning myself and others. It is my intention that you will read this and take what has been said into consideration for the new year and also for years to come.

I would like to write at this time regarding bicycle routes. I feel that Utah is in need for bicycle routes. During the summer time my friends and I always want to go to the mall and other places, but we usually can't do so safely. I live in Sandy and in order for me to get anywhere without a drivers license and a car, I have to ride my bicycle. When we go to the store we have to ride along Creek Road, which is a very busy road that leaves my mother worried whenever we want to go anywhere, because it's not safe. That is one of the reasons why I feel we need to have more bicycle routes. I also feel the bicycle routes should be for other things like rollerblades etc. and not just for bicycles. My friends and I have found a safe way of transportation by taking the bus, but the bus costs 65 cents each bus we need to take to get us to where we would like to be. This is a fairly good way of travel but it can end up to cost quite a lot after a while.

I am very pleased with the new smoking law and so are many others I have talked to. I would like to thank you for passing that law and hope it continues without to much controversy. There is still one more thing about smoking that I do not like about Utah. That is that police officers nowadays cannot do anything to teens that are smoking on or off public property. The law states that you must be 18 years of age to smoke. But what I see a lot around my school is teens that have one too many cigarettes a day. This disappoints me because I know it influences other teens to smoke which is breaking the law. I would really want to see a change in our society with smoking teens and the influence they have on others.

I also would hope to have more talk about gangs and the influence and scare they put upon society. I know they are trying to do a lot about gangs, and I thank you and them for doing so, but if more could be done to help decrease and growth of gangs I would be extremely thankful. For example on how to help decrease the scarce gangs put on society was the Brady Bill which I completely agree with and hope to have more laws similar to this one be enacted upon.

I would like to thank you for reading this essay and hope you will take what I have said into consideration, for my part and for others who live in Utah.

Sincerely, Brady Pope

Taylor Orton
Salt Lake County

Age N/A; **Birthplace** N/A; **Occupation** N/A; **Religion** N/A; **Race/Ethnicity** N/A

Lake Powell—I go there evrey Summer. Lake Powell is vary big and it is fun Jumping off the houseboat. I can swim without a floatie.

John Summerhays
Salt Lake County

Age N/A; **Birthplace** Salt Lake City; **Occupation** Student; **Religion** L.D.S.; **Race/Ethnicity** White

Living in Utah means living in Utah. I need to write about what it means to me. It doesn't really mean much to me except for I don't live in Arizona or South Carolina or San Francisco. I was born in Utah, I've never really been far away from Utah so I don't have outside experience in other places so that I could compare.

Living in Utah does mean somewhat good weather. It also means that you can go to the nearest market without worrying if some guy is going to stick a knife in your back. I'm not saying it's perfectly safe but it is safer. It means having a friendly argument about sports with your family or friends. It means hunting in the mountains, then fishing in the lakes, then skiing on the great snow, then watching professional basketball, then grabbing something to eat on the way to a tubing trip through the Grand Canyon.

Utah is a smoke free state and it's elegal to gamble that is very important to me. It also reduces the chance of dying of lung cancer and get killed because you can't pay debts on a poker game.

Utah is a great state. I was wrong at the beginning of this report. Utah means a lot to me and I'm glad to live here.

Ben Rutherford
Salt Lake County

Age 13; **Birthplace** Utah; **Occupation** Student, Boxer, Baseball player; **Religion** None; **Race/Ethnicity** Whight

Dear Future person,

I'm probably dead when you read this if not come and find me. I promise I won't be a geeky old man. Well, I better shut up and tell you about the past, well, your past my present. Yester I got a new video game (you guy's probably have virtural reality systems) but if not try looking up Nintendo or Sega. I have a pet hampster. Do you have a pet? I'm in sixth grade. We rotate teachers like Mrs. Jimas for social studies, Mr. Walker for math. You guys might not have to go to school you might get Brain implants oh well. If you do have time machines come back to 9:00 a.m. Sandy Utah 10245 Butter Cup Dr and come to Ben R.'s room January 24, pleas contact me, come back in time bring me back to life anything!!!!!!

Yours truly, Ben Rutherford

P.S. I'm enclosing picture of my hampster on the back of this paper.

My name is Kung Lao I am Ben's hampster. I like to eat corn, raisens, and peanut's. I am 2 years old and was born on September 28th. I am a cream colored hampster.

Submitted by Brandon O'Keef, Grand County.

Submitted by Ruth Ann Eggli, Davis County.

"Strawberry Reservoir: Valerie and Wayne Alder. September 1, 1958."
Submitted by Marie Hunter, Salt Lake County.

To me, Living in Utah means Skiing!

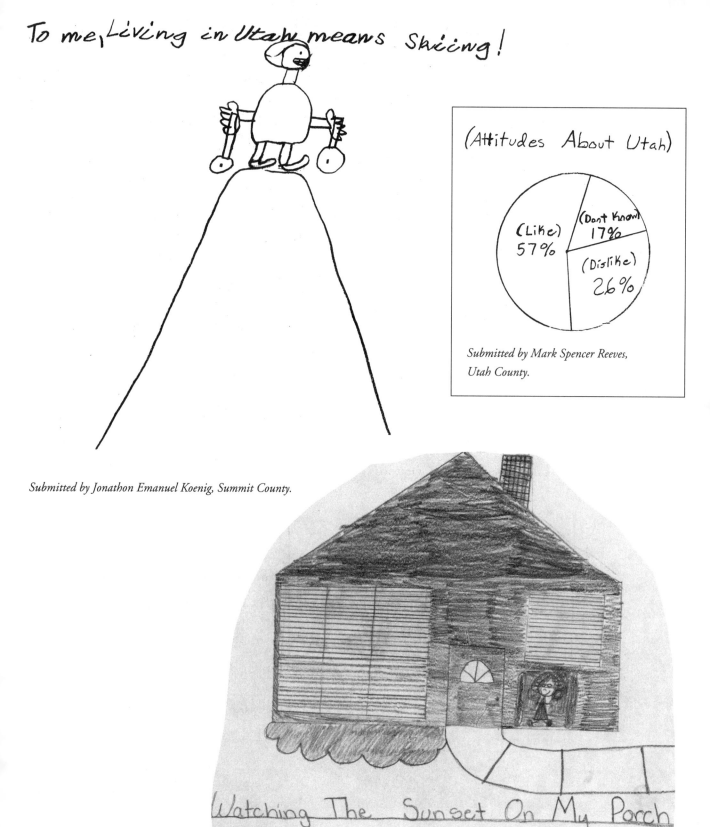

(Attitudes About Utah)

(Like) 57%

(Dont Know) 17%

(Dislike) 26%

Submitted by Mark Spencer Reeves, Utah County.

Submitted by Jonathon Emanuel Koenig, Summit County.

Watching The Sunset On My Porch

Submitted by Ashlin Virginia Gunn, Salt Lake County.

Elizabeth Kidd

Salt Lake County

Age 16; **Birthplace** Murry, Utah; **Occupation** Student; **Religion** LDS; **Race/Ethnicity** Caucasian

I wrote this paper as an English assignment, but I wanted to make sure you got a copy so I'm sending one to you, with a brochure that we handed out at my 14th birthday party. The picture of the clown on front is me. I volunteer my time to Primary Children's Medical Center as a clown now that I am well. I hope you enjoy reading my paper.

I'd like to talk about the medical aspects of Utah. The hospitals of Utah are always on the cutting edge of new technology, i.e. life saving procedures such as surgeries, organ transplants, and bone marrow transplants. The University of Utah Hospital is one of the few medical facilities throughout the Intermountain West that has a Bone Marrow Transplant Unit. LDS Hospital has one, and Primary Childrens' Medical Center just recently opened a new state of the art Childrens' Bone Marrow Transplanting Unit.

I know this information because I had a Bone Marrow Transplant on November 10, 1992 at the University of Utah Hospital. I was diagnosed with Acute Myeloblastic Childhood Leukemia (AML) on June 12, 1992 and was given a 30% chance of survival, or approximately only two weeks to live. My only chance at life was to have a Bone Marrow Transplant. My brother, Russell Kidd, donated his marrow to me. Miraculously, his blood antigens matched mine perfectly, it was a 6 out of 6 match. Dr. Beatty, University of Utah Hospital Oncologist, says that to match this well is remarkable, usually only identical twins match as well as we did. Russ had his bone marrow surgically extracted at St. Marks Hospital, then it was rushed up to the University Hospital in a special container. I was in isolation for 39 days. My brother's marrow engrafted, which meant that my body accepted the transplant. My life had been saved.

I met a young man from Billings, Montana. He was diagnosed with Aplastic Anemia. He had to come down to Utah to have his Bone Marrow Transplant to save his life. He was split from his family for over one hundred days so that he could have his medical treatments. I don't know if I could have gone through such an ordeal and been away from my family too.

I am extremely grateful that Utah has had the vision to encourage and enhance our medical community. Our hospitals have saved many lives, not just mine. We are fortunate to live in a "Medical Mecca" in this beautiful valley. I am sure that our forefathers would be pleased to know that the fruits of their labors have produced such world-renown technology. Our childrens' hospital, Primary Childrens' Medical Center, is one of the best in the nation. One of my many doctors, an anesthesiologist, came from Florida just to work at our hospital here in Utah. He said how lucky we are to have such remarkable facilities.

Family is one of the most important parts of everyone's life—no matter where you live. Utah's availability of medical facilities enabled me to have my treatments for two years and still be able to be with my family. I believe that being able to have my family near me, helped me get well. Family is where love and caring begins. Through love and caring, we will flourish as a people, and as Brigham Young stated: "this valley will blossom as a rose." If we can keep our families together—in sickness and in health—caring and love in Utah will prosper. If we can keep caring and love together here we can share it with our neighboring states. By sharing it with our neighboring states we can share it with this great nation.

I was pronounced cured of cancer on March 2, 1993. This is what living in Utah means to me. LIVING IN UTAH SAVED MY LIFE!!

Submitted by April Martinez, Grand County.

Jeff Cryer
Sevier County

Age 17; **Birthplace** California; **Occupation** Student; **Religion** Luthern; **Race/Ethnicity** White

Living in Utah means a second chance, because the last couple of years I've screwed up. Now I'm back in school and Utah makes me feel good and happy with myself. All the people are way too nice. Also I hope to give back to Utah what I know it's gonna give me.

Emily Steele
Salt Lake County

Age 14; **Birthplace** Provo, Utah; **Occupation** Student; **Religion** L.D.S.; **Race/Ethnicity** Caucasian

A Dreamer in Utah

I didn't always dream of going to the Olympics as a figure skater, but that dream has grown in me. That very first time I was with my cousin and we were bored. I don't

remember who suggested it, but we ended up ice skating at the Bountiful Bubble. It cost $2.00 to skate and $1.00 to rent skates. At first I held on to the wall, but after awhile I got going and started to try some "tricks." I was ten at the time and thought I was pretty neat stuff. I was sad to leave, but I visit my local rink (Murray ice rink) often in the winter. I have my own skates now and can do spins, small jumps, and other fun moves. When I skate it's like a different world the ice just glides freely under my skates, it makes me feel elegant and graceful like a swan.

I think it would be neat if I could be in the Olympics if they come to Salt Lake City, but I've only been skating for four years.

Maybe you'll read this some day and look and see if I was in the Olympics and maybe I will have won the gold medal.

Charles Noyes
Wayne County

Age 16; **Birthplace** Richfield Hospital; **Occupation** N/A; **Religion** Church of Jesus Christ of Latter day Saints; **Race/Ethnicity** White/Caucasian

I am very pleased that I am now living in Utah. I have traveled to other states and lived in other states, but it isn't quite the same. Utah has a special heritage, and to me it is even more special because my ancestors traveled across the plains with Brigham Young to live here in peace. This is a choice land, and a land where families can grow up together in love and fellowship. I live in a small valley near large and beautiful mountains. I love to live here, where I am free to go fishing on Saturday mornings or to go spend an afternoon with my family. I live very close to nature and I have many opportunities to watch animals and nature perform.

I have many goals and dreams that I want to accomplish in my life-time and I feel that living and working here has put me closer and closer to my dreams. This is where dreams come true.

Deirdre Joy Pitts
Salt Lake County

Age 11; **Birthplace** Nephi, Utah; **Occupation** Student Alta View; **Religion** L.D.S.; **Race/Ethnicity** Caucasian

Some of the things about Utah I like are the mountains, and the Indian culture. I will tell you how they have shaped my life in the next two paragraphs.

I've lived in Utah all my life. Right now I live in Sandy where I can see the mountains well. They look so beautiful in the winter, each peak capped with snow. I enjoy fishing in the summer time. In fall my family and I go look at the brightly colored leaves. In spring, is the best, when the mountains are full of life, and flowers.

Also, I like Indian culture. My dad is part Navajo. So occasionally I get to go down to the reservation, Montezuma Creek, and go see my relatives. I also like to go to Lake Powell. I go hiking and sometimes see things that look like they belonged to an Indian.

Those are the things I like in Utah. Next time take a second glance at the mountains and Indian culture. Utah is educational and fun!

Utah is my window to the Wonderful world of life.

Above: "Great pioneer stories like the one about the seagull and the sego lily." Below: "Learning about dinosaurs and their history. I like visiting the dinosaur tracks, a few miles from my home." Submitted by April Ann Jones, Washington County.

I enjoy Snowboarding in Utah

Submitted by Brad James Knickerbocker, Salt Lake County.

"Mary Marie Prisby, age 3 ½, in Joseph, Ut." Submitted by Marie Hunter, Salt Lake County.

I Like the plants and the people and the things and the gramos grapos and I Love my mom and I Love my Dad

Love
Tyler Hardy

Submitted by Tyler James Hardy, Millard County.

help save wield animals.

Submitted by Adam Scott Turville, Salt Lake County.

You could have more freedom to go to church in utah.

Grace Babtist church

Submitted by Micah Anthony Vargas, Salt Lake County.

FACES OF DEVOTION

THE FACES OF OUR RELIGIONS

Utah among all of the states is unique. It's uniqueness arises from the religious heritage established by the Mormons when they came into the area as the first group of permanent, white settlers.

The members of The Church of Jesus Christ of Latter-day Saints came to the Great Basin with the purpose of establishing a religious sanctuary. They were seeking a place where they could be left alone to practice their religion, a Zion.

Although the Mormons sought geographic isolation, it could not be maintained. Soon fate and world events intervened. The transcontinental railroad, the California gold rush, and the Civil War all brought non-Mormons to the territory. With the influx of a non-LDS population came difficulties; although their numbers were small, their purposes were different.

Soon a power struggle began, unique to Utah. Although some of the early colonies had been established for religious purposes, by the time of their admittance to statehood, they had no dominant religion. Utah in 1896 remained eighty percent LDS. The battle between LDS and non-LDS that ensued for control and power was not just religious, but affected all walks of life. It was economic, educational, and cultural—a classic conflict of the rule by a clear majority, with the minority fighting to have some say in the government, economic life, and the education of their children.

The struggle for Utah's statehood illustrates the willingness of the LDS majority to compromise. The seventh edition of the state constitution submitted to Congress for approval showed a willingness by the majority religious block to end divisiveness, to join the mainstream of American life, and to provide a representative government with the religious minority.

Today, Utah is still unique. A strong religious majority remains and the state continues to struggle with the perceptions and realities of majority rule. In many ways the century-old differences of majority rule, but minority consideration is present in Utah even today. The essays in this section testify to the ongoing differences.

—Shannon R. Hoskins

Sister Stephanie Mongeon
Weber County

Age 63; **Birthplace** Rolette, ND; **Occupation** Hospital—Mission Community Rel; **Religion** Catholic; **Race/Ethnicity** White/French

I am pleased to be more inclusive than writing on a personal level. We Benedictine Sisters are proud to be a significant part of creating history and affecting the lives of others in a positive manner. With our Catholic Heritage we work side by side with all other religions. We are united in a common goal and that is to spread the love of God to everyone. Living in Utah is a growthful and rewarding experience. We are committed to continue our service in respectful collaboration with the good people of this state.

This is a wonderful idea. God bless you with success and joy.

Tafta J. Watson
Millard County

Age 46; **Birthplace** Salina, Sevier, UT; **Occupation** School Teacher/Elementary Education/Special Education; **Religion** L.D.S.; **Race/Ethnicity** Caucasian

"Momma," asked Askel, "May I take my dog with me to Utah?"

"No dear," said Mina Jansen, Askel's mother.

"Momma," asked Askel, "May I take my toys with me to Utah?" "No dear," said Askel's mother.

"But momma, what may I take?" asked Askel.

"Askel, my dear, you may take your dreams. Take your faith, your dreams, and your ability to work. That is what you may take to Utah with you," replied Askel's mother.

Thus, it was with faith, dreams and an ability to work, that my great-great-grandmother left Norway with three small children to come to Utah. She came without her husband, who did not believe as she did.

Meanwhile, back in the states, other ancestors were also following their dreams, living by faith and working hard as they moved from place to place, driven out by mobs who did not agree with my ancestor's religious beliefs. They suffered hunger, hardships, cold, and cruelty and they tenaciously clung to their dreams and their faith as they moved from place to place.

Some of these great-great grandparents entered the Salt Lake Valley with Brigham Young. I have a legacy of people who had the courage to come to Utah with little more than their dreams, faith, and an ability to work.

To me, living in Utah means holding on to *my* dreams, *my* faith, and working hard. I dream of helping to make Utah a better place for my children and grandchildren to grow up. I have the faith that the things I am doing will make a difference, and then I set to work to see that it happens.

I want education, culture, and faith for my children and others around me. I think these are parts of living in Utah to me.

I was able to go back to school, with seven children at home, and get another degree because I could dream and I had the faith that what I wanted would become a reality because of the work I was willing to do.

I am helping my children by taking them to church, having them help us keep our yard clean, and encouraging them to help others.

I teach special education in our elementary school. I am an officer in the Fillmore Community Theatre and our Fine Arts Guild.

I try to live my life so others seeing me will know I believe God and live as He would. My life is a reflection of my dreams and my faith.

As I go out of my door and look up at the mountains to the east, I remember that others gave up their homes and security, so that I could be in Utah and nurture my dreams and my faith. It is now up to me to work and help others fulfill their dreams too.

Living in Utah means dreams, faith, and work.

Josie Ralphs
Emery County

Age 11; **Birthplace** Utah; **Occupation** Student; **Religion** Mormon; **Race/Ethnicity** White

I was born and raised in Utah. My ancestors go all the way back to my grandpa's grandpa.

Some of the things that I like about Utah is the influence that we, the Mormon's have in the state. Not everyone likes it, but we try to let people know that it's not good for you to use such things like tobacco or alcohol. Utah is also the state that broadcasts General Conference world wide, twice a year. The magnificent Mormon temples can't be forgotten either. They are so beautiful to go and see. There are a number of temples in Utah including St. George, Manti, Provo, Jordan, Salt Lake, Bountiful, and Logan. My mom and dad were married in the Logan Temple and one of my goals in life is to be married for time and all eternity in one of them.

You can't find another state with the varied outdoors that we have in Utah, especially in southeastern Utah where I live. We have the beautiful sandstone shores of Lake Powell. Just up the road from Lake Powell is Goblin Valley where you can play among the stone likenesses of Goblin's or Smurff's. We have the San Rafael wilderness in our own back yard, and if you look really close you'll find that it's very unique in its own special way. Then you can go West from the town of Ferron and be in the lovely Manti

Forest. My family has spent many wonderful afternoons touring the skyline drive, fishing at Ferron Reservoir, and boating at Joe's Valley Reservoir. My dad, uncles, grandpa, and brother have spent many hours in these mountains hunting for the elusive mule deer and the magnificent elk.

Another thing that I like about Utah is that most of my relatives live here. Being in the same state helps create a closer relationship between us all.

I'm glad that I live in Utah because there is a great influence here for me. I'd have to say that it's a pretty great state and I wouldn't want to live anywhere else in this world.

Linda H. VanWagenen
Salt Lake County

Age 41; **Birthplace** Grand Jct., Colorado; **Occupation** Special Education Teacher; **Religion** Unitarian; **Race/Ethnicity** Caucasian

I am 40 years old and have lived in Utah since 1967. It is still difficult for me to claim Utah as my home. My family moved around the intermountain west as my Dad's employer, the Denver and Rio Grande Railroad, transferred him frequently. In twelve years of schooling I attended twelve different schools, but did have the chance to settle in at Orem High School for the remainder of my High School education.

Living in Utah has been very trying for me. Moving as an eighth grade non-Mormon to Utah Valley was gut-wrenching. All I remember about the move was driving from Boise, Idaho where we previously lived, through North Salt Lake where one of the oil refineries was on fire, past orchards and into a valley filled mostly with lake. The signs were ominous for a lonely teenager trying to wend her way through a different and difficult culture. Memories of my public schooling include many instances of religious persecution. Mormon prayers before all assemblies, even locker room prayers before our drill team marched, release of students (after watching on screens in the auditorium) for one of the Mormon President's funerals. My High School experience was that of being one of a handful of non-Mormons in a graduating class of over 600. What little dating I did was done as a conversion project. My 20 year class reunion was a bitter reminder of growing up in Utah. The opening prayer was given by the person who became the seminary teacher. Only in Utah! The religious intolerance I felt as a young adult has left deep scars which will always make my experiences in this state jaded.

This whirlwind relationship with Utah culture changed slightly when I moved to Salt Lake City in 1972 at the age of 18 to attend the University of Utah. I lived in the dormitories on campus and was immersed with an out-of-state population that helped me to develop into the person I am today.

One interest I developed was a deep love for the topography and natural beauty of Utah. My first backpacking experience occurred my Freshman year at the University of Utah. This opened up a whole new world of Utah for me. I found I could not only hide, but also find myself, in the back country of this state. I fell in love with Canyonlands National Park and took my fiancee there for his first desert backpack. Which is ironic, because he is a native Utahn, growing up in Carbon County. For more than 20 years we have backpacked, hiked, skied, snowshoed, driven, walked, etc. over vast portions of this state. We have been involved in numerous naturalistic and environmental groups.

The most difficult decision I have had to make about living in Utah is that of whether or not to have children. My husband, growing up in a portion of the state that I keep telling him should have been annexed to Colorado long ago, had none of the persecution problems I experienced and had no qualms about raising children in Utah. I very much did not want my kids to have the same experience I did. Luckily, as more out of state people move into Utah the state is becoming more diverse and religious persecution is not as easily tolerated. We do have two children now that tag along on all our excursions. They both started backpacking at the age of four. We have found a church community we can be at peace with even though my children still experience the pains of being a minority religious group.

Utah has much to offer. It is a beautiful country, filled with sandstone deserts to high alpine meadows. I never get tired of what she has to offer. The culture that exists in this state is Utah. If one lives here then you have to find your own way of accepting and being accepted. For Utahns of the future I wish them religious tolerance and encourage them to continue to fight for the protection of the natural environment which makes this state so unique.

Shirley Foreman Bartley
Salt Lake County

Age 68; **Birthplace** Grand Island, Nebraska; **Occupation** Postal Clerk/Library Assistant; **Religion** Methodist; **Race/Ethnicity** Caucasian

I was just informed that the alumni of the East High graduating class of 1945 are planning a 50th reunion. At that time East was the premier high school sitting regally on its hilltop site. I was privileged to be one of that "Gold Medal Class" who eagerly embraced a future which seemed so full of hope as World War II came to an end.

I am proud to say that I am a Utahn. But when I arrived in Salt Lake City on August 6, 1942, little did I dream that I would be living the rest of my life here. Uprooted by the war, we expected this move to be only temporary.

I remember my first glimpse of the Salt Lake valley as we left Emigration Canyon. What I perceived then to be a huge metropolis is no comparison to the urban sprawl of the present day. Nevertheless, I was completely enthralled by the unique geography and history of my new home.

I recall the first time we stood on the steps of the Utah State Capitol and gazed down State Street with the Wasatch Mountains on the east and the remnants of ancient Lake Bonneville on the west. Where else in the world is there such a sight? Visiting relatives were always taken there first followed by a tour of Temple Square and an organ recital in the Tabernacle. We also rode the Bamberger Train to Lagoon to swim in "Water Fit to Drink" in contrast to floating on the Great Salt Lake at the old Saltair Resort.

At that time, there were no malls and since most of the necessities of life could be found in the central down town area, it was a busy, bustling scene where you always encountered a friend or two to chat with. This was indeed an exciting place to shop, dine, and go to the movies. Newsboys stood on the corners shouting "Extra! Extra!" whenever there was a late breaking story of which there were many in those days. Of course, this was before television.

The First Methodist Church which I attended for twenty years is still located down town at 203 South 200 East, now dwarfed by the towering U.S. West Building. At that time, I remember the shocked expression on the face of anyone who inquired "What ward are you in?" when I responded that I was a Methodist. Some of my Mormon acquaintances have also been surprised when I told them that Brigham Young was once a Methodist. Many outsiders are amazed that it is possible for a member of a minority religion to live happily in Salt Lake City. I now attend Christ United Methodist Church at 2375 East 3300 South, which was once called the country church when it was built forty one years ago. As we look forward to the statehood centennial, I recall the Centennial Days of '47

Parade and the musical *Promised Valley* performed at the University of Utah stadium to commemorate the coming of those first brave and hardy pioneers. As my mind flits back over the many events since then, I realized that the people of my generation have been pioneers of the second one hundred years. We who have worked, studied, raised our families and supported our community activities have also contributed to the development of this great state. There has been phenomenal growth and change in the last fifty years. I am so grateful for the opportunity I have had to live in Utah and participate in the life of these times.

Angela Jensen
Salt Lake County

Age N/A; **Birthplace** Starkville, MS; **Occupation** Teacher; **Religion** LDS; **Race/Ethnicity** White

Living in Utah means that I am closer to my heritage and have a greater opportunity to learn more about these pioneers who suffered great hardships to settle this valley and this state.

Utah has a great heritage which most states do not have; a heritage which I hope both LDS and non LDS can share in. It is the story of a people who left much behind, suffered and lost many on the way, but continued on because of their beliefs and their belief in the right to worship their God according to their own dictates.

Today Utah is more diverse religiously than ever before. Yet all can share in the belief of those early Utah pioneers that all have the right to worship their God according to their own dictates.

Living in Utah also means that I can enjoy many diversities in nature. Utah has beautiful, awe inspiring mountain ranges; clear blue lakes nestled within mountain valleys; sage brush covered hills; vast sand dunes; dry desert stretches; unique stone monuments; and snow, snow, snow. I don't believe there is any other state that can rival Utah in its diversity of nature. No matter what season, the Utah landscape is breath takingly beautiful.

What living in Utah means to me is that I have an opportunity to live near people of my same religious convictions and learn of my religious roots; I can still breathe in the beauty of nature; and still be relatively close distance wise to my family.

Perris S. Jensen
Salt Lake County

Age 93; **Birthplace** Heber City, Utah; **Occupation** Lawyer (retired); **Religion** L.D.S. (Mormon); **Race/Ethnicity** White: British and Danish

First, let me introduce myself, and set forth some of the reasons why I feel qualified to speak on the subject "What Living in Utah Means to Me" with a background which enables me to make comparison.

My name is, as indicated above, Perris S. Jensen. I was born 93 years ago at Heber City, Utah. I have lived in Utah all my life except for five years in Europe: three years in Holland and two years in Wales and England. I have travelled extensively: in all fifty states of the U.S.A. and forty six other countries, including all of the major nations, all of the continents. I have visited Europe six different times, and spent time in Israel and the Mideast in 1926 and 1961. I have found good people, wonderful people in all areas, and I have found scoundrels everywhere. I feel I have an excellent background for comparing Utah, with its favorable lifestyle, with anywhere else in the world.

Let me outline some of the favorable factors which, in my opinion, make Utah the ideal place to live, to prosper, and to rear a family:

Environment: With its distinct four seasons the climate of Utah is as near ideal as can be found anywhere. The temperature is moderate, neither too hot in summer nor too cold in winter. Many, who know no better, dream of tropics, the rainy season brings heat and moisture stifling in intensity, and I can never forget the bugs, vermin, the hordes of little crawling creatures that get in the clothes, into the food and have driven some missionaries assigned to such areas, to utter destruction. Tornadoes, hurricanes, floods, volcanoes are almost unknown in Utah …

Cultural Facilities: Utah has always had a high reputation for its high cultural standards. Its Mormon Tabernacle Choir and its Symphony Orchestra are world renowned. Many of the earliest Pioneers were top quality musicians and artists from the cultural centers of Europe. Hardly had they become settled in these mountain valleys until they built the Social Hall. The first theatre between the Mississippi and west coast. This was shortly followed by the famous Salt Lake Theatre, a structure without peer in the theatrical world in its day. That love of culture has been passed down to the present generation.

The entire state is divided into ecclesiastical groups called wards, each ward consisting of a few or several hundred members. Each ward has a "meeting house," sometimes shared with an adjoining ward. These meeting houses are not only places for Sunday worship, but each includes a cultural hall in constant use for social gatherings, for athletics, drama, aerobics, and social and cultural activities for young and old.

Business and Industry: Utah is rapidly becoming a world-wide leader in industry, particularly in the chemical and electronics businesses. It is growing faster in export business than any other state in the union. In 1994 only Utah and South Dakota showed export growth in excess of 30%. Part of this expansion of export business is due to the large reservoir of its young men, returned from foreign missions with a knowledge of foreign languages and foreign customs …

Its People: Notwithstanding the advantageous features mentioned above, without any question Utah's greatest asset is in the high quality of its citizenry, its people. California received its first great influx from those seeking gold. Other states became populated by those seeking free, or virtually free land. Utah, like the early colonies of New England and other eastern states, was populated by those seeking religious liberty, the freedom to worship in accordance with their beliefs, and to escape persecution because they insisted in putting those beliefs into action.

This great intermountain area was a desert, unwanted by anyone else. Inspired by the high concept that they were creating a "Zion" in the wilderness, by strenuous and coordinated efforts in building canals, the first use of irrigation by anglo-saxon people, they caused the wilderness to blossom as the rose. Their stern habits of thrift, hard labor, and a strong desire for education, they have passed on down to the present generation.

Perhaps the greatest problem facing the United States today is the break-up of the family and the loss of family values and standards. Three doctrines and practices taught to and observed by members of the predominant church in Utah, deal with this problem head-on. From the time of the earliest settlement "Home Teaching" and "Visiting Teaching" were everywhere taught and observed, and to these practises was added, over half a century ago, "Home Evening."

What are these fundamental teachings and practices of the Mormon people, faithfully carried on, not only in Utah but wherever members of the church are found, throughout the world? Every worthy holder of the Priesthood, which includes virtually every male, in addition to any other assignment or calling in the church, is called and set apart as a Home Teacher. Working in pairs, each pair is assigned two, three or occasionally more other families for whom they become responsible. Periodically, at least once a month, they visit the family in their homes, with a spiritual lesson. They are also responsible for that family for their moral, spiritual, material and physical well-being. At the monthly meeting they meet with the entire family, to not only teach them but to learn of any problems and to assist in any way possible, calling upon the resources of the entire church if necessary.

Visiting Teachers are the ladies counterpart of the Home Teachers. They, too, are assigned in pairs, to visit and look over a certain number of families. These they call upon at least once a month, to bring a spiritual message, but also to detect any need which the family may be too proud to mention, and to report to the Bishop of the ward any who are in need.

The Family Home Evening is a practice introduced in the church more than half a century ago. Every Monday evening is Home Evening. The entire family meets together, to discuss any family projects or problems, to participate in a spiritual lesson, to play games or some form of entertainment, and finally to top it off with light refreshments. Each of the various responsibilities is rotated from week to week. Even a child may preside over the events of the evening, with the aid of an older member if real young.

With such activities the family remains a close unit, with high ideals and standards, highly educated, and naturally trained as leaders, and with a keen sense of responsibility for themselves and for others.

In view of the foregoing it is easy to see why I regard Utah as the ideal place to grow up, to become established, to raise a family, and to achieve success to the fullest extent of my ability.

Simone O'Neil-Fraser

Sanpete County

Age 22; **Birthplace** Gunnison, Utah; **Occupation** Writer; **Religion** Christian; **Race/Ethnicity** Scotch-Irish/French-Dutch

I grew up in Utah. That doesn't mean that I have an undying love for the state or anything like that. I spent years of my life dreaming about leaving Utah—or at least Sanpete County. I used to hang pictures of cities like San Francisco, Chicago and Seattle on my bedroom walls and dream about what life would be like if I lived there. Oh, I had heard the stories of the horrible things that could happen in these cities—but that didn't make any difference. I was sure that somewhere in one of those cities was my niche—a place where I belonged. I certainly didn't belong in Utah. The people in the town were I grew up had certainly made that clear. I was different, I was alien. In classes I took at high school (the ones my parents or grandparents couldn't teach) I was thought to be odd because I wore a cross, didn't wear fashionable clothes and didn't go to one of the two Mormon churches in our town on Sunday. Even as a little girl it was that way. I was told by one little girl who lived a couple of houses away "I can't play with you because my parents say you're not Mormon." She said it with sincere regret, but the stories of her parents were a different story.

So I grew up eccentric, I fell in love with the public library—I could find a world of my own there, a world where my friends weren't just the outcasts and pariahs … In my world I was friends with Sherlock Holmes and the March Sisters, I rode the range with the Sacketts and traveled through the vastness of Middle Earth. I had long talks with Socrates and Plato … I walked through the ever widening pages of history.

Due to my excessive reading. I intellectually outclassed practically the entire high-school and in a culture (American not just Utah) that idealizes even idolizes stupidity and mediocrity, that made me even more of an outcast … but, through my reading I also discovered that in the outside world there were actually havens for people like me … I had felt a tinge of regret that in order to leave Utah I would have to leave my beloved mountains—and certainly if I went back East, say to Chicago, there would be no mountains.

That is one thing I like about Utah—its stunning natural beauty—the rampant flora and fauna, the awe inspiring sunsets, the peaceful spring mornings when the birds serenade me from the tree outside my bedroom window. With a stab of guilt I realized I'd even miss the snow. I had a friend make this comment "Utah is a place I plan to bring my children to show them how beautiful nature can be—but I don't want to raise them here."

I still dream about leaving. The only thing I think will stay with me is the intense bitter taste in my mouth upon remembering the people who treated me as they did, and the warm memories tied up in her magnificent beauty.

Sheika Elaine Leale

Emery County

Age 15; **Birthplace** N/A; **Occupation** N/A; **Religion** N/A; **Race/Ethnicity** N/A

I haven't lived in Utah all of my life, in fact, I haven't even lived here for a whole year yet. I haven't been everywhere or seen everything there is to see, but I guess you could say that my whole life has changed.

When I first flew in, I looked out of the airplane window and wondered what I was getting myself into. I had spent four hours in a plane with my dad wondering what new and exciting things were waiting for me in what was to become my new home. We landed in Price, and I hate to say it, but my first impression of Utah wasn't good.

I learned soon just exactly how ignorant my judgments of Utah were. Coming from California, I thought I knew a lot more than the "hicks" out here in Emery County did. I laughed at the size of Castle Dale compared to the big city I was from, but as long as I am judging by size, let me say that the hearts of the people here are bigger than three times the "big city" I'm from.

I haven't yet gotten to the part about my whole life changing, but I feel it appropriate to say that when I first got here I was very closed minded and judgmental of anything that was new or different. People say that ignorance is bliss, but I disagree because I wasn't happy at all.

I moved in with a Mormon family and thus, I went to church. At first I wasn't happy about this arrangement, in fact, I thought of it as a big bore. I couldn't believe the irony of me going to church. It seemed so ridiculous to me that I didn't even stop to think that I might be mistaken, about a lot of things.

Well, after several months, I began to realize that I was wrong. It wasn't easy to admit, but after some serious thinking, I asked to have missionaries come and give me the discussions.

After only one discussion, I was asked if I would be ready to be baptized the next week. It shocked me that I didn't have much time to decide, but I knew that it was right. Elder Gaspar and Elder Cutler (Elder Cutler was transferred and Elder Lonergan took his place) were my missionaries and in October of 1994 at the Castle Dale Stake Center.

That is mainly how my life changed. That is in fact a major change. Since then my goals have changed, my relationships with others have changed, my values and morals have changed, even my grades have changed. I was ignorant when I got here, perhaps I still am to some degree but for the most part I have "seen the error of my ways." If I hadn't come to Utah, I probably wouldn't have changed at all, and looking back, that is a rather scary thought. I suppose living in Utah means new beginnings, a clean slate. A chance to start over and make it better the second time around. Living in Utah means friends, happiness, and love.

Mark Lynn Merrill
Utah County

Age 12; **Birthplace** N/A; **Occupation** N/A; **Religion** N/A; **Race/Ethnicity** N/A

When I think of Utah, I think of the snow, the church, the love, and the joy we all share. Utah is peaceful, and it's where my parents, my grandparents, my aunts and uncles, and my cousins all grew up.

I feel most peaceful when I go to church or visit the LDS temples. I love the mountains, the neighborhoods, the people, and the gorgeous views, the love of indoor and outdoor sports is great. My whole family loves sports very much! Our baseball park is the best in the state. It's name will soon be changed to the Russell Swenson Memorial. I love going to Jazz games at the Delta Center.

One particular cemetery I like is the Payson City Cemetery, because that is where my dad, my sister, two of my cousins, and my aunt are buried. I used to cry about my dad's death but I realized where he went, and that he went there for a reason.

I have 6 brothers and 7 sisters who all grew up in Utah. I've lived in Utah 12 years and I intend to live hear the rest of my life. My mother has been a widow for almost 8 years. She works at home and likes it. I was 4 when my dad passed away, so I don't have many memories of him. I was blind and deaf when I was born, my dad gave me a blessing and within 3 months I could see and hear.

I like shopping at most places, and the movies are fun to go to. Every year we go to the Festival of Lights at

Canyon View Park. During the Christmas season, there is usually snow on the ground. The church office building is in Salt Lake, which is also very special to me. I enjoy writing and I enjoyed doing this. See you in 100 years!

Olivia Trujillo King
Davis County

Age 49; **Birthplace** N/A; **Occupation** N/A; **Religion** N/A; **Race/Ethnicity** N/A

My parents were originally from the San Luis Valley in southern Colorado. Their families were ranchers and very tight knit Hispanic families. My mother and father married very young and left the valley with hopes of a wonderful future here in Utah. Beginning here was difficult because many men were out of work and being Hispanic and not really comfortable with the language was difficult for my father. He took many different types of jobs to provide for my mother and us children. To some people we were poor but in parental love we were extremely wealthy. I am the 7th child of 8 children, my parents have suffered the heartache of losing 3 children in death but the great joy of having 22 grandchildren and soon to have 21 great-grandchildren added to the Trujillo family along with the importance of honoring our Hispanic heritage. We were encouraged to participate in school activities; student government, the arts, academic scholarship, athletics and to be faithful to our religious beliefs. There were very few Hispanic students who were also LDS and sometimes that was difficult. I have personally only felt the pain of prejudice behavior by others on a few occasions but the sadness of it still remains. My parents took time to explain to us the destructiveness of prejudice attitudes and to have pity on those who limit themselves in getting to know other races and nationalities. They taught us to be proud of our Hispanic heritage. We have been here for over 400 years in North America, our ancestors were colonizers, Native Americans, honest workers and pioneers in many ways. They taught us to be thankful for our bronze skin and beautiful brown eyes and to share our heritage with all that would listen, for we were of great importance to them and to our God. I feel that I grew up in a safe clean town (Layton), attended excellent schools in Davis county, received scholarships to colleges in Utah (CEU and WSU) which helped me to future my secondary education. I had the privilege of marrying my sweetheart 27 years ago in the SL Temple and blessed with 3 children and two foster daughters. They have all excelled in their schooling, community and religious service. We as a family enjoy the beauties of nature here, the accessibility to cultural events, the strong family values, work ethics, religious freedom, and high quality of life we are privileged to enjoy. I have had the opportunity to be involved in my church, community and public schools; having a voice to vote for what I know to be true and good. I have actively tried to enlighten others to the benefits of learning about other cultures and the importance of recognizing all people as Gods children. We may be a small state but I have had a good life here and I echo the phrase, "UTAH … A PRETTY GREAT STATE."

Barbara Guy
Salt Lake County

Age 35; **Birthplace** N/A; **Occupation** N/A; **Religion** N/A; **Race/Ethnicity** N/A

I am an only child, born to parents forty years old. In Salt Lake City, Utah in the 1960s this just wasn't done. Whenever I told anyone I was an only child they assumed one of my parents had died. My parents looked like everyone else's grandparents.

When I was very small we lived on a street full of elderly people. The only other family with kids were the Oswalds. They had a girl Michelle, who was my age. We became friends but she was a Mormon and she couldn't play on Sunday. She couldn't play on Monday night because of Family Home Evening and she couldn't play on Tuesday afternoon because of Primary. At all these times she was accompanied by a gaggle of sisters, but when she was away from me, I literally had no one.

I loved Michelle and I loved playing in our clubhouse we made in my backyard from an old chicken coop. We'd play house and take turns being the mommy (the good part) and the daddy (something to do until you could be the mommy again). The mommy had a lot of speaking parts, things to do with cooking and cleaning and household maintenance as well as an enormous selection of loving and encouraging things to say to her children. The mommy always had more than one child.

The daddy's part was to kiss the mommy and the imaginary kids in the morning and leave until nighttime when he would come in, kiss the mommy and kids and sit down to read the paper. The daddy's role had to be beefed up to be anywhere near as interesting as the mommy's role. We'd make him come home sick. We'd make him forget his lunch or briefcase and come back in. We'd make him get fired. But even when his script brought him into the house for longer periods, he had little to say to the wife and kids. We just couldn't think of what he would say.

I remember saying "jeez" at Michelle's house one day and she and her sister sat me down and earnestly explained, "You can't ever say 'jeez' 'cause it sounds like 'Jesus,' you can't say 'gosh' 'cause it sounds like 'God' and you can't ever say 'sheesh' 'cause it sounded like, well you know. Only bad people talk like that and our dad says we can't be friends with bad people." I eagerly took this little lesson to heart and did my best to comply. After all, Michelle and her sisters were my only friends. I loved them and I needed

them. I couldn't afford to disappoint them.

Michelle always asked me to come to Primary with her. I really wanted to go but my mother would never let me. I was being raised Methodist and went to Sunday school most weeks, and my mom intended to have me remain a Methodist. She saw an invitation to Primary as the first step toward indoctrination, but I saw it as a chance to fit in, a chance for acceptance and a chance to play with a lot of other kids my age.

I said my prayers while kneeling next to my bed every night and my dog would kneel with me until I was done. It got so that everynight I would ask God if I could just please be allowed to be a Mormon. In the dark next to my iron bed, Bandit the dog knelt by my side, whining as I cried.

When I was ready to start the third grade we moved to a house on a circle where everyone was Mormon but us. There were ten houses on the circle, and lots of kids. I was delighted to be around so many kids for a change. On the first day of school, the teacher asked anyone who wasn't Mormon to raise their hand. Without thinking about it I raised my hand. I was the only one. If I'd known that, I probably wouldn't have done it. This makes me think there might have been a few others, possibly with older siblings, who knew not to raise their hands. My fate as a novelty item, THE NON-MORMON, was sealed.

One afternoon, a family friend whose kids went to another school was in my school's parking lot waiting for me. She gave me a ride home where I found my mother in tears. Her mother, my grandmother, who had been living with us had just died. I did my best to comfort my mom and I sat there listening to the grown-ups talk for quite a while. Finally I went outside and saw that most of the neighbor kids were in the front yard next door. We had just lived there a few weeks and I was still getting acquainted. My grandmother's death was news of the year. Some of the kids had even seen them take her away. This is why my mom's friend had picked my up, so my mom could tell me herself. We kids sat around watching water run past us in the gutter, sometimes sending sticks downstream. Someone asked if my grandmother had been a Mormon. When I said no, they said, "That's too bad, 'cause this very minute she's on her way to hell." This wasn't said with malice particularly, more matter-of-factly.

Someone else added, "And the worst thing is, you'll never see her again. When people in *your* family die, they're just gone forever and no one gets to see anyone else ever again. When *we* die we go to the celestial kingdom, and one by one our family comes to be with us and we live just the same as here."

"Even better," someone added.

Julie, the girl next door came out carrying a can of spray paint. We had seen our mothers get interested in "dried weeds" as a craft item and at Julie's suggestion we scavenged the neighborhood for the most interesting looking dead weeds we could find. All the kids took turns spraying their weeds with black paint and then they delivered them, still sticky and pungent, to my mom as a token of sympathy. She still has them and whenever I visit, they remind me of that afternoon.

How can children thoughtful enough to make a gift for a grieving woman not even notice when their words ripped through the heart of a little girl?

I was constantly coached by kids about how great Mormons are and about how they have "the one true church." My church spent a lot of time encouraging us to love our neighbors and be kind to those different from us. Mormons seemed to spend their time teaching children to be cliquish and exclusionary and to criticize anyone or anything different from ourselves and their beliefs.

Little phrases pepper my childhood memories, "Mormons don't bet," "Mormons don't swear," "Mormons don't drink coffee," "Mormons don't play on Sunday," "Mormons have the one true church," "Which ward are

you in?"… and on and on. At the time, I felt all these things were aimed at me, pointing out how different I was from all of them, and how inferior.

The ward house was right next to my elementary school and there was a steep paved hill that was the boundary in between. On really windy days we could unzip our parkas and hold the hems of them way over our heads behind us, stretching our arms far out to the sides. If the wind was good enough and we got a good running start, we could actually fly. If it was windy in the afternoon, kids would stay at school until dinnertime, flying.

One day in the third grade, a new girl joined our class. Her clothes were funny and she had the longest, blackest hair I'd ever seen. She was huge, much taller than the rest of us and her skin was brown. She was Native American. No one else in the whole school had brown skin, and I was still eight years away from meeting my first black person. This girl was so *different*.

Our teacher, Mrs. Cook, who I hated because she'd always single me out as the non-Mormon who could stay after school and clean erasers on Primary day, introduced the new girl to us. "Class, today we have a new student joining us, a Lamanite named Regina Begay." Kids snickered. At recess, everyone was talking about her name and making jokes about how she must be gay. This was said with derision although I'm sure no one really understood what it meant. To make matters worse, Mrs. Cook had introduced her as if her name rhymed with vagina, Regina. The poor girl Regina didn't even bother to correct the pronunciation of her name. She must have been mortified. I was much more interested in the word Lamanite, which I had never heard before. I asked someone in the group what it meant and they said it had to do with the color of her skin and how God hated her so he turned her brown. I had always thought that skin color had to do with how long a person spent in the sun, so this was a surprise to me. I remember asking my mom about it that night and she told me that God loved all children and paid no attention to what color they were.

Regina wore medallions around her neck made of seed-beads with brightly colored Indian designs and she wore necklaces made of apple seeds. I was so relieved to have someone in class who was different, even more different than I, someone to be the new center of attention, negative as it was.

I'd like to say that Regina and I became friends and our friendship overshadowed all the cruelties perpetrated on us by Mormon kids, and that together we learned that being accepting and kind is what God wants from little children; that God is not impressed by children who inflate their sense of superior morality by being hurtful to others. The truth is, except for one time, I avoided Regina like the plague and hope the other kids wouldn't see how alike she and I were. With the big Indian girl Regina around, it was much easier for me to fit in, once I learned all the rules, and I was mostly content to let her suffer the sore thumb fate alone.

One time though, I did invite her to stay after school with us on a windy day. She accepted and seemed eager to join us, but it turned out she was too heavy to fly.

Christopher F. Krueger
Salt Lake County

Age 27; **Birthplace** Ft Bragg, NC; **Occupation** H.S. Social Studies Teacher; **Religion** Non-Affiliated; **Race/Ethnicity** White

When I was small, I used to always wonder what my classmates were talking about when they threw out words like *primary* and *mission*. I'd ask my parents, and they would tell me that they were Mormon words, and that I should not worry about them.

But that's impossible, isn't it? To grow up in Utah without knowing what a *Ward* or a *Stake* is would be equivalent to burying your head in the sand and pretending that Utah is not as it seems. That, in fact, Utah is just like everywhere else in the United States, with people from all sorts of religions, no one getting too wrapped up in it.

It was hard for me, really. Going to public school where everyone else in your class was somehow part of a big club that you didn't belong to is troubling for an awkward kid who was incredibly lacking in his social adjustment anyway.

Mind you, I never felt *discriminated* against, at least not on any conscious level, so I was never bitter about not being LDS in our pretty great state. I never, as my parents often recommended, chose to enter private school. *Why not?* I wonder now, fifteen years later, and I conclude that I must have been, in some way at the very least, happy. But on some larger scale, I do suppose I felt that I was missing out. I had not been chosen to be in this group, a leftover piece of meatloaf abandoned for months in the back of the lower shelf of the fridge.

In junior high school, I actually came pretty close to converting. Why again, I don't know. I remember going to church a few times, playing Ward basketball and volleyball with my LDS friends and thinking it was pretty cool. It was a place where I felt accepted, and anyone that remembers, really remembers, their adolescence knows how valuable that feeling can be. My parents, strangely did not seem to care one way or the other, and they were very good parents. Their friends who often forbid their own children to play with LDS kids, would stare blankly with disbelief at me when I defended my LDS friends against their frequent jokes and occasional tirades.

Then, in high school, there were suddenly many kids that weren't LDS, and although I didn't isolate myself from Mormons, I found myself spending more and more time with those that weren't. As I neared graduation, I noticed, with some degree of wonder, where all my LDS friends had gone. Had I gone away, or had they?

During this time, I had also convinced myself that I wanted to get out. My gentile friends and I all left, some to the West Coast, some to the East, swearing we'd never come back. We didn't hate Utah, mind you, we simply thought we had outgrown it, thought the prevalent religious situation was stifling our growth and our fun.

But at college, and the other years I was away, I began to realize something that is very difficult for me to explain. Utah, I guess, isn't just about being Mormon. The people here really are a little nicer, and more genuine, but that really doesn't begin to cover it. I really do feel like I belong here. I am comfortable with my lack of affiliation with the predominate power structure, and they, I think are comfortable with me teaching their children.

It's funny. Of the six of my closest friends who all left Utah back in 1987, five of them have returned, for good, including my wife. The other one is coming back as soon as he can convince his girlfriend.

France A. Davis
Salt Lake County

Age 49; **Birthplace** Burke County, Georgia; **Occupation** Clergyman; **Religion** National Baptist; **Race/Ethnicity** African American

LIVING IN UTAH HAS BEEN AN EXCITING EXPERIENCE. I STARTED WITH A JOB AND STUDY OPPORTUNITY AT THE UNIVERSITY OF UTAH, WAS INTRODUCED TO THE LOCAL COMMUNITY BY A LANDLORD'S DENIAL OF A PLACE TO LIVE, AND JOINED THE CALVARY BAPTIST CHURCH. THE COMMUNITY WAS BEHIND THE TIMES IN ITS ATTITUDE TOWARD MINORITIES ESPECIALLY THOSE OF AFRICAN HERITAGE. RACISM WAS ALIVE AND WELL ALTHOUGH NOT TALKED ABOUT VERY MUCH. THAT ATMOSPHERE PROVIDED ENDLESS OPPORTUNITY FOR INVOLVEMENT AND ENGAGEMENT WITH THE POWERS THAT BE TO BRING ABOUT POSITIVE CHANGE. WITH SOME OF US WORKING OPENLY AND OTHERS AGREEING NOT TO FIGHT AGAINST OUR EFFORTS OPENLY, MUCH HAS BEEN ACHIEVED.

CONSEQUENTLY, THE HISTORIC CALVARY BAPTIST CHURCH IS WELL-KNOWN FOR HER LEADERSHIP IN COMMUNITY BETTERMENT AND CULTURAL AWARENESS. THE PUSHING THROUGH OF A MARTIN LUTHER KING JR/HUMAN RIGHTS HOLIDAY BILL AND THE HONORARY NAMING OF A MAJOR STREET SIGNAL THE PRESENT GROWINGLY INCLUSIVE ATMOSPHERE. BY WORKING TOGETHER, WE ARE ALL JUST A LITTLE BIT BETTER AND MORE HUMAN.

PERHAPS, THE GREATEST THRILL FOR ME HAS BEEN THE PRIVILEGE TO SERVE AS LEADER OF THE OLDEST PREDOMINATELY AFRICAN AMERICAN CONGREGATION, TO TEACH VARIOUS COLLEGE AND UNIVERSITY COURSES, AND TO NOW BECOME BOTH A REGIONAL AND NATIONAL LEADER. THE FUTURE BRIGHTENS A LITTLE EACH DAY. MY CHILDREN ARE FILLED WITH THE POSSIBILITIES OF PERSONAL INTEGRITY AND SELF-ESTEEM. SO, WE DREAM ON.

"St. Joseph's Church, 24th Street, Ogden, Utah." Submitted by Robert Beckstead, Weber County.

Stephanie W. Jensen
Salt Lake County

Age 27; **Birthplace** S.L. County; **Occupation** Teacher @ Kearns Junior High; **Religion** L.D.S.; **Race/Ethnicity** Caucasian/White

Ever since I can remember, there has been unrest, debate, controversy over the lack of separation of church and state in Utah. And although I feel that the L.D.S. church does exert undue influence in governmental issues in which it has no business, I can't say that this influence makes Utah a bad place to live—for Mormons or non-Mormons.

We enjoy one of the most scenic landscapes in the country. With just a short drive, we can change that scenery to almost anything else—sagebrush covered desert to alpine forest, red sandstone to parched salt flat. The population is as varied as the land. A wealth of cultures are represented and celebrated. And, in spite of the racially defined gangs, the cultures share with each other in a myriad of festivals and fiestas.

In fact, because of the L.D.S. church's influence we enjoy air in public places free from second-hand smoke, tough laws regulating alcohol, and a society free from such addictive temptations as gambling. Because of the influence of "the church," I feel relatively safe in my home, safe allowing my son to play outside in our neighborhood. And I know that the values, morals, and ethics I try to teach my children will be reflected and reinforced in society.

Utah, however, is not utopia, as some would have you believe. Our natural environment is rapidly being "developed," California-style gangs have gained a foothold and violently make their presence known. Fear is beginning to creep into our neighborhoods to govern our lives. Mistrust runs rampant.

In spite of all this, I can't think of a place on earth I'd rather live.

Cynthia Harris
San Juan County

Age 11; **Birthplace** Moab, Utah; **Occupation** N/A; **Religion** Mormon; **Race/Ethnicity** White

The reason I like living in Utah is because it is mostly a Mormon state. And also I like living here because Utah is the state that Brigham Young and Joseph Smith started. I think it is fun living in Utah because of all the National Parks and because of all the mountains.

It's fun to go to all the national parks. I like Utah because most of my relatives live here. There are a lot of reasons that I like living in Utah for.

Donald R. Seamons
Cache County

Age 23; **Birthplace** Ogden, Utah; **Occupation** Student; **Religion** Latter-Day Saint; **Race/Ethnicity** Caucasian

It doesn't seem very long ago that I had friends who hated living in Utah. They blamed all of their problems on the state and felt that there was some force holding them down and keeping them from doing the things they wanted to do. Life in the state of Utah was void of the kind of excitement and opportunity that they felt they deserved. I thought I understood at the time what their gripes were all about. Utah is not conducive to the person who desires instant gratification, nor is it the type of place where the average Joe can make a fortune in a short amount of time. It's relatively small and is isolated geographically from the more exciting places in the nation like Los Angeles or New York. But the more I thought about it the more I realized that what my friends meant was that the people and the overriding values of the state were not tending to accept their desired lifestyle. Geography was not their problem.

Their conflict was with the establishment.

One could say that I didn't have a problem with Utah because I was part of the establishment. I adhered to the basic principles of Mormonism and my thoughts and philosophy were fully in line with what the Latter-day Saints teach. So much so, in fact that I resented my friends' moanings as an attack on my cherished beliefs and way of life. What I couldn't understand was their perspective. They were living in a society that had a history of hostility between social and religious groups. Early on, no one felt that hostility greater than the Mormons did. Here in Utah however, the majority of the hostility was directed not toward the Mormons but toward the non-Mormons. Whether intentional or unintentional, the religious minority was often snubbed by the majority.

It wasn't too long ago that my perspective changed. As a Latter-day Saint I had always wanted to serve a mission, and that desire didn't change after I received a notice that I was to serve in Chicago. I was terribly excited about the fact that something I had always wanted to do was so close at hand and that I could do it in such an exciting place. It never occurred to me that I would have the experience of being a "minority."

During the course of my two years of service, I was in about every type of living situation one can imagine. I lived in farming communities, and walked the streets at night of Gary, Indiana, a city which a few years ago had the highest black on black murder rate in the nation. I've knocked on doors in some of the richest areas of the nation and rode the famed "L" trains through downtown Chicago. I've also lived in some of the poorest areas in the nation. I've been referred to as a honky, a white boy, and an FBI agent. I was told often that I should go back to my white neighborhood, and frequently reminded that "white men can't jump." I've been asked how many wives I had and if people in Utah really wore black hats, rode in horse-drawn carriages and lived without electricity. In short I've experienced life on the other side. I've been a minority.

Although this experience was new and challenging, it was also rewarding. Aside from all the other things I learned in Chicago, I learned how much we all have in common, religiously and culturally. My eyes were opened as I associated closely with African-Americans, Latinos, Filipinos, Koreans, and Poles, and loved them as if they were my own brothers and sisters.

Since it's admission into the Union, Utah has made a slow, methodical, 180-degree turn. It wasn't too long ago that Mormon Utah considered itself an outsider in the United States, a state where the majority held "peculiar" beliefs and didn't believe they could be understood by mainline America. I was shocked to read that even in Mormon Utah the evils of segregation were present until the civil rights movement that culminated in the '60s brought legal segregation to an end. As more people started moving into the state, more Mormons were introduced to different religions and cultures, and subsequently have been able to understand them, and conversely, to be understood.

Today, Utah is known as largely a friendly place; a place where people all over the world can come and enjoy the rich resources and cozy atmosphere. We're seeing a great influx of not only tourists but new residents who are adding new dimensions to our culture. Utah's progress has hinged on understanding, on tolerance, and on openness, and its appeal as a great place to visit and live has come not only because of its physical environment, but also because of its virtuous environment. Utah is seen as a great place to raise children, to live and to work.

My minority experience in Chicago gave me perspective that I had never had before. I lament that I had to leave the state to have such an eye opening experience, but I'm thankful that it helped me to understand how left out people can feel, and how defensive they can get when their culture or religion is challenged. It also helped me to realize

"Five generations in Utah." Submitted by Julia E. Barrett, Cache County.

"Touching four states at one time." Submitted by Kelli.

"Father Herlich Magen celebrates the baptism of Meghan Mendez." Hand-colored photo by Robert T. Beckstead, Weber County.

Plate 17

"Greg Hansen and son, Matthew, celebrate the 1994 USU graduation." Submitted by Pamela K. Neilson, Cache County.

Above: "Rural Utah." Submitted by Sheldon and Lucile Proctor, Garfield County.

Left: Submitted by Loretta Frei Adams, Washington County.

Plate 18

"Pioneer Days Parade, Salt Lake City." Submitted by Judith Ann Blain, Salt Lake County.

Above: Submitted by Jennifer Davault, Salt Lake County.

Left: Submitted by Loretta Frei Adams, Washington County.

Plate 19

Submitted by Loretta Frei Adams, Washington County.

"Native American Culture Presenter (teacher)." Submitted by Leo Shepherd Jr., Iron County.

"Former USU President Stanford Cazier prior to the 1994 graduation ceremonies." Submitted by Pamela K. Neilson, Cache County.

Plate 20

"Other parents: Norman and Lavon Gubler." Submitted by Loretta Frei Adams, Washington County.

Submitted by Gene Harkins, Salt Lake County.

Plate 21

Above: Submitted by Marian Bonar, Salt Lake County.

Left: Submitted by Judge Ray Uno, Weber County.

Submitted by Loretta Frei Adams, Washington County.

Plate 22

"Victoria and son, Joseph E. Harkins, stand in front of Mormon pioneer—3rd great-grandparents—in Kannaraville, Utah." Photo by Gene Harkins, Salt Lake County.

Plate 23

Submitted by Loretta Frei Adams, Washington County.

Submitted by Loretta Frei Adams, Washington County.

"Going to work with Grandpa Frei." Submitted by Loretta Frei Adams, Washington County.

Plate 24

that I have a self worth that is inherent in me, and that all people have that same inherent value. Living in Utah is a celebration of differences and sameness. Admittedly, there isn't a wide variety of ethnic groups in the state, but we do have a good amount of religious diversity. We Utahns, no matter what we believe or where our roots are, have too much in common to concern ourselves about divisive issues. We've built together a state that is conducive to family and to peace and to goodness. Let's spend the next hundred years maintaining what we have made, while building bridges of understanding and acceptance.

Julianna Boulter
Utah County

Age N/A; **Birthplace** Texas; **Occupation** N/A; **Religion** Mormon; **Race/Ethnicity** N/A

I like living in Utah because I think it's fun. I think it's fun because it snows alot. I lived in Lubbock, Texas and I hadn't seen a mountain in my whole life except for when I went to my cousins house in Salt Lake. The mountains are beautiful. There's Timpanogas Mt. and it's so high and pretty. Once my grandma came and hike up to Timp. Cave with us. Timp. Cave is so pretty. When you go inside you can't touch anything except some rocks that look like salt and pepper shakers. Our state bird is the sea gull. There's a story about it.

Some mormons had a big field of crops. Then some crickets came and attacked their fields and sea gulls came and ate the crickets.

And that's what I know about Utah.

Natalie Weight
Utah County

Age 15; **Birthplace** Provo, Utah; **Occupation** Student; **Religion** L.D.S.; **Race/Ethnicity** White

The three most significant possessions in my life are my family and friends, my religion, and my education. Living in Utah helps me to have more freedom and in having these things.

My family and friends supply me with lots of happiness and joy. Without them my life would be dull and lifeless. They are always there to help me up when I am down and encourage me to do the impossible. My friends are always there to make me laugh and are always ready to have a good time. They always join me in doing outrageous activities which include playing hide-and-go-seek in stores and having laughing contests. I love going and doing things with them—even if it sometimes turns people's head's. They are my inspiration for everything I do.

My religion is another key importance in my life. I belong to the Church of Jesus Christ of Latter Day Saints. Growing up with the gospel in my life has helped me stay morally clean and helped me to live a happy life. I would not be the person I am without the church in my life. Living in Utah allows me to enjoy living in the church.

My third importance in my life is my education. I strive to work on making my knowledge grow and strengthen. I want to make my life the best it can be, and without education it could never reach its full potential. I would never be able to enjoy my favorite hobbies—reading, playing the piano, writing—without an education. Living in Utah has helped with my education through providing all of the materials for a successful learning process.

My life would be nothing without these three possessions in my life. Living in Utah has helped me to make these things easier to obtain and enjoy.

Isaac Sanford Clarke

Utah County

Age 18; **Birthplace** Kahuku, Hawaii; **Occupation** N/A;
Religion (LDS) Church of Jesus Christ of Latter Day Saints;
Race/Ethnicity N/A

Living in Utah means most importantly these three things: family, religion, and beauty.

Living here I am always close to family. Originally, my parents' families are what motivated mine to move here. My parents felt that it was more important that we, their children, were able to live close to and get to know their families than it was for my father to make more money in his profession than he might have elsewhere. I am glad that we did because some of my best memories are with my extended family. The people here just make me feel as if I were family. The communities seem to put so much effort into trying to become better acquainted with another. They would give you the shirt off their back if you needed it. This is one thing that makes Utah so great, everyone is family, one way or the other.

Living in Utah has allowed me to live in an LDS, or Mormon, community. These communities share the same high standards that I and my family have. I believe that the LDS church is the major source of these values. I feel that not being persecuted by others because of these values are shared by the majority is truly unique about this state. As a result of the good value system here, this state has a relatively low crime rate in comparison with the rest of the nation. It is those standards that make the quality of life so good here. Utah has these great standards mainly because of the high importance which we put on obeying our religious standards always.

These are [several] things that I think make living in Utah so great: family, and religious atmosphere, and its natural beauty.

"Talmage, Utah." Photograph by John A. Calk, Utah County.

LIVES DETERMINED BY VALUES

Is there a common value structure unique to Utah? While there seems to be a majority opinion, there are also paradoxes and exceptions. For the most part, Utahns express themselves as pragmatic realists. This means they portray things honestly and base their values on utility and practical common sense with a strong overlay of Christian thought.

There is a strong emphasis on "family values" such as traditional role models, traditional family units, and moral teachings that include honesty, loyalty, caring, and civility. Equally important are "community values" that stress responsibility to neighborhood, town, state, and nation, and respect for education, safety, fairness, and freedom of expression. At the same time, there is considerable fear that the status of these values is eroding, threatening the image of our geographical place as a refuge from negative outside influences. Recent immigrants, however, are less fearful than longtime residents concerning such change.

One paradox is the contrast of "rugged individualism" with the concept of "obedience to authority." On one hand Utahns think of themselves as law abiding, yet acceptance of central authority is sometimes undermined by the ideas of individualism and self-reliance that have been transmitted through our historical struggles for survival in a harsh, spacious environment. Like any other group of people, we are complex in our diversity, but Utah may be distinguished by the extent to which common values are shared.

—Delmont R. Oswald

Bette Grace Cole

Lincoln County, Idaho

Age 71; **Birthplace** Levan; **Occupation** Housewife; **Religion** L.D.S.; **Race/Ethnicity** White

For nearly seventeen years I lived in Utah. For nearly fifty four years I have lived in Nevada. It is a great source of pride to me to be able to claim the wonderful heritage of both states. "What living in Utah means to me" is a multitude of things. There were seven of us in our family. We lived in a small four room house with no indoor water. We carried all of our water across the street from the neighbors. We were very poor during the depression but we didn't feel poor. We had food and raimant enough but most of all we had each other; parents, grandparents, uncles, aunts and wonderful, wonderful neighbors and friends.

We had love and security. We were taught honesty and moral values and to practice the golden rule. We learned to be resourceful, to work hard and to expect to work hard. To count it a blessing to learn how to work and be able to do so. To be helpful to all and concerned for others.

Many good teachers both in and out of school taught us how to think and be responsible. To do our best at all times.

We learned of God. To believe in him and his teachings. To trust in him, rely on him, love him and serve him.

We learned to love our country. We often sang, America, the Star Spangled Banner, America the Beautiful and other patriotic songs both of country and state. We learned to feel the greatness of this land. To know it is the best land in the World. Not that it would take care of us but that we would take care of it. That our great responsibility was to maintain freedom for all. We went to war and sent our loved ones to war to do what had to be done. Keep this land free.

We grew up with total confidence in our fellowman. We knew we could trust and rely on family, friends and neighbors with our very lives and never fear.

Yes living in Utah means to me that my character of trustworthiness, dependability and integrity were instilled in me there and I am ever grateful for this wonderful heritage to pass on to my loved ones, as it was passed on to me by staunch pioneers who settled this western land.

F. Gayle Higgins

Salt Lake County

Age 39; **Birthplace** SLC, UT; **Occupation** Homemaker; **Religion** LDS; **Race/Ethnicity** Caucasian

I woke up this morning and looked out my bedroom window at a snowy, quiet world. I am 38 years old and the wife of a wonderful man. I am the mother of four wonderful and challenging children. I am able to be the kind of woman that I want to be. As I looked out at the white peace that was there, I couldn't help but feel so grateful for all of it! You see …

I can send my children off to their respective high school, middle school and elementary school classes and know that they are facing some trials and they will have to stand firm on their values. But they will not face an over abundance of drugs or weapons. My tall, strong sons won't have to fight off muggers to keep their shoes. I can know they do not risk being shot by a sniper in the hills or bombed by an enemy that wants them exterminated. I can dream of their futures and believe with all my heart that they have great lives ahead; rather than wonder if they will live through starvation and disease.

I can kiss my sweetheart as he leaves for work. He isn't going out to fight off invaders of our country. He has a good job that he has earned. He didn't have some government official tell him what his vocation would be. I am so proud of him that I could burst because he works hard to give us a good life. Not long ago, I was driving home from the store and I realized how very lucky I was to be able to go shopping. My thoughts were with those in countries overseas where their lives are so tenuous and their liberties are so few.

So, you see, I feel so grateful. Living in Utah means so many things to me. As a child, I had the opportunity to live in different places and cultures. There were interesting things to see and do. But when I think of the different living conditions I was in, it was here in Utah that I felt the safest and most comfortable. As an adult, I have become more observant of just what the differences are. I have been to other places and felt disapproval because our family consisted of more than requisite one or two children. I have friends who moved to other parts of our country and go month after month trying to fit in and make a friend. Because in so many other parts of the country, there is an indifferent or, at least, distrusting attitude that is hard to get past.

Utah isn't a perfect place. There is *NO* perfect place on earth. I have heard lots of complaints about our state. But one thing that I noticed all the time—*those who complain about our smoking laws or our liquor laws or the lack of gambling and 'adult' entertainment; these are the ones who came here because they liked our lifestyle!* They came because they want their families safe. They came because they wanted to walk down a street at night and not be completely fearful. They like what we have and they just do not understand what makes it the way it is! In time, they will. But for now, I just pray that our leaders will not buckle in to the complainers and can stand firm for the ideals that make Utah what it is!

Our family visited Southern California recently. We thoroughly enjoyed the fun things we did there. The children commented once or twice on how nice it would be to have that in Utah. But not *once* did they say, "Oh, I wish we lived here!" They couldn't wait to be home in their own state where they felt safe and secure. It was rewarding to my husband and I to see that they liked the amusement parks enough to want them home but not enough to move *away* from home to get them. We knew then, beyond a doubt, that our family was living in the right place. We have had job opportunities that were in larger, much more populous cities. But when we prayed and thought hard about what was best for our family, we knew we wanted our family here.

Utah is growing at a record pace. As more and more people recognize what we have, they pour in. I love living in Utah. And my prayer for the next one hundred years of our state is that we can maintain the standards that our forefathers set in place. I am not talking about the old laws of not dancing after midnight or not leaving your horse double parked or what ever they were. I am speaking of the standards of cleanliness and purity of thought. The standards that provide a wholesome place to raise children that can grow strong and ready to serve their fellowmen. I pray that we won't give in to pressures from big-money groups and others to be more "cosmopolitan" or to "move into the 21st century ahead of the pack."

Utah is like any other state in that we can't please everyone. *But we can stay true to the roots that have given us the great place that we live in now.* I am grateful for Utah and I like it here.

Sandi S. Graff
Washington County

Age 34; **Birthplace** Winslow, AZ; **Occupation** Homemaker;
Religion LDS; **Race/Ethnicity** White

Living in Utah means building. The pioneers built cities out of sagebrush, towering temples out of mountain stone, and a thriving economy out of dust. Whether it's a new economic base for a floundering town, or computer chips, or Olympic venues, we're still builders.

Living in Utah means loving children. We respect, them, we spend most our taxes on them, and we have a lot of them. We enjoy them, learn from them, pass on our values to them, and stay young because of them.

Living in Utah means accepting any and tolerating all, asking only that they reciprocate. Brigham Young gave land to other churches, that all might worship here. He walked down the aisle at church and declared one side Republican and the other Democrat. He amalgamated people of diverse nationality. People still come here from all over, and Utah learns from them, welcomes them and adopts them. Thus new residents who never heard of a handcart, are imbued with the spirit of those who came here on one.

Living in Utah means being different. The early settlers were persecuted because they were "odd," and in today's culture of declining morality, rising crime and me-ism, we're still "odd." Thank heaven.

Living in Utah means giving. Early settlers ground their fine china to make windows for community buildings. Now we contribute and fast and share and volunteer. From our sports heros to our big businessmen to the busy parents who lead Scout troops or teach church classes, we remember that charity never faileth.

Living in Utah means being healthy. Okay, we drink a lot of pop and down a lot of sugar—we even eat green Jell-o. But statistics reveal that our lifestyle, values, and attitude make life long and active in Utah.

Living in Utah means being thrifty. The earliest native Utahns turned caves into homes. Pioneer women put a few pounds of possessions into in a trunk, carried it across the country, then used those few items to rebuild a whole life. In business, government and our homes we make do, start with a little and make a lot.

Living in Utah means doing. We don't just gripe about it, we don't just talk about it. We fix it, help it, vote on it, study it, improve it, do it.

Living in Utah means having hope. Some of our towns are growing too fast and others are dying away. We have gangs (mostly because sometimes we fail to love children, tolerate, or care) and crime is up. Poverty, illegitimacy and divorce are more common than they should be in this great state, and in places our land and air are polluted.

Most of our ancestors, however were immigrants. They left everything they knew for a dream they could only imagine, and only true, bone-deep, clear-to-the-genes hopeful people do that. They overcame worse odds than any of us now face, and look what they built, because they had hope. How much more can we do? Like those pioneers, we believe there really isn't a mountain range or force or army or social trend that can stop us from having our very own promised land.

That's why living in Utah means taking pride, and a lesson, from the 150 years while expecting the next 150 will be even better.

Vicky Janet McCombs
Cache County

Age 42; **Birthplace** Idaho Falls, Idaho; **Occupation** Wife/mom/day care; **Religion** LDS; **Race/Ethnicity** White

"Home Is Where You Hang Your Heart." Nine years ago I "hung my heart" in Utah. We chose to live in Cache Valley because of the peace, beauty and security we felt here as we'd visit. I have grown to love this state. I have found a sense of well-being and belonging here.

The people we have met over the years have been kind and giving. We have made many friends and our five children have felt welcomed. Utah is a friendly place to be. Warm smiles, handshakes and greeting from the heart characterize those who live here. We have been blessed to be recipients of all that Utah has to offer.

I am so thankful for the beauty I see here each day. Not only from the caring of people but from the scenery of life. The shouts of children throwing snowballs, watching the grace of ice skaters, hearing the crunch of the leaves in fall, and sliding down the twists and turns of the waterslides in summer.

I have been to St. George, Manti and most places in between and each county in our state has its own seasons and beauties to soothe our souls and bring us peace and enjoyment. Bear Lake on a hot summer day, the canyons in autumn, snowfalls in winter and the glorious spring flowers are just some of my favorite things here.

My family loves the sports programs offered in Utah for the youth. The shouts at soccer games, the crack of a baseball bat, the pace of basketball games, and all the other activities our children can participate in. They are able to learn sportsmanship, endurance and meet new people as they also grow in self-esteem. We love the Jazz games and the BYU sports programs. We love going to Temple Square and feeling God's presence there. He has surely blessed our state and been a guiding influence in its growth.

As a mother I appreciate the education our children are receiving here. I am grateful to the teachers who not only teach but who care. They are positive examples to the youth of our communities. In Utah we have found ancestors who helped shape this state. They came across the plains, fought in the Mormon Battalion, worked, loved and died here. We feel their presence and appreciate the sacrifice they gave for us.

It takes not only earth, scenery and buildings to make a state. It takes caring hands from people who love where they live to make a state a home. This state is growing so fast because people from other places are finding a peace and welcome here they have been seeking. They are finding a place to grow, a place to put down roots. Utah is a state for all seasons, all reasons and all people. It is a place to "HANG YOUR HEART AND CALL HOME!"

Mike Anderson
Tooele County

Age 48; **Birthplace** S.L.C., UT; **Occupation** Industry; **Religion** LDS; **Race/Ethnicity** Caucasian

Living in Utah means:

—Long Indian summers, served with lemonade on the front porch.

—Family deer camps, where the old timers tell you how many deer there used to be.

—Opening day at Strawberry, waiting for your turn to launch, and hoping there is room for one more boat.

—High school basketball games, where the home team almost always wins.

—Vacations to the National Parks, once, when you're too young to remember, and again when your kids are too young to remember.

—Late summer evening watermelon busts on a church lawn.

—Boy Scout Camp in the high Uintahs.

—Beauty Pageants in early July, where the whole family thought your sister should have won.

—A thousand small Pioneer Day Parades followed by one BIG one.

—Game booths on the park lawn on the 4th and 24th of July, hosted by the local Volunteer Firemen or Lions Club.

—The night of the 3rd of July all night dance, where as a kid you believe Uncle Charlie must be sick, because he keeps falling down.

—Watching the clock in church, as some long winded speaker, speaks, and the Denver game starts at 2 p.m.

—Just settling down for a good after dinner cup of coffee, and the home teachers call.

—Going to the Baptism of a second cousin, on Saturday.

—Proudly baptizing your own child.

—Being unlucky enough to listen to Paul James or Bill Marcroft on a Fall afternoon.

—Being lucky enough to be at the game on Saturday.

—Utah by 5.

—Rise and Shout, forever.

—Thankful that Frank and Barbara Layden chose Utah for their home.

—Second guessing Jerry Sloan, after a loss.

—Praising Jerry Sloan, after a win.

—Getting to shop for new school clothes if you're a girl.

—Having to shop for new school clothes if you're a boy.

—Proud to be an American, lucky enough to be a Utahn.

"Fairfield, Utah." Photograph by John A. Calk, Utah County.

Keith L. Wilson
Utah County

Age 27; **Birthplace** Salt Lake City; **Occupation** Student; **Religion** L.D.S.; **Race/Ethnicity** Caucasian

Living in Utah is …

… In loving, having, and being with a family, and in helping and relieving the burdens of the poor and the needy, of friends and neighbors, and of other families and loved ones;

… Being a good neighbor in belief and by example, in cheering and blessing the deprived and unfortunate, and in living true religion as well as hearing the teachings thereof;

… Being a doer of the word of life, opening the minds of the uninformed, and in guiding and teaching the meek and willing, the humble and contrite, and the inquirer after truth;

… Imparting life, hope, courage, and good will to the unfortunate, the weak, the ill, and the discouraged and forsaken; renewing their faith and self-esteem, and rejoicing with them in their redemption and happiness;

… Representing the cause of the people in low-profile daily labor, as well as in the public eye; in believing without seeing; in doing good without compulsion or constraint; and in honesty of heart without shame or disgrace in the powers of heaven and the blessings of repentance, with grateful appreciation for the goodnesses of life in their eternal perspective;

… In environmentally responsible and wildlife-conscious enjoyment of our outdoor natural wonders, of our mountain vales and scenery, and of our reservoirs, lakes and valleys; and in fishing, hunting, camping, and family gatherings;

… In acceptance of all that is edifying, virtuous and lovely, and changing continually for the better with each step of determined progress on the way to life eternal.

Living in Utah can be a worthwhile challenge and a blessing forever.

Matthew F. Stevenson
Salt Lake County

Age 10; **Birthplace** Salt Lake City; **Occupation** Student; **Religion** Mormon; **Race/Ethnicity** White

"Living in Utah means to me" having fun being joyful and happy. Making friends of all kind. Working hard and playing. Making people feel wanted and helpful. Going to school and learning from our good teachers. Having fun in all sports. Feeling needed. Saying things that are nice and good. Getting jobs and working hard at them. Having fun with friends. Making people feel comfortable at all times. Growing food and crops. Doing your best at everything. Being the best you can.

Elisa Anne Goold
Salt Lake County

Age 12; **Birthplace** Salt Lake City, Utah; **Occupation** Student; **Religion** N/A; **Race/Ethnicity** N/A

WHY DO PEOPLE GAMBLE
Why do people gamble and gamble?
I would rather ramble and ramble.
A few people win.
But the smart ones never come in.
Gambling equals no money.
Wouldn't you rather have money, honey?
When people gamble their money away,
I'm glad Utahs not that way.

Daryl S. Yardley
Utah County

Age 9; **Birthplace** American Fork; **Occupation** Student; **Religion** N/A; **Race/Ethnicity** Caucasian

I like Living in Utah because it is free and I like evryone. We are different, but we like each other.

Jeannine F. Crabtree

Davis County

Age 57; **Birthplace** Kermit, Texas; **Occupation** Elementary School Principal; **Religion** LDS; **Race/Ethnicity** Caucasian

What living in Utah means to me is "High Expectations." In Utah we expect people to work hard, to keep their cities and properties clean and in good condition, to be good neighbors, and to live up to high moral and ethical standards. We have high expectation of our elected officials also. We expect them to pass laws and allocate tax monies so that the needs of the citizens will be met. We expect that our wilderness areas will be protected and properly used. We expect the symphony and the arts to be supported. We also expect provision for sporting and athletic events. We expect our highways to be in good condition. We expect law enforcement to be adequate, and we expect that people have been brought up to be law-abiding citizens. We expect our schools to give our children a world-class education, and we expect that children will come to school with the attitude that education is a top priority. Of course, we fall short in many areas and in many ways, but the high expectation is there, the goals apparent. And I believe that we are working toward achieving them. I love living in Utah.

Connie Bon

Davis County

Age 53; **Birthplace** Salt Lake City, Utah; **Occupation** Homemaker; **Religion** LDS; **Race/Ethnicity** Caucasian

Living in Utah means that I am living and have lived most all of my life—in a state that allows me to feel secure in my chosen profession. Motherhood. This is and has been more than a full time job to me. I know that in Utah motherhood is respected and honored. I have 12 children and am raising a 5 year old Granddaughter. I have not been made to feel like I needed to be a career woman in order to matter. I have given my time to my children and freely done so. It has been important to help them develop their talents and interests. Even though they have not all stayed in Utah now they are married, I am secure in the knowledge that growing up in Utah has given them a good foundation. They respect nature and people and have a secure religious knowledge also. I am also grateful for our schools. As many problems as we have, ours are few when compared to other states. Living in Utah is contentment to me. Thanks Utah!

Submitted by Guadalupe Rodriguez, Salt Lake County.

Jacob Zollinger Hess
Davis County

Age 18; **Birthplace** Provo, UT; **Occupation** N/A; **Religion** LDS; **Race/Ethnicity** Caucasian

Grandma Zollinger died six days after Christmas one year ago. Grandpa still lives in the house he built, the house they lived in as newlyweds and ultimately raised their seven kids in. Grandpa symbolizes what living in Utah means to me. This includes family, security and hard work.

Sometimes, family life in Utah is humorized because of family size, or different beliefs. But this is a great strength to Utah. Utahns have a strong pioneer background which provides pride and stability. Utah is famous for its large network of families. Family bonds help to strengthen the whole state and provide a great moral force in the state. Difference is good—especially for the better.

As mentioned, families provide security. A strong religious life also gives Utahns security. These two factors make Utah a very safe place relative to the rest of the United States. A strong community spirit is inherent in Utah. Service is a key part in this community spirit.

Utah has the greatest old people in the world. They have done a good job in passing on their values to their kids. One of the most important values is work. The deep work ethic in Utah began obviously with the pioneers. It continues today in many youth of this generation.

Let us all hope Utah will *always* be different, and never blend into the rest of the depravity of the world.

Kathleen Mary Capels
Cache County

Age 45; **Birthplace** Syracuse, New York; **Occupation** Editor; **Religion** Roman Catholic; **Race/Ethnicity** Italian-American

As an "incomer" to Utah, rather than a native, I can write only about what six years of living in this state means to me, rather than a lifetime here. It has indeed been a unique experience, one filled with more contrasts than in any other of the many places where I've lived (New York, Florida, California, Pennsylvania, Michigan, Illinois, North Carolina, Georgia, Texas, Wyoming, and Massachusetts).

Utah is in the West, and yet this state isn't really of the West, in that its traditions have been dairy farming and agriculture, rather than the cattle ranching which still dominates the rest of the region. In some ways, it shares the Western ethos of stubborn independence, with a group of pioneers who scrabbled a toe-hold in an unforgiving land and clung to their religion in the face of intense oppression; yet the independence of individual thought, a Western hallmark, is subsumed by Mormonism's doctrine of un-swerving obedience to authority.

Utah has more national parks and monuments than any other single state, and a choice of landscapes for enthusiasts of natural beauty, from the austere slickrock country of southern Utah to the steep, narrow, wooded canyons and mountains of the north. My experience here has been that it's not primarily native Utahns who are out among the state's splendors in droves, but tourists and those who, like myself, are adopted residents of the state. A large number of the people I see who are lifetime residents of Cache Valley stay in their houses with most of their shades drawn all day, and enclose themselves in the steel and glass cocoons of their cars when they venture outside their homes. Then again, perhaps the fact that generations of Utahns have been forced to wrest their living from the out-of-doors means that the current set of natives enthusiastically embrace an alternative to what was their ancestors' only choice.

Above everything else, what dominates my experience of living in Utah is the way I've needed to think here, more than in any other place I've lived. The fact that I am part of a small minority of gentiles, and accustomed to patterns of living that are very different from those of most of my neighbors, has made me look at many of my values, and define both what they are and which of them are truly important to me. I've found that what I prize most is independent thought, listening to and looking at what's around, but coming to my own decisions. I could not survive if I was not able to think, and then act on *my* beliefs. It's something that's tested here at times, and isn't the norm for many people I know, but it still is possible, for which I'm grateful.

So thank you, centennial project, for giving me a chance to write down some of what I think about living in Utah, and to pass it on for posterity.

Orrin Hatch
Salt Lake County

Age 61; **Birthplace** Pennsylvania; **Occupation** Senator; **Religion** LDS; **Race/Ethnicity** Caucasian

My Utah-born dad and my mother relocated to Pittsburgh where my father could find work as a metal lather; so that is where I was born and where I grew up. Pittsburgh is a very nice place, but it is not the place I ultimately chose to make my home as an adult. Almost all of my heritage is in Utah.

I first moved to Utah to attend BYU. And, after seeing a little more of the United States on a church mission to the Great Lakes region, I came back again. After I graduated from BYU in 1959, I was fortunate enough to receive a full scholarship to the University of Pittsburgh

Law School and graduated in 1962. I hung out a shingle in Pittsburgh for a few years, but my heart was in Utah. It wasn't long before my wife, Elaine, and I moved our family back to Utah for good.

They say that home is where you make it, and to some extent that may be true. Certainly my parents managed to import Utah values to our home in Pittsburgh. But, I believe there is a natural "fit" to a person's home town. Some people thrive in big cities; others, in smaller towns. Some people enjoy the wide open spaces and breathtaking scenery; others prefer urban centers with night life and theaters. Some people are happy in an impersonal environment; others, like Elaine and I, appreciate the neighborliness of Utahns … We came back to Utah and chose to raise our family here because it fit.

To be sure, Utah's natural beauty is unsurpassed. Ranging from spectacular mountains and forests to breathtaking red canyons, Utah's geography is hard to beat. Utah is simply a photographer's dream. I sometimes feel sorry for my Senate colleagues from states with drab and uninteresting physical features.

Furthermore, Utah is a cultural mecca for the whole of the Intermountain West. Who can not appreciate the marvelous opporunities we have in this state to enjoy the arts and to learn at our great universities.

And, as our state motto indicates, Utah is industrious. As we excel in the arts and humanities, we also excel in the sciences and in commerce. This success has brought us an enviable level of prosperity compared to other states and sets the stage for a stable future for our chilren.

… The 19th century French political scientist Alexis de Tocqueville observed: "I sought for the greatness and genius of America in her comodious [sic] harbors and her ample rivers—and it was not there … in her fertile fields and boundless forests—and it was not there … in her rich mines and her vast world commerce—and it was not there … in her democratic congress and her matchless constitution—and it was not there … not until I went to the churches of America and heard her pulpits aflame with righteousness did I understand the secret of her genius and power. America is great because she is good …"

I agree. Utah is great not because of our postcard-quality scenery, our universities, or our many successful industries. We are great because our people have made us so. We are great because of the values we share and have put into practice.

Utahns, regardless of religious affiliation, hold solid values in common that I believe are essential to the quality of life anywhere—a strong work ethic, honesty, charity and compassion, thrift, perseverance, and respect for the family. There is a positive, "can do" attitude in this state that is irresistible and refreshing.

Some may say that we are not a diverse state. They are wrong. Some may say that these common values do not provide for differences among us. On the contrary, I believe Utahns' inherent sense of fairness and order inspires tolerance and respect for others.

Utahns do not apologize for this value system. That Utahns have insisted on these standards for over 100 years is why Utah is a great state. It is why we have not succumbed to the moral blight that is eating away at the fabric of society in other parts of our country. It is why Utahns will never give up the fight against those destructive influences that have broken so many other communities.

These Utah values and the people who believe in them are the reasons why we made Utah our home 32 years ago. That is why we chose Utah as the place to raise our children. That is why I am so grateful and so proud to represent Utah in the United States Senate.

Kim R. Burningham
Davis County

Age 59; **Birthplace** Salt Lake City, Utah; **Occupation** Centennial Commission Director; **Religion** LDS; **Race/Ethnicity** White

Today is January 4, 1995. Besides being the 99th birthday of Utah's statehood, it is also the date of my mother's death. She died at 10:00 this morning. I have been reflecting upon those two things: my mother's death and Utah. And in a way, I recognize a similarity in the two.

As I reflect upon my mother's 90 years of life, I am impressed with three qualities that characterized her life. She had a *positive outlook,* an *independent spirit,* and a *caring heart.*

Mother always saw the bright side of things. When arthritis added agony to her walk, she still smiled. When her son and later her grandson tragically died as children, she simply said, "Well, you can't let it get you down. Life goes on." Through myriad challenges, Mother always faced those challenges with a positive approach. As age advanced on her, she simply kept going, and only in the last two months when death flung her to the mat did she give in.

She was independent. She drove her car until she was in her 80's, lived in her own lodging until three weeks before her death, was still working until a few weeks before death, never asked much of others, but handled her own needs. She was the epitome of independence.

And mother cared about us. She listened to us. She agonized with us. She loved us.

Mother lived her entire life in Utah. For over 90 of the State's nearly 100 years she was here. She is typical of the people of Utah: positive, independent, and caring.

How has Utah influenced me? In the same way that my mother did. Its spirit has taught me to be positive, to have hope, to address challenges with optimism. The soil beneath and the air above have preached the sermon of fierce independence. And its people—my family, my neighbors, my classmates, my community—have taught me to care.

I shall always remember my mother with fondness, and her memory will remind me of the positive, independent, and caring strength that is Utah!

Cecily Huefner
Davis County

Age 22; **Birthplace** Bremerton, WA; **Occupation** Student; **Religion** LDS; **Race/Ethnicity** White/Caucasian

Outside my bedroom window grows an apple tree with a trunk just right to sit in. Its leaves, like flannel, touch my window in the wind; its autumn branches are straight and long, just right for roasting marshmallows. Until last year, I only appreciated my Utah apple tree for what it gave me—fruit, rest, memories, peace. One experience in Russia during 1993 taught me the true value of apples—of Utah—of home. After joining a family for a Russian meal one night, I was sent off with a bag of small, wormy, polished apples as a token of their gratitude to me. How often have I thought of those apples, given in complete love from absolute poverty.

Returning to Utah, I was astounded at the space, the open air, the blue sky of home so different from the crowds and filth of Russia. I was astonished at the apples of Utah—their size and their sweetness and their tight red skins.

I went out to my apple tree one afternoon—rubbed its branches and looked for its fruit—I *smelled* it. Autumn spiced and warm. Perhaps every region claims those blessings of homey apple trees. But to me, they represent *Utah,* in all its bounty and goodness, containing and giving life from within itself. Those memories of Utah, of Russia, of *love* will remain in me always, to be rekindled with every bite of apple—dear *slorcho*—that returns me to the homes within me.

Clinton Anderson
Salt Lake County

Age 13; **Birthplace** Salt Lake City, Utah; **Occupation** Student; **Religion** Mormon; **Race/Ethnicity** White

Living in Utah means freedom. Even though the whole U.S. has freedom I think Utah is freer in different ways. Like in other places you might get a horrible senator and he may make different rules.

I'm glad I live in Utah because I am a Mormon. I don't have as many things to make me do bad like Casinos. In UTAH your not allowed to gamble, There's not much violence either …

Utah is not a very violent state. We are one of the states that has very few gangs. I don't think I've ever seen a gang in my life. When I lived in Heber, you could leave your bike out on the lawn overnight, and it most likely wouldn't get stolen …

John Allsa Cutler
Davis County

Age 17; **Birthplace** Salt Lake City, UT; **Occupation** Male Stripper; **Religion** LDS; **Race/Ethnicity** Mexican-American

Living in Utah means that 3 out of every 4 cars I pass on the freeway is a mini-van.

Trisha Eaton
Salt Lake County

Age N/A; **Birthplace** N/A; **Occupation** N/A; **Religion** N/A;
Race/Ethnicity N/A

Will put most bad people in jail but not all of them.
I hope my children aren't in gangs or don't end up in jail!

Submitted by Trisha LaNae Eaton, Salt Lake County.

Michael O. Leavitt
Salt Lake County

Age N/A; **Birthplace** N/A; **Occupation** N/A; **Religion** N/A;
Race/Ethnicity N/A

Today, I see Utah in the context of the world. But for the first 18 years of my life, Utah was my world. It was a world of security for me. It featured fishing with Grandpa, Little League and scout troops, summers at Navajo Lake, building fences, hauling hay, taking the water turn. It was the school song at a ball game, walking the familiar path home from school and family vacations. Now that my perspective has broadened, I have come to understand how wonderful it was to grow up on 700 West in Cedar City. While the larger world struggled with the cold war, amidst the family by family struggle for health, happiness and financial viability, the world was secure for me. I learned and grew. I developed values. I realized that those values, formed then, are still my values and evolved from many of the things that still make this state a wonderful place to live. Let me speak of some things I cherish.

Living in Utah means the enjoyment of small wonders. The evening sprinkler change, watching the shadow creep from Ponikee to Thousand Lake. Golfing on a summer evening. I call it the glory time; the sun has set, there is no wind, and less passionate golfers have long since gone home. Fly fishing the Green River, deer hunting on Parker Mountain. Skiing, everything from a rope tow in Cedar Canyon to a quad lift at Park City. Walking at night, in Loa. On the stretch from town to our house there are no street lights, only the glow of the ranch house in the distance to walk toward. No carbon monoxide filter separating me from the stars. And there are more stars than you can remember.

Living in Utah means cold watermelon at Melon Days in Green River, the magic of the Christmas Light Parade in Richfield. The great Peach Day parade in Brigham and Onion Days in Spanish Fork. Thanksgiving with Jackie's family in Cache Valley, or with mine in southern Utah.

For me, living in Utah means taking the cows to Parker Mountain with my brothers; the smell of new cut hay; the beauty of a field with all the bales gone.

It means participation in the long cultural tradition. The Shakespearean Festival brings memories; when it was just those of us from Cedar City, sewing on sequins. The Freedom Festival in Provo; the Utah Symphony playing Mozart's Four Horn Concerto, or James Taylor and Chicago in the mountain air at Park City.

It means teaching your children a work ethic that you learned from your father and he learned from his … even when it would be faster, cheaper and more effective to hire it done.

Living in Utah means living among people who care about each other, watch over each other, and are motivated by their sense of neighborhood. That same sense of community is found in Murray or Magna, in Monroe or Manila. It is found in every town and city.

In December of 1993 our home burned. Our clothing, our personal belongings, even our anticipated Christmas gifts were gone. Within an hour, people had come with offers of shelters, food and clothing for our family. It was high-profile misfortune, it was the Governor's Mansion, and some might feel that explains the outpouring. But not for me. You see, it had happened to me before.

In 1965, our family home in Cedar City caught fire. The response was exactly the same. Within minutes our neighbors had taken us to their home and people were coming from all over town, again with tangible offerings to fill our needs. People with boys our ages brought some of their children's sweaters and jeans, and by the next day our sense of security had been reestablished by the extraordinary care of the people of Cedar City.

Living in Utah means coming under the influence of willing-hearted people who contribute from love of serving. The smell of Utah air at six in the morning still reminds me of Little League baseball practice every summer, when Tom Cardon and Blaine Betensen picked up sleepy-eyed boys and hauled them to the ball park in the backs of their pick-up trucks. …

Utahns have a unique connection with our heritage— an awareness of the costs of our comforts, which heightens our enjoyment of them. I drive into any agricultural valley and exult in the sight of fields nourished by sprinkler irrigation systems. Then instantly comes the image of my grandpa, struggling with a shovel and a canvas dam. When I experienced with my wife a traumatic delivery of our little daughter in a sterile hospital, I think how profoundly grateful I am that we are not doing this in a log cabin.

On the 24th of July this year, I took my son and six of his 10-year-old friends to a hill overlooking the Salt Lake Valley. It was Brigham Young's grave site. He must have chosen that spot, because from there you can see the whole valley. I realized that all the things that I enjoy are based on the sacrifices of those remarkable pioneers and those who came after for 150 years. How different than then, it must look today. Yet how well they planned for us. Ours is a tradition of visionary people …That day I stood looking across the same valley Brigham Young had seen from that viewpoint. I looked beyond and saw other valleys and imagined that he looked beyond his time to see the needs of future generations. I marvel at his insights.

Today, in evidence of their planning, we enjoy wide streets and communities spaced to allow future generations to flourish. I have thought, as we approach a time when the Salt Lake Valley becomes crowded and we are challenged by bulging populations of people who clearly see "this is the place," there is little question that we have benefitted from their remarkable vision.

Future generations depend upon the clarity of our view and the courage of our actions. As we plan for the years ahead, it will be a time to reflect upon the values that make living in Utah desirable. It will not be a time to strive for the biggest, fastest or loudest. It will be a time to cultivate a sense of quiet, competent quality. Our aim must be to make life in Utah steady, safe and secure. Perhaps our greatest challenge will be to rekindle the sense of personal responsibility and community feeling that made possible the legacy of strength the settlers left for us.

As we move progressively forward, we must also look thoughtfully back, to find in the lessons of yesterday, values with which to steady our course. As pioneer men and women hoisted onto their shoulders the children of those who faltered on the trek, our success in keeping this place nourishing and safe will depend greatly upon the measure of personal strength every Utahn is willing to lend. Looking forward, I predict wonderful years ahead!

Submitted by Cynthia Heath, Davis County.

FACES THAT CAN'T BE IGNORED

Some of Utah's faces are smug, fraudulent, and cruel, as the following essays reveal. After years in Utah some people find themselves still strangers and aliens. A frequent complaint is that those belonging to the predominant faith consider all others to be outsiders or gentiles. One writer speaks of a high school counselor who told the writer's daughter, transferring from out of state, that newcomers are not welcome. Another newcomer, disillusioned by fraud, likens a particular Utah city to a carnival where hucksters lie in wait to cheat the unsuspecting. Others associate their private misery with the state. For example, an angry youth finds the adults of Utah to be overbearing and dictatorial. He can't wait to grow up and depart.

One writer, long a Utah resident, laments that "centennials tend to celebrate illusions." Centennials, she maintains, ignore the social problems of the state—"school children who are hungry, drunk, illiterate, dark-haired, depressed, pregnant, diseased, or drugged up on methamphetamines." Unquestionably, Utah has its share of loneliness, failure, and tragedy. Its history includes the Mountain Meadows massacre and the Scofield mine disaster. Newspapers report auto accidents, bankruptcies, murder, rape, and child molestation on a daily basis. One does not escape the human condition merely by living in Utah.

—Levi S. Peterson

John J. Seay
Weber County

Age 53; **Birthplace** Montgomery, AL; **Occupation** Warehouse Worker; **Religion** Jewish; **Race/Ethnicity** Jewish (Hebrew)

There are several appropriate words and phrases to describe "What Living in Utah Means to ME," e.g. (i.e., in MY opinion) [one of seventy-eight examples:]

"Landing party to Enterprise! One to beam up, Mr. Scott! Report = Utah—class H planetoid; hostile plant life; NO detectable humanoid life forms: Mr. Scott! Have Mr. Sulu set a course for the next galaxy: Notify the Federation to request no further contact with Planet Utah! We've wasted enough time here!!"

Ms. Ursula Jourdan
Tooele County

Age 57; **Birthplace** Germany; **Occupation** Retired; **Religion** Lutheran/Christian; **Race/Ethnicity** White

I moved here 1½ years ago, and have never been accepted by the Mormons. I have been verbally and mentally abused ever since I arrived. The neighbors killed 2 of my cats. I have lived and worked all over the world, and this is one of the worst, if not *the* worst, place I have lived. I have been told that Grantsville people do not want "newcomers!" I have tried *very* hard to be everyone's friend, and have many, many friends all over the U.S.—*all except here in Utah!* I even have several Mormon friends elsewhere—all who say the Utah Mormons are very different and do not live by the Gospel.

The mountains and red-rock country here are spectacular, but the Mormons who live here make it a very miserable place to live. This is not only my opinion—I've heard it from many people who moved here.

For medical reasons I've had to stay here, but as soon as possible, I plan to leave.

P.S. I've never seen as many illiterate persons anywhere as I've seen around here, Salt Lake City seems to be much better because they have allowed "outsiders" to live there.

T. Jones
Iron County

Age N/A; **Birthplace** N/A; **Occupation** N/A; **Religion** N/A; **Race/Ethnicity** N/A

They say you can't go home but what they mean is it will hurt. The memories of simple life devoid of "things" and pressure seemed so alluring.

Yet the return to the land of the 18–19th Century has been traumatic. The land has been used by our people to satisfy their lifestyle of farming where they shouldn't hunt to kill anything that moves in spite of laws and common sense, mining for temporary jobs, lumber where it can't be sustained, use of very limited resources for the quick buck, postponing the complete lack of any jobs rather than a few.

Poor to no work ethics excused as time with the family—large families who can't be supported except thru others—47th in wages and 14th in taxes. Never did our family previously understand that we don't have "thinking or reasoning" here. Utah is now a 3rd world country exploited by big business because we don't know any better and refuse to listen to "outsiders." Coming home really hurts!!!

No Name

I moved our family to a small town in Utah in 1965. It's a pretty town. Red hills, warm weather. I had great hopes and dreams. Soon many of those were crushed. The first day of school we took my daughter to enroll at the High School. The counselor looked at the transfer form and said, "You certainly won't be an asset to us, *we don't like new comers.*" My daughter was hurt deeply and lost much confidence. It took a long time to feel accepted and to convince her that she is *ok!* Being from another state where my children didn't have opportunity to go to college, I moved them to this small town just for the college that is located there. It did turn out to be a real opportunity. We were different than most people there. We were Democrats, had somewhat of a Southern accent, were new members of the L.D.S. church, our back-ground had been in owning and operating Night Clubs and Farming. We didn't have ancestors who came to Utah with the early pioneers. We often felt like our differences couldn't be accepted as good. We were a close family, we loved our God, our country and our fellowmen.

My son was the first boy in that small town to grow hair down over his ears. The city fathers judged him as "bad" because of his hair. Their threats of throwing him down and shaving his head *terrified* him. Their age, size, and the number of them was so overwhelming. He came home crying often. They didn't know the scars would be so deep and long lasting (emotional scars). But he knew that because he was in a free country he would be able to have hair over his ears and continued to suffer it through. Now all the young men in that town who want their hair over their ears are free to have just that.

There's much good in Utah. I guess our experience with a small town that had a hard time accepting differences of new comers had to happen to teach us and them.

"Life is a long hard lesson in humility." We all must learn to live with and love people who are different than us.

But I worry about what we are teaching our children. One of my daughters has a friend who long ago attended East High in Salt Lake City. This girl often was "left out" because of her clothing. She said students would pull back the neck of your shirt, blouse or dress to see what "label" was on it. If it wasn't bought at a certain store, you were mocked, not allowed in "the in crowd" and not accepted. Unfortunately her mom bought her clothing at K-Mart.

As Martin Luther King said, "the content of character" is what really should matter. What are we teaching the children.

I'm not going to put my name because my children (all but one) are doing well. I don't want to bring-up negative experiences with their names attached; now that they are feeling a "part" of Utah. May we just remember that along with *all* the *good* in Utah, we have much yet to explore.

Valerie Cohen
Iron County

Age 48; **Birthplace** Pasadena CA; **Occupation** Artist; **Religion** Atheist; **Race/Ethnicity** Caucasian

Propaganda for the "Living in Utah" project illustrates precisely why living in Utah has been so bleak for me.

Centennials tend to celebrate illusions. Publicity for the Centennial Portrait include TV clips of fair-haired school children lisping "It's so fun to go hunting with my Dad," "We can go snowmobiling and jet-skiing," or "In Utah we can have holidays with our families."

Apparently, it never even occurred to the advertisers of the Centennial Portrait that the historical record should also show school children who are hungry, drunk, illiterate, dark-haired, depressed, pregnant, diseased, or drugged up on methamphetamines. Most of the kids I just described are Mormons; those who are not Mormon may be crying in the corner because other kids told them they were going to hell.

It's not that I expect Utah to be able to solve problems—but we could acknowledge that we have the same problems as the rest of the country. We could acknowledge that those who suffer are us, are not outsiders, are citizens of Utah's society.

I have lived in Utah all my adult life. I find the dominant culture closed-minded and cruel. I've always participated in local politics: I do this because it's my way of paying society back for my expensive California education; I do this to help "my" town protect itself against environmental dangers; and I do this because I want to be part of the community.

My reward is that I have been publicly attacked: "Hey, you're not from around here, are you?" (I've been here for 21 years). I have been reviled for being a Jew (I am married to a Jew; my own ancestors came over on the Mayflower). Consider that the entry form for the portrait provides space for one's "race" and "religion"… could not the U.S. Census Bureau provide this data? I sent my only child out of state for high school, so he could be part of a community. I am afraid to grow old here, because then I would be as alone as if I were already dead.

David Lewis
Cache County

Age 38; **Birthplace** Ogden, Weber County, UT; **Occupation** Assoc. Prof. of History, Utah State Un.; **Religion** No thanks!; **Race/Ethnicity** Caucasian

As a historian and lifelong resident of Utah I feel compelled to say something for this Centennial project about life in Utah. In my 37 years I've thought a great deal about what it means to live here and away from here. I also think I bring a certain amount of studied historical perspective to the subject—understanding the present as a product of cumulative experience. I'm going to write this in a free-flow of thought, so don't expect polish. Hold on to your hat and sense of humor!

Utah has so much to offer people in terms of opportunity, environment, and quality of life. There is a hidden potential here that outsiders see, but many of us locals miss. And there is greatness we recognize that outsiders don't. It is a "pretty, great state," even a pretty and a great state, but it is not the utopia many will describe in this survey.

Utah is, at present, a very prosperous state economically, but that is probably because the rest of the country is doing so poorly. We are attracting high tech industries because of our relatively well-educated work force, but also because of our cheap land and cheap labor, almost non-existent zoning laws, and a government willing to bend over backwards to give tax breaks and benefits to any business willing to come here. We seem to think any growth is good growth, even the possibility of housing or destroying toxic wastes (unless, that is, if the Skull Valley Goshutes want a MRS nuclear waste repository in Skull Valley; then the white elite scream bloody murder—it's a racist paradox that eludes most Utahns). We need to be more careful of development, to develop wisely and not at any cost to our land and people.

Living in Utah means making less money. Average pay in Utah is 85% (or less) of the national average—women do even worse. Cost of living is only 97% of national average, so we are still falling behind. We have a higher than average percentage of working poor—working families who still fall below the poverty level. Part of this is attributable to large family size. The other part is because of the high proportion of minimum wage jobs and the lack of a significant unionized labor force. Unions never made it big in Utah, especially among the Mormons—an interesting phenomenon given the communitarian background of Mormonism and early Utah. What unions we have in the state are relatively small and weak. No wonder Utah workers are treated poorly. Unions aren't as strong as they once were, and they may not be all good, but Utahns need to realize the benefits they take for granted come from 100 years of union struggle nationally to improve pay and working conditions for all workers. We need to work toward those goals again here in this state because those hard-won benefits are being eroded ... With "right-to-work" (anti-union) leaders like Sen. Orrin Hatch in power, Utah government will be of little help either. We are witnessing an influx of higher paying jobs as companies move into the state, but those are being kept by employees arriving with the companies, accelerating the disparity between Utah wage earners and newcomers. The resulting hostility growing in Utah as these newcomers up property values and monopolize resources/jobs is counterproductive, but it does point out the relative instability of Utah's economy.

Living in Utah means listening to conservative Utahns complain about government regulation of any kind. Yet these same people are very quick to support the regulation of Utah society in accordance with Mormon Church dictates. It is interesting to witness the "regulate them, not me" attitude generally in this state, especially if it has to do with moral issues—smoking, drinking, abortion, pornography, etc. Perhaps these do deserve regulation, but the state has gone overboard on many issues with poor results—witness our defense of Utah's abortion law, parts of which were clearly unconstitutional, costing taxpayers over a million dollars; witness fraud/corruption in highly regulated Utah liquor Commission in 1960–70s; witness the Sunday closing laws that were finally thrown out; witness attempts to censor the TV airwaves of adult entertainment. Our leaders seem to miss the point. Gov.

Mike Leavitt just testified before the Senate Judiciary committee and asked Congress to quit imposing unfunded federal mandates on states. Sen. Joseph Biden then pointed out that Utah itself imposes over 320 unfunded mandates. Leavitt had no comeback, impaled on his own myopia!

Living in Utah means putting up with the anti-government rhetoric that passes as political insight ... Gov. Leavitt has become a national leader of the new states' rights/Sagebrush Rebellion, calling for a return of land to state control, for government to get out of local affairs, failing to see how essential that presence is for western states. They don't realize that the same issue was hashed out in the 1930s, and that Governor Dern and other farsighted officials fought against a return of federal lands to state control because of the costs involved in keeping and rehabilitating those lands—lands ravaged by years of unregulated grazing, mining, and neglect—something we still face in this state. They have already forgotten what the Reagan years (the New Federalism) meant to states—more programs turned over to states without enough funding, leaving states with the economic burden of running such programs. Likewise they forget about the presence of federal facilities, especially military bases, the IRS, national parks and forests, etc., that bring so much money into Utah from the government—forget until the government tries to trim the budget by closing military bases in Utah; then they howl that the govt is not doing enough for us, that we need their presence. Utah Republicans/anti-govt reactionaries in general fail to see the paradox of their position. Overall, Utahns receive more money back (@108% last I checked) from the federal govt than we pay in in taxes. We receive more money in "in lieu of" funds for federal land holdings than we could get leasing or selling those lands ourselves. Indeed, recent revelations about the mismanagement of state school lands trust funds in Utah suggests that we don't do a good job of taking care of what we already have ... Local control is not always best and businesses do not always have the PUBLIC good at heart. We need to can the rhetoric and find a better balance in this state.

Living in Utah means paying taxes and listening to the anti-tax rhetoric that pops up each year. No one likes taxes, and Utah is a high tax state, but that is a function of the demographics of the state which are a function of religious beliefs and an uncanny fear of birth control—too many kids, too few taxpayers. Property taxes are high here, but assessed values remain low. Income tax rates are high too, but given the higher-than-national-average family size and tax breaks for dependents, Utahns with children don't pay that much, especially when it comes to educating their children. You don't hear much about the tax on alcohol and tobacco which is very steep and discriminatory because it doesn't affect the majority (but it does educate their kids—so drink up). Utah Mormons are particularly susceptible to this anti-tax sentiment because they are already paying out 10% to a church that builds buildings and returns only a very small percentage to its members in worldly form. Since Utah's founding investment capital has been lacking, drained off 10% at a time by a church that spends much of that OUTSIDE Utah. Utah has always relied on outside capital for development and that continues today, furthering the capital drain. Mormons are overtaxed, but not exclusively by the state or federal government.

Living in Utah means coming to the realization that Utah is not and never will be a strong force in national politics, not just because of its small population, but because it is a one party state. This hurts Utah politically and affects our lives. Neither party takes us seriously because one can't get us and the other can't lose us, so neither cares to invest any time or attention to our needs. The recent rash of federal military base closings is a case in point—no help from the Democrats or Republicans, even now that the Republicans control both houses of Congress for the first time in 40+ years. You would think that Utahns, and particularly Mormons, would understand this situation given their history—the experience that standing outside national politics or courting only one party is a dangerous game. 100 years ago the attitude was that you couldn't get to Mormon heaven being a Republican. Church leaders worked hard to change that at the time of statehood, directing members on two-party voting. Now the sentiment is that Democrats have little or no chance of getting to heaven. Perhaps Church leaders should work on it again … We will never have significant political power until we learn and practice the balance of party politics. And all Utahns will suffer the political consequences of conformity.

That leads to the issue of Mormon Church domination of the state, socially and politically. Although many would deny it, this is a fact of life in Utah. It affects life for member and non-member alike—always has, probably always will. While every community has the right to make choices and legislate for the good of the body of citizens, they need to recognize minority rights. We also need to be fully aware that church and state are to be separate, constitutionally—something that held Utah from statehood 100 years ago, and despite changes, still rears its head in the tyranny of the majority today. Utahns live with the subtle and not so subtle direction of civil decision making by church leaders—a direction that subverts the idea of an open public voice. Nearly 90% of state legislators are L.D.S. in a state where only 75% of the population is. Legislatures openly look to the church for guidance on public issues/legislation more than to their constituents—there is a difference.

Non-Mormons are excluded from local decision making, not totally or always, but routinely and in many subtle ways. Public meetings become church forums with deference paid to the local bishop's opinion. Meetings take on a patriarchal air where women especially can be treated as 2nd class (witness Jim Hansen's treatment of Bobby Coray in the 1994 1st district congressional race). I never thought this existed to any great extent until I came back to live in the state after graduate school. I've seen this personally in local town meetings, and irrigation district meetings, even university meetings. I've attended public meetings where leadership and elections are run, not according to Robert's Rules of Order, but like LDS ward meetings—where leaders are called and then sustained without discussion. Being a ward member is all the endorsement many need in order to vote for that particular candidate, and word is clear from the pulpit and private conversations who wears the right underwear.

Non-Mormons are kept out of the loop whenever discussions occur in places where they cannot participate freely. Holding state legislative hearings in the Logan Tabernacle in 1994 is only the grossest of examples. More commonly, public business is conducted in informal conversations at priesthood meetings and in church cloak rooms. Decisions are pre-made and then open discussion goes lacking. Even the language used reinforces and excludes: "Brother so-and-so," "Bishop," etc. It is unconscious and therefore more insidious. Insiders laugh it off when it slips out in civil forums, but the point has already been made clear to all present. It has an excluding effect that Mormon insiders fail to recognize.

Again, I've seen this from both the inside and outside—growing up within the church and looking at it critically with an outsider's perspective. Growing up we systematically excluded and ostracized non-Mormon kids. In school, scouting, dating, school clubs, etc., religion was always an issue, always present (consciously and unconsciously) in organizing and acting. I didn't realize how insidious and destructive that could be at the time, but now that I have kids and am experiencing it myself, I'm beginning to understand the impact that it has on their development. I see my students blowing off what I say in class

(especially Utah History) because they think I'm not a Mormon, even when I'm giving them the perspective of good Mormon historians like Arrington, May, Alexander, Peterson, etc. They do the same to fellow students who voice different opinions and experiences. They think I don't know their religious history, organization, and beliefs because I don't practice their faith at this point in my life, after having lived it longer than many of them. They take critical analysis of individuals and institutions as criticisms of faith. I see this particularly in young women who have so much to lose if their faith is challenged, and much less in returned missionaries who seem to have a broader perspective and firmer faith tested under fire. It is an attitude that affects my teaching, that affects their learning, that affects life in Utah.

What I'm trying to describe is a smug insularity that pervades life in Utah. It even negatively affects non-Utah Mormons. Mormons from other states tend to be treated like second class Mormons/citizens once they get to Utah. Every year in my Utah history class I hear this repeated over and over again by both Utah Mormons and non-Utah Mormons—the "I'm better than you/know more than you because I grew up closer to the SLC Temple" routine. This also seems to be a symptom of BYU attendance—those who attend BYU thinking they are better Mormons than those who don't. This holier-than-thou attitude really puts off non-Utah Mormons and is part of a little-understood division within the church. I hope people will talk about this and confront the growing divergence of Utah/non-Utah Mormon experiences with leadership and the faith.

Other divisions have gained more recognition recently as the church is strengthening its demand for personal and doctrinal conformity from its members and outsiders. Threatened on the right by fundamentalists and polygamists, threatened on the left by intellectuals, the church is demonstrating the depth of its tolerance by retrenching and turning inward, cutting out the diversity needed to evolve (as it has since the death of J. Smith). It is a sad situation that will weaken the organization (and, by extension, the state) by leaving a mediocre corpse of blind believers. An underground of intellectual dissent will remain and will hopefully serve as a night light for those looking to the future rather than living in the past. The growth of the New Mormon History [NMH] is particularly important at this time and needs integrating into the church educational (seminary) system. I find more people who profess to know Utah history who have no idea of anything beyond church history (and then imperfectly). The two are interwoven, but the former is much larger. The NMH has the potential of expanding the focus by addressing Mormonism and Utah as LIVED history, warts and all, rather than simply as faith—a hagiography that defies the more complex human reality.

There is more than a little truth to the joke that Utah is still living in the 1950s—that golden age of consensus and conformity and idealized families that the church likes to think has and will always exist ... We still have a hard time admitting that divorce among church members is higher than the national average; that child and sexual and spouse abuse is as prevalent as in the general population; that women in Utah must work outside the home in higher proportions than in the rest of the nation in order to help support their families, and not simply stay at home as their leaders command, forsaking even education to bear children. Mormons show an amazing deference to authority—a blind faith that is both scary and impressive at the same time. This can lead to lock-step conformity on issues and behaviors. It can also lead to great public works—outpourings of community action in response to disasters like the floods of 1983, or to local tragedies like a home lost to fire. This is part of Utah's heritage, part of the success of the communal experiment and part of its failure. The sense of shared community is even grudgingly accorded to non-members in need (not on a daily basis). But it is there,

something that many parts of the country have lost. It is something to be proud of.

If I have spent an inordinate amount of time discussing religion, it is because of the overwhelming impact the church has on nearly every aspect of everyday life in Utah for both members and non-members. One hundred years from statehood, and we are still dealing with issues that were a stumbling block back then. With their own innate sense of uniqueness and persecution, Mormons didn't realize it back then, and many refuse to recognize its persistence today. Religious issues (belief and struggle) still pervades life in Utah, and Mormons make up the majority. Some may call this critique an example of paranoia, anti-Mormonism, or whatever—that's a good way to deny the reality of my experience and reimpose your own. So be it, administer another dose of conformity. Some will say, as I have heard too often, "love it or leave it." Well, I do love the state and will fight that kind of closed mindedness in order to try to improve it for everybody. My critique is not of faith, but of individuals and institutions that limit/impact my life without consent or due process. It is not a blanket critique, although some will see it that way in order to rewrap themselves in the rag of persecution. Mormons and Mormonism are fine. I value my Mormon heritage, family, and many of the basic values I learned. But I see the blind conformity and the imposition of that belief/morality on others without their consent as a problem—a problem that needs to be (at least!) recognized by all involved. Even then I have little hope that it will ever change ...

For me, living in Utah is about educating people. We need to quit complaining about the costs of public education if we choose to continue having so many children and just do it right—invest in the future instead of trying to find trendy new cost-saving programs that deliver an impersonal, watered-down educational experience. We need to invest in libraries, books, and bricks-and-mortar as much as an electronic superhighway. We need to find ways to instill the desire to learn, not just the desire (that I see in some students) to get a grade and degree with minimal effort. We need to improve the quality of teacher education and offer support and better incentives to retain good teachers and researchers. We need to work harder to include all students regardless of race/ethnicity. We need consistent funding, not centennial school handouts and words of praise from a leader who hasn't demonstrated a commitment to or understanding of quality education despite his rhetoric. We need to turn off the TV, read to our kids, get involved in their education, and give them every opportunity. We need to speak up and act against an establishment that won't fully fund public education, let alone higher education. A well educated public should be our goal and most valued asset as a state—people trained with skills as well as the ability to analyze, think critically, write coherently, express themselves and their studied opinions, and then act, work, and return that investment to the state and citizens of Utah. That's what we should pursue, at any cost, as the best means of dealing with all other social ills.

Some of this may get pretty far from a narrow consideration of "what living in Utah means to me," but I see it as part of the larger issue of what life should be like in Utah, what Utah should become, and, when you read this, what life in Utah has become. Cheers!

Ty Busch and Donna Busch
Salt Lake County

Age 47; **Birthplace** Longview WA; **Occupation** Teacher; **Religion** LDS (Christian); **Race/Ethnicity** Native Am.

As a newcomer I am seeking a place of peace and tolerance. My wife and I came here in refuge and respite because we were the victims of *"racial intolerance."* We felt in Utah there would be peace and tolerance. Peace and tolerance to us means respect for common dignity and the equality and parity of the sexes consistent with my ethnic heritage. Since being here in Utah I have found people to be warm and open and generally respectful within my own faith. "Outside I have found intolerance bigotry and hate to abound." *Utah needs alot of work in the areas of brotherly love and tolerance.* The dignity of the human *spirit* needs to be worked upon. As the character of Utah changes so will the people have to change or Utah will not be a refuge but a battle ground of indifference. The Mtns can't hide the rest of the world forever. We are going to confront the realities of the 21st century very soon, if we haven't already. I feel the indifference is due to the failure of Utah Citizens in accepting the inevitability of change and the change that has become a reality!

When Mormons settled Utah it was to escape persecution. We have to take the lead in respecting the dignity of everyone, man, woman, children. We have to respect the brotherhood/sisterhood of our Mormon and non Mormon friends. We should not be afraid of ideas, especially ideas that challenge our principles of faith for if we are strong and remain strong we will truly grow in grace. The patriarchy should teach from respect of diversity not fear of difference. The role of women and children in the church in the past, present and the future should be affirmed. Tolerance of difference in life style orientation should be the rule rather than the exception. Even though conservatism/fascism is flowing over the land Utah should take the lead and *reject what has evolved in the current congress.* It will divide people, genders, classes, racist further if we succumb to this brand of ungodly fascism. If LDS see their salvation in the coldness of this new movement *"we deserve to perish."* Realizing what I have said may be termed radical, I cannot apologize; it's the duty of everyone to be his brothers keeper. (Bro is gender neutral). When we can move to a higher level and view people as equal then we will be truly in perfection. Our trouble has been in viewing we are better than someone else; black, white, oriental, man, woman etc. (xenophobia must cease too).

Where we have learned, respected and lived diversity and tolerance we have truly evolved as a victim of hate. I know of what I speak. As a survivor of "Mississippi burning" and as an ex-civil rights worker I have confronted death and lived thru the K.K.K. I recently confronted and have temporarily survived hate at SLCC Redwood Campus. I say to those who committed hate and racism upon me that I forgive you; however, I will bring the Civil and Criminal forces upon you without further Ado. ... My strength and dilligence in god will endure and see me in the right on this. ...

BONDING WITH THE LAND

To be rooted, to live and love one's surroundings, to know the names of things, to carry the stories of our ancestors in our bones—this is what it means to inhabit a place. And the narratives which follow are a celebration of these things.

Utah is a state of mind. We are born to its diversity of forms: mountains, redrock canyons, the salt desert. These various landscapes create a people with character, and character rooted in this country creates culture, a culture that doesn't take itself so seriously because we know what it means to stand in the presence of grandeur.

Wallace Stegner, native son of Utah, writes in *Mormon Country,* "Another age, with different values from the age in which the Mormon country was first settled, is likely to find that country much more than the Mormons found, certainly more than the Gentiles who went through it like a high wind. It is a good country to look at, and with the initial hardships out of the way a good country to live in. There is even glamor of a kind. As it offered an opportunity for the Mormons to escape the United States, as it gave Marle Ogden a place in which to build her spiritual kingdom, as it offered the wide vision of an unknown world to mountain men and explorers and scientists, and the vision of fabulous wealth to miners and promoters, as it offered impregnable sanctuary to outlaws from the Hole-in-the-Wall to the Blue Mountains and raised up a fantasy of unutterable loveliness for Everett Ruess, so it has offered a refuge to the floating myths and the undying legends. That desert has in very truth been sanctuary to outlaw and zealot and artist and scientist and Indian and Nephite. For all its homey domesticity and its tradition of laborious piety, it is a country that breeds the Impossibles."

As we celebrate our centennial, perhaps it is the individual voices that give us the most insight into who we are and what we value. The testimonies in this collection are honest renderings of what living in Utah means in our one hundredth year of statehood.

We are a people who deeply love this land. We are a people who understand democracy as both the right and responsibility to embrace beauty of thought and country. We are a people who believe in community and the practicality of good sense. We are a people who cherish our posterity and it is for our children that this centennial is perhaps most meaningful.

May they know that we considered them, that we worried for them, that the reason we felt it important enough to tell our stories, to speak about what we love at the end of the twentieth century is that it is their legacy to care for these incomparable lands, that these lands created the culture they belong to, that nothing can be taken for granted, that if we choose to be good and loyal stewards and take care of these lands, these lands will continue to care for us.

May we listen to these voices.

—Terry Tempest Williams

William L. Furlong
Cache County

Age 59; **Birthplace** Garland, Utah; **Occupation** University Professor; **Religion** LDS; **Race/Ethnicity** White

As a child living in Ogden, I remember traveling to Southern Utah to visit relatives almost every summer. I remember the spectacular scenery of the region. For many years, we stopped at Big Rock Candy Mountain. It was beautiful with its colors of yellow, red, and green. The Lemonade Spring was flowing and the environment was serene. We would also visit Red Canyon (beyond Panguitch) and picnic there. Bryce Canyon was my favorite and still is. Zion Canyon with its stunning mountains, its long dark tunnel, its narrows and streams were all planted early in my mind.

As a sophomore in college, we were introduced to a part of Utah I had not known before. We went to Arches National Monument in 1960. There were no paved roads or established camp grounds, no water. This was a real out of the way spot then. On that same trip, a geology class field trip, we went to Dead Horse Point, Natural Bridges, the Narrows of the Green River and Mexican Hat.

My children grew up also traveling to these locations. We have tried to visit a National Park within the state or neighboring states every year since we returned to Utah in the late 1960s to live. We have visited nearly every national and state park and national forest in Utah and we hope to continue to do so for the rest of our lives.

Utah means to me, spectacular scenery, marvelous mountains, dry salty deserts, green canyons, lakes in the Uintahs, and empty lands in the Levan desert (before irrigation). Utah has more variety of landscapes and extraordinary vistas, fantastic seasons and breathtaking panoramas than most people could see in a lifetime. It also has the beauty of Salt Lake City and its surroundings.

Although I have traveled throughout most of the States in the Union, and have visited over thirty countries, I still believe that the variety and beauty of this state is not surpassed.

My concern today is that my grandchildren may not be able to enjoy some of these areas in tranquility and peace. Too many people now visit Arches. Some want to close or sell off wildlands and wilderness areas. Some would destroy the desolate and frightening drive over "Hell's Backbone" for mining and exploitation. This seems shortsighted to me. I fear that the pressing needs of the present may destroy the needs of a larger more urban society of the future. As cities grow, as traffic becomes more congested, as the most spectacular parks become more crowded, the quiet empty lands of the present may become the only refuge for people like me.

We need to protect our state heritage. We need to be better stewards of the beautiful areas God has made for us to enjoy. We need to be concerned about the present, but we need to protect and conserve for the future. We need not, and we had better not, "waste Utah."

Christine Layton Graham
Salt Lake County

Age 43; **Birthplace** Syracuse, New York; **Occupation** Homemaker (writer, editor); **Religion** LDS; **Race/Ethnicity** Caucasian

When I was a little girl in Utah, I knew at least two things about it. It was my mountain home, and it was not part of the West.

The West was cowboys and Indians, maybe the Lone Ranger and his faithful Indian campanion. It was sagebrush and red rock. Sagebrush for me belonged up in the mountains below the pine trees, and the red rock I now love was hours away on vacation and seemed desolate and ugly. There were cowboys and rodeos in my valley, but I didn't know them. I grew up in books filled with fireflies and English gardens, and almost every father in my neighborhood was a professor.

My home was a college town with a big whitewashed Y on the foothill where the June grass turned brown by the time summer started …

Would my children say they lived in the West? I'm not sure. They seem much more aware of such issues than I was. Their literature and textbooks are less bicoastal and British, but probably not much more Utahn. We live in the Avenues in Salt Lake City, an area full of Utah history, old houses, big trees, and cultural diversity. In some ways it looks and feels more like the places of my childhood reading than any other part of Utah I know.

Last summer my children and I spent many hours volunteering at Pioneer Trails State Park. On the way home from being pioneers in Old Deseret, the children would pretend the car was a time machine, reacting in mock amazement to all the modern innovations in "their" valley.

What amazes me sometimes are the things that do not change and the ways the assumptions of our lives are shaped by our surroundings. Quirks of climate like bread quickly drying nearly to toast on the kitchen counter or the cabin table. Crackers left out open when a coastal woman would seal them away to keep crisp. The constant protective presence of mountains that leaves me always vaguely uneasy in wider country. Virga on summer afternoons when everything longs for rain. The proverbial January thaw and the late frosts after backyard fruit trees have blossomed.

The Utah of my ancestor's childhood, and mine and of my children's looks different in many ways. But the place shapes our lives in ways that are fundamentally the same.

Theodore W. Shumway
Washington County

Age 66; **Birthplace** Phoenix, Arizona; **Occupation** Attorney; **Religion** L.D.S.; **Race/Ethnicity** Anglo-Saxon

"—it is a goodly sight to see what Heaven hath done for this delicious land." Lord Byron

———————

No combination of natural beauty, moderate climate, and genuine people matches the blend of these qualities I find in southern Utah where I have made my home for the last 15 years. I have lived near the sea, in the middle of the desert, greener places, hotter and colder places, and in the midst of good people from the Pacific to the Great Lakes. The finest quality of life ever offered to me is just across my doorstep.

Drawn originally by the irresistible beckon of its natural beauty, I have been able to hike and explore an unending variety of leafy canyons, sculpted redrocks, wooded mountains, and sandy washes with an ease unmatched anywhere else in the world. These things, visible out my window and accessible by a short drive in any direction, have proven to be the antidote to a stressful world and balm for a weary spirit.

Living in Utah to me means the opportunity to avail oneself of the delicious natural bounties dreamed of by Lord Byron, together with the opportunity to contribute to and share in a community that cherishes moral and personal values. Utah, for me, has indeed proven to be Byron's "rainbow to the storms of life."

Annie Marie Mutsaers

Weber County

Age 10; **Birthplace** Ogden; **Occupation** Student; **Religion** L.D.S.; **Race/Ethnicity** Caucasian

What living in Utah means to me is not polluting the air. Don't litter and clean up around the area you're in or at. WE should keep it clean, you know, because it's the only Utah we have. There is not going to be another one. So we should keep it clean, clean, clean! If I am somewhere and I see a paper I will clean it up and not throw a piece of paper or something because I want to live in a clean area not one that is littered. That is why I will keep Utah clean.

Elfriede Schmitt

Salt Lake County

Age 60; **Birthplace** Mainz, Germany; **Occupation** Housewife; **Religion** LDS; **Race/Ethnicity** White

"This is the place" for me as it was for Brigham Young. I emigrated 36 years ago from Germany to America, Utah. As I looked out the window of an airplane, I was impressed by the majestic mountains, the Rockies and fell in love with this country right away. I have run a few Deseret News Marathons. The route takes you through the canyons and I am still in awe and think about the pioneers and how hard they had it. Here, running on the 24th of July, Pioneer's Day, it is easy just to follow the winding road to the finish in Liberty Park. However it's hard too because 26.2 miles have to be covered! You get exhausted too. But it makes you feel good because of the accomplishment and it feels like a real little pioneer. I live close to the mountains and enjoy the daily view from my home. Wouldn't like to live anywhere else for "This is the place"!

Bonnie Lynn Nelson

Salt Lake County

Age 16; **Birthplace** Salt Lake City; **Occupation** Student; **Religion** Latter Day Saint; **Race/Ethnicity** C

I would like to bring up the two topics of religion and nature, both are highly important to me. When people hear "Utah" they automatically think "Mormon State" and in many ways that is true. Utah was set up by the Latter Day Saints and its a part of history. The majority of people here are Mormons, including myself, but there's nothing wrong with that. People believe in different things and I wish more people would accept each other, no matter what their differences may be. However many people do accept each other, which is great.

Off the religious side, the environment of Utah, which I have lived in for over fifteen years, I couldn't imagine life without. There are many sides to Utah. There's the hot blistering desert side, and the cold freezing side. Both are highly enjoyed by many. Utah provides the beauty of nature which many of us so desire. In the winter we are able to enjoy the snowy mountains which fulfills our needs of skiing, snowboarding and many other winter sports. In the Spring, many Utahns head to Southern Utah where great hiking, rock climbing, four wheeling, boating and many other luxurious activities take place. In the summer, camping in the mountains is a favorite. In the Fall, you could just about do anything also. Yes I am grateful for the nature which has surrounded me.

The only complaint I have would be that of pollution, which has recently so highly risen. It saddens me how ignorant and destructive human kind may be. I worry about the environment for our future generations. Will they not be able to enjoy the nature so much as I have. Nature is a fragile thing, we need to treat it so. But because of the greed and selfishness of mankind, we are not leaving Utah as we found it.

Once so pure and once so clean
Now the stars, they can't be seen.
Covered in smog and creations of man
Why don't the pollution they stop and then ban
They're destroying our home can't they see?
Where's the answer that will set us free?

Kent Mason
Coconino County, Arizona

Age 63; **Birthplace** Aurora, Utah; **Occupation** Truck Driver
Ret; **Religion** LDS; **Race/Ethnicity** Caucasian

This is my Utah
From the majestic high mountains
where the pine trees kiss the sky
To the deep rugged canyons
where those wild eagles fly
From the salt flats to the sandstone
Beneath the blue skies above
This is my Utah
Land I always will love
Sitting at night around a campfire
far from the world's famines and wars
The glow of my contentment
could outshine the stars
where the world's still as God made it
And I want it always to be
This land my Utah
Where I can always be free
I feel I'm next door to Heaven
And I want always to be
Here in the homeland of my Father
And his before him
Where my heart, my eyes can see forever
From the high canyon rim

Here in my Utah
Her beauty will never grow dim.
I hear the wind sigh thru the cedars
Just before dawn on the trail
There in a million miles of sagebrush
I hear the lonely coyote's wail
Where the World's still as God made it
And I want always to stay
so if God will allow it
I'll spend all of my Days
Here in my Utah
Land I always will love

Edith Rauh
Salt Lake County

Age 58; **Birthplace** Hof, Bavaria, Germany; **Occupation** Housewife; **Religion** LDS; **Race/Ethnicity** White

I live in Salt Lake for nine years.

Living in Utah means to me to experience nature. Nature how I can find it nowhere else. In spring and fall I wake up in the morning by the voice of wild geese, flying over our house. In which other big city can you find this?

When I walk two minutes from our house to the Jordan River I'm on a wilderness like place, where I can watch a little pond with ducks, all kinds of birds and even beavers. I don't know if anybody knows this place and the existence of beavers there. You have to make your way through shrubs to get there. I worry very much about this place because there is the beginning of a street pointing at that area. I hope this place will not be made "beautiful" like other Jordan River Areas I saw. With lawn, walk ways, and trees which are not native to Utah and do not produce food for native animals especially birds. And where is no dirt left for swallows to build nest.

When you drive through Utah the landscape is changing constantly. There is the hot desert and not far away mountains with forest and green meadows and the higher mountains with rests of snow all summer.

Last year the colorful wild flowers in the mountains were just a dream.

Even I do not ski. I like to be in the mountains at wintertime. On some days the sky over the white snow looks like dark blue ink. (A lot more beautiful then the dark blue sky in Italy)

And then there is Antelope Island. This Island is a paradise by itself. All this birds, the white sand on the shore, and the wonderful clear blue water.

When we take visitors from Germany there, they cannot believe this place is not crowded. If this Island would be in Germany you could not find enough space on the shore to put a towel on the ground. Our visitors can't stop watching the seagulls, running with the beak wide open, to catch the little black flies. Our German visitors love this Island and think the sunset there is just breathtaking.

Our friends here call our house Hotel Ranch because of the many visitors we have from Germany. They just keep coming back, because they love the wild beauty of this lands nature and the feeling of freedom this landscape gives them.

Sometimes I think people who grew up here don't know and appreciate what they have. Some do not teach their children to respect small animals, insects and plants. I just love this beautiful land, and I wish, I could protect it.

Laurali Noteman
Kane County

Age 46; **Birthplace** Pasadena Calif.; **Occupation** Payroll Clerk; **Religion** LDS; **Race/Ethnicity** White

Springtime in the Country

See the sun there on your meadow?
The refracted light, there on the grass,
A green that's almost transparent,
With a glow as crisp as glass?

The wind whistles down your canyon,
The breeze flutters in the leaves
The eagles soar on the currents,
And clouds change forms as they weave.

The air is clean and vibrant,
As I sit and watch the day.
A doe with her fawn cross the valley,
With a buck up the draw just a way.

Oh God, how I do love your country,
Your canyons, valleys and glens.
The colors of nature surround me,
With the sounds of the earth on the winds.

See the groundhog on the tree stump,
Why! there's a chipmunk in a pinon pine.
A squirrel scrambles up that tree branch.
Your stream just sparkles and shines.

The ponderosas with all of their grandeur,
And the oaks with their scraggly bends,
The aspens' leaves are quaking.
As a day begins so must it end.

Original drawing submitted by Shalom Allred, Salt Lake County.

Above: "The Narrows in Zions National Park." Submitted by Jason Wertypora.

Left: "Bryce Canyon." Submitted by Jason Wertypora.

Plate 25

Submitted by Michael Spencer, Weber County.

"Hiking the Mountains in Goblin Valley." Submitted by Lynn Shepherd, Salt Lake County.

Plate 26

Submitted by Erica Traube, Salt Lake County.

Two-time world middleweight champion Gene Fullmer, in 1957 and currently. Submitted by Gene Fullmer, Salt Lake County.

Plate 27

"Lee and Landon Frei get ready to load cows." Submitted by Loretta Frei Adams, Washington County.

"L.D.S. Temple, Manti, Utah." Submitted by Della Downs, Salt Lake County.

Plate 28

"Horses in Red Butte Canyon." Submitted by Guadalupe Rodriguez, Salt Lake County.

"Decker Lake." Submitted by Jared Kades, Cache County.

Plate 29

Submitted by Erica Traube, Salt Lake County.

"Rodeo State Finals." Submitted by Shari Lynn Feekes, Salt Lake County.

"Swiss Days." Submitted by Loretta Frei Adams, Washington County.

Plate 30

Submitted by Alyssa Bilanzich, Salt Lake County.

"Clair Hafen works in his lot." Submitted by Loretta Frei Adams, Washington County.

Submitted by Jennifer Davault, Salt Lake County.

Plate 31

Submitted by Jacob Gregory Glissmeyer, Salt Lake County.

"Lynettie Farr Beckstead and 84-year-old father, Morris Farr, set out with Brandy, his dog, for morning feeding of calves." Hand-colored photo by Robert T. Beckstead, Weber County.

Submitted by Kelli Marie Nelson, Salt Lake County.

Plate 32

And in the twilight of your evenings,
As your stars begin to glow,
My mind wanders through my memories,
Where images of your land still show.

SENTINAL OF TIME

I have stood here, watching for ages past,
From my home upon this hill.
In silence I have held my place,
My hold, a noble vigil.

I have offered shade in summers heat,
And a haven from the wind.
Lives have used me, when in need,
To some I have been a friend.

I knew one life that comes to mind,
That sat upon my limb.
She was young and agile on my branch,
She would come and think of him.

She played and giggled as time went on,
She grew along with me,
She sat and thought of things to come,
And enjoyed serenity.

As branches grew and strength set in.
She found maturity,
She brought him here to share our place,
Their love was pure and free.

They would come and talk, beneath my boughs,
On life as it changed its ways,
They brought the family as it grew,
We shared both nights and days.

After years had come and years had gone,
The kids no longer came,
It was just my couple once again,
But their thoughts were not the same.

Years they passed, visits less,
As time demands they do,
My branches broke, my colors changed,
My life was changing too.

Verle P. Peterson
Sevier County

Age 81; **Birthplace** Redmond, Utah; **Occupation** Retired Educator, Merchant; **Religion** L.D.S.; **Race/Ethnicity** N/A

What living in Utah, for eighty years means to me? It means peace, tranquility, security, opportunity and beauty.

The rugged mountains, always in view, seem to be a place one can back-up against when facing lifes problems. Many times visitors from the plains states are terrified by the steep mountains, the deep canyons. Not me, I see the gnarled pine firmly rooted in the crevasse high on the granite cliff. Tenacious, productive—shade for the hiker, home for the hawk, holding back the heavy snow. Its roots hold back the spring rain. Perhaps I too can overcome adversity, survive, thrive and be of some use in this world!

On the gentler slopes of the Utah mountains, cattle, sheep, deer, and elk grope on lush foliage and grass. Fishermen follow the streams, line the banks of high mountain lakes. The oak and aspen trees play their symphony of color along the hillsides in the fall of the year. Winter brings an abundance of snow held back in hills until it is stored in fishable reservoirs. Fertile valleys thirst for the moisture. Irrigation systems and spraying utilize the precious water. Nature teaches conservation and if I will work I will eat.

Utah has a large rural population. As children growing up in families of four or more, we had responsibilities. We were too busy to be bored or mischievous. We learned there was dignity and satisfaction in helping in the home. Neatly folded towels, making the bed with "army corners" and no wrinkles, gathering the eggs, washing and drying the dishes etc.

Today numerous schools of higher learning are up and down our state. They stress physical, moral and intellectual excellence. The best talents in the country visit our state, the theater, ballet, symphony halls or sports arenas. I can partake of any of it by driving two or three hours. Our medical facilities rate highly in the nation. Our red rock country in southern Utah is as scenic as anywhere in the world.

Yes, I thoroughly enjoy living in Utah. Its physical attributes are enhanced by its quality of opportunity, security and tranquility.

Patricia G. Cutting
Salt Lake County

Age 65; **Birthplace** Raleigh, North Dakota; **Occupation** Teacher—philosophy; Writer; **Religion** Presbyterian; **Race/Ethnicity** Scandinavian-British

This is the second time around for me. My husband Dale and our family—Paula, Beth, and David—were introduced to life in Utah in the 1960's, living in the Salt Lake Valley from January of '61 to August of '66. In January of 1981 my husband and I returned to the house in the sub-division of Manhattan Terrace that we had left rented for almost 15 years.

When we left to follow Dale's work in the mining industry the house was in the unincorporated Granger area, near the Hunter boundary. When we returned it was in newly formed West Valley City. The area has changed a great deal, becoming more densely populated and more urban. Gone are the fields behind our home, replaced by rows of houses with carports, garages, and cars spilling into the streets. Gone is the old Monroe Elementary School with its tall ceilings and two stories, replaced by a sprawling one-story building a half mile away.

We came back to sell the house, but we stayed. Dale, officially retired, was offered a part time job as consultant for Goldfields Limited, and other companies, who had their gold refined at Johnson Mathey Refinery in West Valley City. And I developed camaraderie with poetry writers through Crafthouse Poetry Classes, Westminster Poetry Series, the Utah State Poetry Society, and my alma mater the University of Utah. (I received a B.S. in history and philosophy from the "U" in 1966 and went on to get a Masters (1971) and doctorate (1976) in philosophy from the University of New Mexico.)

My family enjoys returning to Utah to visit with former friends and neighbors, and to meet new ones.

I have chosen to stay in Utah after Dale passed away in February 1986, because of the bonds I have built with neighbors, friends, and fellow writers of all ages. This has been possible in part because of the respect for older people that is pervasive in the state and because of the classes offered senior citizens through the universities and colleges, as well as the public school districts.

I have a rich life here, full of opportunities for writing and for recreation, including water and snow skiing, theater, ballet, art exhibits, and sight seeing in the canyon lands, mountains, and along the shores of the Great Salt Lake. And, as in all states I have lived in, there are many loving, caring people.

Early Spring at Farmington Bay
For Jo Townsend, 1930–1994

Ducks molting into spring plumage
gather in the tide water pool
lined with jetties
both natural and man-made
last year's grasses
and telephone poles strung
with Violet Green swallows.

Three Northern Shovelers
black heads glossed with green
blue shoulder patches bright against
rufous sides
muttering to themselves and each other
circle a mottled brown fourth
bills gently bobbing in her direction

Four Pintail ducks
whistling and piping
needle tails held high
slim necks alert
white feathers flashing
near black sterns
dash about each other
in chaotic patterns
like kids in a game

A lone Glaucous gull
chalky white
translucent windows barely visible
at the wings' outer edges
floats quietly
    far from her nest
    on a rugged Arctic cliff

Marilyn Openshaw Chapman
Utah County

Age 66; **Birthplace** Salt Lake City, Utah; **Occupation** Freelance Writer; **Religion** LDS; **Race/Ethnicity** Caucasian

National Park Heritage and a College Degree

In 1946, Southern Utah's National Parks were experiencing a revival after World War II's restrictions on gasoline and travel had kept tourists away. The Union Pacific Railroad was operating the franchise and I had been hired to serve as a waitress at Bryce Canyon, with a goal to earn enough money to pay my tuition to the University of Utah. I rejoiced! My wages were $45 a month—plus an average $9 a day in tips—more than enough to cover the $25 a quarter cost of attending college in Salt Lake City.

Utah is the keeper of a national treasure, and working at Bryce Canyon kindled in me a love for the place that has never wavered. I could never forget the sight of those strange rock shapes rising towards the sky. Their color changes with the light. Rain intensifies the blush of the pinks. Shadows created by sunrise and sunset give the ledges of the rock formations a life of their own.

Kids from Kanab, Hurricane, Tropic, Paragonah, Circleville, Cedar City, Provo, Salt Lake, Ogden and Logan worked at Bryce as bellboys, cabin maids, receptionists, food servers, horse wranglers, tour bus drivers, cooks and office workers. Lasting friendships were made. We cared about each other. Some of us were homesick. But we weren't melancholy for long. United in our efforts to show the tourists all the beauties of the Park, we, too, fell under its spell.

On our days off we visited Zion National Park. There we looked up instead of down from a rim. The spectacle of the majestic Great White Throne looming above us was awesome.

Back in our dormitory above Bryce Lodge we ironed our uniforms and prepared to answer questions about Utah that the astonishing visitors always asked.

After dinner, we Bryce Canyon employees entertained the tourists with songs and dances. We sang, "We're the crew and we work for you, but we have our fun when the work is done. We can't go swimming so we all go rimming."

Promptly at ten-o-clock we were free to go and run up and down the trails through the canyon. We had to be back at the dorm by eleven. Doors were locked, then.

Breathing deeply the tangy air from the pine forests along the rim we hurried down the trail that meanders through Peek-A-Boo canyon. We would pause only for a moment to view the odd sandstone shapes that rise precipitously into a black velvet night sky that is thick with stars. Often we would hear the voices of tourists echoing over the edge of the rim above us proclaiming something we heard a thousand times, "Isn't this an incredibly beautiful place?"

Utah is the keeper of a great national treasure. Bryce Canyon and Zion Canyon attract people from all over the world. They are amazed at these startling natural wonders. And I am grateful to have earned a Bachelor of Science degree—paid for with the wages I earned while working at Bryce in the late 1940's.

Marva Jeanne Pederson
Box Elder County

Age 61; **Birthplace** Murray, Utah; **Occupation** Freelance writer; **Religion** LDS; **Race/Ethnicity** Caucasian

The attached collection of poetry which I have entitled "The Touch of the Mountain Sod" represents "What Living in Utah Means to Me."

HILLS OF HOME
(WITH DIANNA JEPPESEN)

Silhouetted in the rosy glow of morning light against
the eastern sky
Stand rugged mountain bulwarks, invincible as stone,
These mighty hills of home.

My hills of home, my hills of home,
The glory of their summits stretching up to meet the
face of God,
Inspires my soul to rise above the limitations of the
common sod.
Thus, anchored firmly in a strength beyond my own,
I'll sing my song of joy forever,
Standing here within the shelter of these lofty hills of
home.

My hills of home, my hills of home,
These mighty towering mountains rear their rugged
peaks,
and guard the safety of the valley home beneath my
feet.
Here within their shadows lies the substance of my
hopes and dreams,
Symbol of my aspirations as I attune my life to higher
themes.

Yes, this is my own country, the spot on earth I love
the very best,
Here beneath these mighty towering mountains in
the valleys of the west.
This rocky mountain grandeur cradles all I call my
own,
My life, my love, my family,
All are here, all are here,
Safely here within these hills of home.

Parker Shaw
Salt Lake County

Age 18; **Birthplace** Salt Lake City; **Occupation** Student; **Religion** Mormon; **Race/Ethnicity** White

I won't claim to know much or anything about the Politics of Utah. I don't know much about our state government at all. But I am really glad to live in a state so full of mountains and deserts.

I am a backpacker and a hiker. I love being able to be at the bottom of a trailhead within about a half hour of leaving my house.

In the winter, if I take a hard hike, I can be above the inversion that covers the city from sight. I can stand on a snowy peak and breathe real air free of exhaust.

In the fall I like to backpack in the Butler Fork Area of Big Cottonwood Canyon. Standing on Mt. Raymond (behind Mt. Olympus) I can look down on aspen forests that are completely golden, with a few dark evergreens poking through for good contrast.

I have sat up on cold nights in Little Cottonwood Canyon listening to coyotes howls echo all around the cliffs.

I have sat in fear watching bull moose watching me during their mating season. I didn't know that these animals lived in Utah mountains until last year and I have visited them several times since.

Living in Salt Lake City, I don't go to the deserts as much as the mountains, but they are a good change. Lake Powell is beautiful, (even though its man-made). But the less populated places are more interesting to me.

While on a roadtrip to Moab with some friends, we visited Arches National Park. When night fell, the moon lit up the sandstones, making the land look familiar to day time, but completely different in feeling. We hiked to Delicate Arch that night (the Arch on the new license plate). I sat right under the Arch for a long time. I felt a lot of power sitting there under the Arch under the full moon. The landscape around the Arch at night made us feel like we were on another planet.

I'm glad to live in a State with such a wide range of places to pitch my tent.

Merle Edwards
Salt Lake County

Age 72; **Birthplace** Roosevelt, Duchesne, Utah; **Occupation** Retired Secretary; **Religion** LDS; **Race/Ethnicity** White

The Utah Centennial means a great deal to me, particularly because my mother, Ella Rose Gagon Roberts, now deceased, was born to her parents, William Highland Gagon and Mary Augusta Goodrich Gagon, on December 20, 1896, in Vernal, Uintah County, Utah.

My great-grandmother, Margaret Ann Vest Kay Harrison, came from England on an ocean voyage which landed the family in Philadelphia on the 5th of May, 1855. William Clover was the captain of this company. Later she and her family walked many miles beside the overloaded wagons and handcarts. They arrived in Salt Lake City on the 25th of September, 1857.

Through the years my husband and I have traveled our great State from North to South, from East to West. There is so much to offer here—at any time of the year—the blossoms of Springtime, the flowers of Summer, the blue skies, the golden colors of the trees, and the fruits and vegetables of Autumn, the snows of Winter. Oh, UTAH! how great thou art!

We have stood in awe as we have gazed at the pinnacles, the spires, the walls, the arches and cathedrals in brilliant colors of red, pink, copper and cream at Bryce Canyon. Do you notice how the colors change with the sunlight?

We have taken time to climb beautiful Mount Timpanogas, relaxed as we have taken a boat ride at Lake Powell, have marvelled at the well-planned campuses of the University of Utah, the Brigham Young University and Utah State University.

We have been enthralled as we have strolled through the museums at famous Promontory Point and Silver Reef.

We have attended many cultural events here in Utah, including the Pops Concerts under the direction of Maestro Eugene Jelesnik, and the Festival of the American West, held on the campus of Utah State University, for twenty years, and we never seem to tire of that exciting and educational production.

And we must mention historic Temple Square and its well-manicured gardens, the world renowned Tabernacle and its outstanding Choir—and just up the hill to the north is the Daughters of Utah Pioneers Museum—and there are many churches and temples available throughout our State.

Besides the variety of scenery here—there is also a variety of faces, of many cultures, who are our good friends and neighbors. Our neighborhood is still safe. We are able to move about freely without fear. People are friendly and are concerned for the welfare of one another.

Say—do you take time to notice the sunsets over the Great Salt Lake—and have you watched a full moon rise over the mountain range?

Here and there, during the travels, we spot our lovely State flower, the white three-petaled sego lily, and the cactus blooms are especially beautiful.

In our travels we visited the "Coral Dunes," near Kanab, where the prevailing winds have heaped and shaped sand into dunes that are sometimes as high as twenty-five feet. This day we encountered an elderly Navajo woman in native dress, struggling to reach the top of a very high dune. She was accompanied by a granddaughter. To climb to the top was a goal she had set for herself—and she had reached her goal. She was wearing a contented smile.

While there we saw long delicate lines across the sand, and learned that these were made by tiny, shiny, quarter-inch scarablike beetles. Their paths went uphill and downhill. These tiny workers were busy everywhere, doing their bit, endlessly beautifying the dunes with their intricate patterns, made by their six legs.

The Utah soil holds the graves of my ancestors. I have a feeling of peace and love when we make visits to various cemeteries in Vernal, Roosevelt and Mona. There is a place reserved for me among them when my days upon this earth are completed. Besides my relatives, there are many of my friends and long ago acquaintances also buried in these places.

It is wonderful to travel to foreign countries, as my husband and I have and to see other parts of the world. We have seen unusual cultures and many beautiful sights, but we are always happy to see the familiar Wasatch Mountains as our plane circles the Salt Lake Valley for its landing, and to know that we are once again home—home in UTAH, the State we admire and love!

Thomas Jefferson Lyon
Cache County

Age 58; **Birthplace** Binghamton, NY; **Occupation** Professor; **Religion** N/A; **Race/Ethnicity** Euro-American

At first, it meant getting used to different, drier air—to a run of blue-sky days—and to the absence of a humid, enveloping, tree-enclosed world. This took some time. Over years, the spareness came to seem beautiful.

Then I began to see that the small town life in Utah was not any sort of denial, but a richness, if one looked properly. You learned not to look for the movies that never made it to Logan, and not to listen for slangy, knowing street talk. These things were simply not there. What was there was a way of pronouncing "trail" as "trell" that somehow made its way into your own speech, and a feeling of nativeness that began to grow—especially when you went somewhere else like California and people betrayed a lack of knowledge of Utah. Then you spoke of Lombardy poplars and washed-down streets, the storekeepers of Logan out in front of their doorways with a hose, spring mornings, and the wind out of the canyon on summer nights.

The feeling of a settlement surrounded by wild space and quiet mountains and canyons is very different from that of one town among many, adjacent. If Utah were sold off, and its wild space converted to mere numbers on somebody's bottom line, it wouldn't be Utah any more. That is why the battle for Utah's wilderness is a battle for Utah's soul. What Utah means to me, living in Utah, is the chance to feel that life of the soul, and to try and help preserve it.

Joy J. Heaton
Kane County

Age 50; **Birthplace** Phoenix, Arizona; **Occupation** One of the few full time homemakers; **Religion** LDS; **Race/Ethnicity** Caucasian

Ever heard of Alton, Utah? It's located just off Highway 89 about midway between Panguitch and Orderville in Southern Utah. If you blink, you'll miss the turn off. The narrow road into town is the only thing here that needs unwinding. And the only thing that's uptight is my husband's working boots.

Life out here is only for the stout hearted—those with true grit who can scratch out a living with a horse and a bale of hay or keep the roads hot going to other places for work.

No traffic jams either. The only jam I've ever seen around here disappeared long ago after the choke cherries were picked and put up.

Kids here think that hard rock is the mountain ridge that frames their homes. In the summertime, they long to ride their horses over those easterly pink cliffs just inches from Bryce Canyon. Too bad about the national parks. The only ones who get to enjoy the parks nowadays are the "foreigners."

I used to think that my husband was one of the greatest environmentalists around. After all, he makes his living from the dust of earth, and keeping the land in good shape is what has kept him out of the red. But don't call him an environmentalist! It's a dirty word around here. And with good cause. The endangered species list has endangered the farmers and ranchers, that's for sure. And wiped out the timber industry and mining operations. It makes you wonder who has the right to pursue happiness any more. The prairie dogs and snails have more rights than we do. The especially sad part about all those people losing their jobs is that they are hard working people who were contributing to the well being of America! They weren't on any government handout rolls!

There is one bright side to the political and bureaucratic mess we find ourselves in today in America. We've got a good ol' country boy for a governor, Mike Leavitt, who's not afraid to work and who uses wisdom and common sense—so uncommon today in the political horse manured arena. He's using his influence to turn things around and we are praying for him.

Pollution? Well, the skies are pretty clear around these parts. Problem is, they want us to have emissions controls, etc. just like the big cities. Why should we be taking aspirin for someone else's headache? The only pollution we get comes from the television programs on prime time. That's why we don't turn it on much.

But would I want to live anywhere else? No way! I'm

extremely proud of my American heritage. I'm related to John Hancock—that great patriot who signed his name in big letters on the Declaration of Independence. I wonder if today's school children even know who he is. I have ancestry who fought in the Civil War and World War II. I don't want to forget them, and I don't want my kids to, either.

I want my kids to remember and be proud of the heritage of Utah. I want them to know as much as they can about the Mormon Pioneers who settled here and sacrificed so much that we can now enjoy the great prosperity that we have in 1995 because of them.

I want them to love the heritage that is ours that came from the establishment of the United Order. Those precious pioneers came to Orderville from the Muddy Mission—a trial that left them in the depths of poverty. But from those humble circumstances by trying to work hard together, by helping each other, and by living the principles of Christianity, they established a communal order of living that lasted longer in Orderville than anywhere else.

The spirit of those Orderville Saints still thrives in the communities of Long Valley (Orderville, Glendale, Alton, and Mt. Carmel). They are the most hard working people I've ever lived around. Not only that, they are the kindest, the friendliest, and the most neighborly.

These rocks and hills and these stouthearted people have truly shaped my life. I want to be like them. Living in Utah is one of the best things that has ever happened to me.

Leo Shepherd Jr.
Iron County

Age 37; **Birthplace** Cedar City, UT; **Occupation** Native American Culture Teacher; **Religion** Native American; **Race/Ethnicity** Native American

Living in Utah means to me as a Native American, many things. We are caretakers of this land. Our Mother Earth has provided us with everything that is essential to our survival as Human Beings.

We (our Native People) try not to take things for granted such as our precious water; clean air; wildlife (game for hunting); the trees, mountains, and all other Gods creations. I was taught to have respect for all elderly people, especially our Native American Grandfathers and Grandmothers.

Living in Utah means to me that our non-Indian brothers and sisters should have respect for our people. Be thankful for all our Ancestors have taught them in living through the harshest conditions in many seasons.

Living in Utah also hurts my heart many times because some people see others for their skin color and not whats in their hearts. They think that they are better than others ... like we (along with other races) don't belong here in North America. I try and remind them of who was here long before their arrival, and never forget it. It doesn't matter how long your hair is, what language you speak or what religion you belong to. What matters is the Love, Friendship, Understanding and Compassion we should all have for one another. There is one who is our supreme/superior being and we worship him as the almighty—he is our "First Maker."

We have no one to answer to but him, we should all strive for "World Peace" here upon this Universe. I'm Red like the blood that connects me to all Gods creations such as the Earth, Trees, Animals and the Web of Life. ... thats what living in Utah means to me (see plate 20).

Leo Shepherd Jr., Paiute and Navajo Tribes

Jessica Marilyn Gleason
Kane County

Age 12; **Birthplace** Preston, Idaho; **Occupation** Student;
Religion Church of Jesus Christ of L.D.S.;
Race/Ethnicity White

WHAT IT MEANS TO ME TO LIVE IN UTAH:

There is hardly any smog, the stars shine so bright. I love the snow here, and so pretty. The mountains are so big and beautiful. And my family, most of them live here in Utah. It is also easier to get animals in Utah.

People very nice in Utah, they go to great extents to help you, every body is very friendly.

The lakes, ponds and rivers are ever so lovely, probably 99% cleaner than pine sol!

I hope Utah will stay beautiful.

Ryan Craig Perry

Age N/A; **Birthplace** N/A; **Occupation** N/A;
Religion Mormon; **Race/Ethnicity** N/A

If you asked me what I think about Utah. You would get the reply **I ❤ ∎**. The number one reason **I ❤ ∎** is that it has alot of wildlife. So I decided to write this true story.

One day, in October we were driving down the highway. As we drove I saw something brownish move just off the highway. I asked my mom to stop the automobile. Just as I was asking if she would, she pulled over and stopped. I told her what I had seen. Then we walked back down the road. And we found a hawk. The hawk could not fly. So we took it home and fed it, even though it was against the law. Pretty soon it was starting to fly a little bit. So we put it in the chicken coop. 1 week later the hawk could fly with ease. Then we let it go free. But it didn't hybernate. It stayed around and ate mice we caut in the garauge. We would put them in a mesh fenced yard. Now the date is January 8, 1995 and the hawk is still hanging around.

Badrun Nahar
Salt Lake County

Age 28; **Birthplace** Bangladesh; **Occupation** Home maker;
Religion Muslim; **Race/Ethnicity** Asian

My name is Badrun Nahar. I am from Bangladesh. I came to Utah with my husband seven years ago. The reason for coming here is for my husband to get a higher education.

We came here in 1987 in the month of December. It was very cold and snowy everywhere. It was the first time I have ever seen snow in my life. It looks beautiful, especially when we came to the University of Utah Student Housing Complex. The circle shaped playground was covered with very thick snow. It seemed like a huge cake, covered with white frosting. I felt like eating it all up. When the snow sets on the bare trees, it seems to me that white flowers grew from the tree, like something special came from another world. It looks so beautiful that I still enjoy seeing that scenery through the window all the time.

I like the mountains. Bangladesh is mostly a plain land. At first I was scared to go down the hill. The first day when our friend was driving up and down in the mountains, I was about to scream. But now I love to go to the mountains. It's fun.

Another thing I find here is the "Dinosaur Park," the biggest animal that used to rule this world millions of years ago. Before coming here it was a fictitious story to me. But now I believe it seeing the real fossils of dinosaurs stuck in the mountain in Vernal.

In Utah I enjoy seeing lots of natural views like falls and rivers that flow between the mountains.

Another thing I find here is the people from all over the world. It gives me an idea about their culture, food and dress from different ethnic people in the world.

In conclusion, I enjoy living in Utah. It gives me a chance to know how the world is different from one place to another. I get to know people from every where in the world. I enjoy the climate, the mountains and other natural and beautiful things. But I still love my country where I grew up. I miss my family and friends. I would like to go back there and have my time with them.

Brady Clifford
Davis County

Age N/A; **Birthplace** N/A; **Occupation** N/A; **Religion** N/A; **Race/Ethnicity** N/A

Utah, it has it all. The canyon lands, such as Lake Powell; the Mountain, Pineview reservoir, and Skiing Resorts. Utah has everything that anyone would ask for; I wouldn't live anywhere else.

Utah has snow every winter and it also has Ski Resorts. There are many Ski Resorts in Utah; such as Snowbasin, Snowbird, Park City, Powder Mountain, and Deer Valley. One Ski Resort that me and my family go to the most is Snowbasin. Utah is a great place for skiing, I think.

Pineview Reservoir is where me and my family spend most of our water recreation. In the early summer boating on Pineview lake, you can view the majestic Wasatch mountains covered with snow on their peaks; it is extremely awesome. Last summer me and my family camped overnight on the beach of Pineview, and enjoyed the sand, fishing, water skiing, and the stars. There are many fresh water lakes in Utah.

The Mountains, these massive, gigantic rock surfaces are one of Utahs wonders. They are used for skiing, hunting, wild life, reservoirs and much more. The mountains protect Utah from tornadoes and other things. Me and my family have mountains to the east of us, these mountains are called the Rocky Mountains. There is a trail that I sometimes go hiking on near my home. We also have hills to the North and South of us. All the mountains and hills that surround our house are a big reason that we live in Utah.

One other thing that makes Utah such a great place is, Lake Powell. Lake Powell was once a big and deep canyon that the Colorado River used to run through. But, men had built a dam in Arizona that blocked the Colorado River to form Lake Powell. This place is beautiful in so many ways. The tall canyons provide alot of shade and are so fantastic. The water is blue as the sky and contains so many species of fish. There are many lizards to catch on the rocks, they are really fun to catch. The water is warm in the summer and is a little cold in the winter. You can do alot of hiking in that country, which is extremely fun. All of these places, and landscapes, are just a few wonderful things in Utah. There is no other place that I would want to live in the world.

Billie Perry Prpich

Salt Lake County

EXCERPTED FROM
"AUTUMN IN UTAH"
© 1968 by Billie Perry Prpich

Who has seen autumn
    Strolling on the hills?
In her brightest costume
    Of gold and coral frills.

Who has seen her dancing
    Gaily in her scarlet gown,
On a carpet of green
    Spread upon the ground?

The mountains and valleys
    Are flaunting their lavish colors.
The gold of the aspens between
    The flaming scarlet maples
With a background of evergreens
    Create a glowing luminous scene.

Who has seen autumn
    In these dreamy October days?
She leaves a trail of beauty
    In a thousand lovely ways. …

LOVE LETTERS TO UTAH

Restless and footloose, Americans are nevertheless deeply committed to place. At the centennial of statehood, Utahns are no exception. Of the half million who responded to the "Centennial Portrait" call, some 98 percent wrote in positive terms. A once-in-a-century poll, the "Portrait" reveals a Utah that is still very much in the making. It is good-hearted and friendly. It is responsible, idealistic, and filled with promise. Extending from young to old and through all walks of life, the portraits suggest that national attachments, worldwide media, and modern complexities notwithstanding, love of home, state loyalty, sense of place, and commitment to civic responsibility still persist. Many themes are repeated—the four seasons, caring neighbors, a textured experience—but the statements reach far beyond the stereotype to feelings tender, frank, and honest that reveal Utah at heart as well as in sinew and bone. Its spirit is the spirit of America twice distilled. Through it shines a conviction that promise and opportunity have not perished. Like thousands of Utah statements collected by the Federal Writers' Project of the Depression era, the "Centennial Portrait Archives" will be consulted again and again by historians in the decades ahead.

—Charles S. Peterson

Bettye Berliner Gillespie

Weber County

Age N/A; **Birthplace** Ft. Worth, Texas; **Occupation** Retired; **Religion** Episcopalian; **Race/Ethnicity** African American

For a woman of African American descent, living in the State of Utah has presented some unique challenges and interesting contradictions. I have always had to remember that I am not only a woman, but black as well, and that the possibility exists that I may be treated differently from women of other races. Yet, I have been able to establish some enduring relationships and contacts through affiliations with, and memberships on some of the State's most prestigious boards. I have served on the Board of Trustees of the University of Utah, and continue to serve on the State Advisory Committee to the U.S. Civil Rights Commission.

Had I lived in a larger, more populous state, I may never have had the occasion to personally express my views to the Governor, or the U.S. Congressional delegation, or any other public official in a high position of authority. Living in Utah has afforded me the opportunity to know these people, and provided them the opportunity to know me.

Emma Lou Thayne

Salt Lake County

Age 71; **Birthplace** SLC; **Occupation** Writer; **Religion** LDS; **Race/Ethnicity** White

Fifteen minutes into the mountains east of our city home is total seclusion. Our family cabin peers out from a hillside of pines and aspen onto the granite outcroppings and numberless greens of summer or the six-foot white of winter that cross country skis or snow mobiles can carry us to.

We can roast marshmallows over the bonfire with cousins one season or sled down for two miles without stopping in another. I can go there alone without fear, my laptop on wooden shelving to plunk away with no noise but birds or squirrels and maybe wood snapping in the Monarch stove.

Nothing essential has changed since my brothers and I hiked to Castle Crags or made rope swings or my doll houses six decades ago, sure that when we sang "Our Mountain Home So Dear, where crystal waters clear flow ever free" in Sunday school on the screened porch, it was we kids who flowed free along with them.

Utah is where I have found the freedom to study and play at a university in the valley where my pioneer polygamous great grandparents came to make homes and find ways to laugh as they toiled or went fishing (women too!). Here for me and mine are symphony and dance, theater companies and a whopping tennis program, all as handy as skiing in fresh powder in March or water skiing among the sandstone wonders of Lake Powell in October.

Here also are variety and naturalness among those who have peopled the committees and nourished the worlds I've been lucky enough to be part of, from the Utah Endowment for the Humanities to the staff of a daily newspaper to peace groups to the Mormon congregation where our five children grew up. Somehow goodness and generosity make their untiring way through forests of activity and dogma, and indomitable spirit through and clashes in ideology either civic or cultural. My wrestling is most often with the multiple choices that spin from a society of doers as well as propounders of so many good words. The diversity is as inviting as the mountains I run to.

Utah is a desert that blossoms and teems with contrasts. Even as I sometimes struggle with the complexities of change, every decade I'm gladder to call it home.

Clark Young
Salt Lake County

Age 100; **Birthplace** Salt Lake City; **Occupation** Medical doctor; **Religion** LDS; **Race/Ethnicity** Caucasian

As the oldest surviving great-grandson of Brigham Young, I am proud of my great heritage. I was born in Salt Lake City in 1895 while Utah was still a territory, and was six months before Utah was admitted into the Union.

I attended the old LDS High School, and went several times to the Lion House to meet President Joseph F. Smith in order to date his daughter. Later I attended the University of Utah, where I sat at the feet of James E. Talmage. After graduating I went to Boston and studied to become a doctor at the Harvard Medical School. I returned to Salt Lake City to practice medicine and specialized in surgery. Also, I am a fellow of the American College of Surgeons.

At the age of 98 I became Utah's oldest writer by publishing a romantic novel, which is entitled *The Gloom and Glow.*

I have traveled on every continent in the world, and I honestly feel that Utah is the prime place to live.

when Utah became the "newest star" on the Union flag, and speaks of many of the things that still make this state unique.

"Land of the mountains high," "Land of the sunny sky," "Land of the pioneers," and "Thy lustre shines afar," are just a few of the phrases from the song that have stuck with me.

In an almost prophetic tone, the song says: "Grow with the coming years, With wealth and peace in store, To fame and glory soar, God-guarded evermore. Utah, we love thee!"

Through the years I have traveled in Europe, Asia, some parts of Africa, and in all 50 states, but have yet to find a place that means more to me than Utah. Nothing so sweet as to come back to Utah after being anywhere else.

In this state of my birth I have been educated and trained. I have had career opportunities that have far exceeded my expectations as a youth. My seven children and 12 grandchildren have all been born here, and I expect to enjoy the remainder of my years surrounded by the beauties and peace of this state with loved ones and friends who add special meaning to my life in this very great state.

I do love Utah, and hope to add my continued efforts to make this state a true jewel among its sister states.

William James Mortimer
Salt Lake County

Age 63; **Birthplace** Provo, Utah County, Utah; **Occupation** Editor and publisher, *Deseret News*; **Religion** LDS ; **Race/Ethnicity** Caucasian

As a youngster growing up in Utah I learned in school to sing the state song, "Utah, We Love Thee." The message of this special song has stayed with me through the years, even though it is hardly sung any more.

The song was written in 1896 by Evan Stephens

Wilmer "Bud" Perry
Weber County

Age 76; **Birthplace** North Ogden, Utah; **Occupation** Retired; **Religion** Mormon; **Race/Ethnicity** White

It's HOME! It's where I was born—where I grew up—where I went to school—where my family is—where my friends are.

It's where I happily returned after World War II—got a wonderful job—met and married my lovely wife,

Fay—and raised two wonderful kids.

It's where my wonderful wife of 46 years is now buried on a hill beneath the beautiful Wasatch Mountains overlooking the far reaching valley to the Great Salt Lake and the distant mountains. Could there possibly be a more beautiful view anywhere in the world!

Add to this the most exceptionally interesting Ogden Canyon, the majestic Ben Lomond Peak (named by my great grandmother, Mary Wilson Montgomery), the landscape—the rivers. What more could you ask for?

It's where the people are friendly—where you can participate in or watch an unbelievable variety of activities—ball games, dancing, socials, musicals, plays—you name it—it's all here.

It's where we have a wonderful climate—never really seriously hot or seriously cold. And it has the four seasons—always something different to look forward to.

It's where I spend a large portion of my time doing volunteer work. Meeting and working with a bunch of great people. What a wonderful feeling when I "Do unto others as I Would Have Them Do Unto Me."

It's where my ancestors, who came to America on the Mayflower and the Good Ship Lion, and who's progeny came to Utah Territory in the 1850's for religious preference, gave me life after they decided "this is the place" they wanted their progeny to live.

And, by golly, I'm gonna stay here as long as God is willing. And I'm going to be buried, next to Fay on that hill beneath the beautiful Wasatch Mountains overlooking the far reaching valley to the Great Salt Lake and the distant mountains.

Robert Foster Bennett
Salt Lake County

Age 62; **Birthplace** Salt Lake City, UT; **Occupation** United States Senator; **Religion** LDS; **Race/Ethnicity** Caucasian

I was born and raised in Utah and never left it (except for a family vacation here and there) until I turned 20. As a result, I had no idea why living in Utah was any different than living any place else.

I spent two years in Scotland as an LDS missionary, which opened my eyes to the way Europeans live. I came home with a much sharpened understanding of the importance of being an American, but still didn't focus on the uniqueness of Utah within the American experience.

Then I went to the Army, with the service in California and Oklahoma. As I met with other servicemen from around the country, I began to realize that Utah was not only different in terms of my own "comfort zone"—an amalgam of family, friends, religion, and familiar geography—but also in a distinctive cultural way that I have now come to appreciate as being something special and significant.

As I represent Utah in the United States Senate, I have many opportunities to hear people from outside the State comment on this. Depending on the background of the individual, the specifics vary, but there is an underlying theme.

I meet with business people who have operations in the State; they tell me of the "unique workforce" that they find in the State, mentioning things like "strong work ethic," "trustworthiness and loyalty" and "highly educated." This last comment always surprises them, since they look at the amount of money spent per pupil in the State and wonder how we do it.

Arts enthusiasts talk glowingly of Utah's support for the arts, from the symphony to the ballet to the theater and finally the countless numbers of local choirs, orchestras, theatrical groups, and dance organizations.

Utah has its racial and ethnic problems, but I'm often told by leaders of such groups that, as a general rule, Utah is more hospitable to their members than most places. Utah politics are vigorous, but lacking much of the mean-spirited nature of politics in many of the places that I have lived. Utahns can support a cause with as much passion as anyone, but elections are fair, the results are respected and duly elected leaders are duly supported in office, even by those who disagree violently with the positions that they take.

The underlying theme in all this is a deep respect for each individual. Utahns believe in self-reliance because they believe each one of us can be relied upon. Utahns believe in education and artistic expression because they believe each individual is worth it. Utahns render a good day's work for a day's pay because they believe the employer is entitled to it.

There are exceptions to this rule, of course, and perhaps they are growing as a percentage of Utah's population. There are many other places in the country where this same rule is followed; Utah is not unique. Nonetheless, I find more of this quality in Utah than I do in the other places where I have visited and lived, and it is the quality that means the most to me. When my Senate term is over, I will live in Utah full-time (not part-time, as I do now) and I will do what I can to see to it that the special qualities of this State are handed down to future generations of Utahns, however long my influence might last.

Ronald Taylor
Kane County

Age 46; **Birthplace** Provo, Utah Co., Utah; **Occupation** Educator; **Religion** Church of Jesus Christ of L.D.S.; **Race/Ethnicity** Caucasian

Edgar A. Guest said it best when he said: "It takes a heap of livin' in a house to make it home." Well, it takes a heap of livin' in a state to make it home. I've done a heap of livin' in Utah and it's home. My roots run deep in Utah's soil. I'm a fifth generation Utahn on all sixteen lines of my family tree. I have been a legal resident of Utah my entire life and although I spent four years in the Air Force and two years serving my church, my legal residence has always been Utah. I was born here, educated in her public schools and her universities. I was married here, raised my family here and hope to someday die and be buried in her bosom.

I've fished her streams, hiked her mountains, and camped in her forests and in her deserts. I've been on top of Mt. Timpanogos at four o'clock in the morning and watched the sun rise on her vast expanse. I have stood in awe at the majesty of her national parks and her hidden beauty. Within a ten hour day I saw her mountains change from black, to pure white, to sandy red, and I didn't have to leave her borders to see such change in scenery. I've ridden her railroads, driven on her freeways, city streets and lonely country lanes. I've flown over her and have seen her spread beneath me like an old fashioned patch-work quilt. Utah's spirit runs deep, oh, so deep within my soul.

The poet, Bob Hilliard said: "I love those dear hearts and gentle people that live and love in my home town." Yes, I too love the dear hearts and gentle people who live and love in my home state. It takes good people, a dedicated governor and other public officials to keep Utah a lovely place to live. For over one hundred years we have had good leaders to govern our state. Her communities and villages have been filled with gentle hearts. People who love her and are grateful to a loving God who allows them to make Utah their home. I've lived in her northern valleys, was raised in her central valleys and make my home now in her southern valleys, and throughout the state I've found dear hearts and gentle people.

"It takes a heap of livin'… and ya sometimes have to roam before ya really 'preciate the things ye lef' behind, and hunger fer 'em somehow, with 'em alus on yer mind." I've left Utah to roam the country as I served my Country and my God and it was during those times that I learned to appreciate the things I left behind and hungered for them with them always on my mind. I'm entering the middle years of my life and with that has come a love to travel and see the sites of the world, but it is always so good to return to the safety and security I feel as a Utahn living in this great State of mine.

I've done a heap of livin' in this state and now it's not just a state, it's my home.

Lucille Bush Hampel
Weber County

Age 71; **Birthplace** Pleasant Grove, Utah; **Occupation** Retired; **Religion** LDS; **Race/Ethnicity** Caucasian

As I travel south on I-15, round the bend at the point of the mountain, there before me is the most beautiful place on earth. As my eyes look skyward, I can trace the ridge of those lofty peaks and see the outline of the body of the Indian maiden I learned about from folklore of long ago. My Timpanogos—it's more than a mountain—it's a sentinel.

I lived in the shadow of that mountain; when as a child I roamed the rocky foothill. What a comforting feeling to know of its protection. Yes, I was born in

Pleasant Grove, Utah, where the birds sang songs of praise to a peaceful valley. I know no other valley so tranquil. We children all thought of it as our mountain, with the very special surprise in the cave inside—the heart of Timpanogos. Wherever I have been; north or south, east or west, that mountain seems to speak to me as if to say, "Your back, back to the place of your childhood—your home."

I felt so protected living near that mountain. Just above our town, in a very special place, was a block "G" painted on the hill. In later years I showed that "G" on the mountain to my grandchildren and found out our Angela, age four, told all her school friends—"there's a big, big mountain in Utah with a "G" painted on it, which stands for Grandma." I never told her any different—would you?

Many times, as we were returning from trips around the United States, our whole family would cheer as we came to the sign that announced "entering Utah—it's still the right place." When we were vacationing near Boston several years ago, all dressed up in our Utah shirts, a lady on the street came up and asked if she could hug me. She said, "It would be just like being home. I miss Utah so much."

Our valleys, our mountains, our changing seasons, our people all make up a state of mind—Utah, the best of all.

Tyrone K. Lopez
Salt Lake County

Age 12; **Birthplace** Salt Lake; **Occupation** Student; **Religion** N/A; **Race/Ethnicity** Native American/Navajo

My name is Tyrone Kee Lopez. I am 12 years old. I am a Native American Indian from the Navajo tribe and I go to Thomas Jefferson Junior High School in Kearns, Utah.

Living in Utah means that everything is different

from the reservation. There are basic things here that I am grateful for, which my grandmother will never have, such as running water. She does not have a telephone or electricity nor does she have nice roads that go to her house. The reservation where my grandmother lives is quiet, the air is clean and there are no neighbors for miles around. Here in Utah, everything is close to where I live, and even if it is far away, I can get there on nice roads. There are beautiful mountains in Utah and during the winter there is a lot of snow.

Living in Utah means having to be exposed to all kinds of nice people. Utah is a place with many different people from different ethnic groups and some from different countries. People are very friendly here. I have made a lot of friends from different minority groups with different cultures.

When you walk downtown, the sidewalks and streets are kept very clean. During the summer the place is kept with pretty flowers and trees. Utah has beautiful scenery and there are many activities going on throughout the year. There is always something that everyone can see and enjoy while they visit Utah. Utah also has a great basketball team, the Utah Jazz.

Living in Utah is never boring, it means a lot of fun and many exciting things to do!

Karen Kofford Huntsman
Emery County

Age 54; **Birthplace** Castle Dale, UT; **Occupation** Homemaker; **Religion** L.D.S.; **Race/Ethnicity** Caucasian

It is looking out my kitchen window at my neighbors and KNOWING them … having loyal friends who do kind deeds but never seek for glory … going to the store or post office and taking a couple of hours because you stop to visit with each one there, for they are your friends … getting up on Sunday morning, going outside and it is so still and peaceful that you can pray without being disturbed … looking up in the heavens at night and seeing billions of stars … to be able to sit in Church each Sunday and thank Heavenly Father for the privilege of living in Utah.

It means being able to walk out over the old County bridge, stopping to listen to the gentle river as it slowly runs by and being grateful for the day … being close to the temple … it is being able to enjoy all four seasons of the year … being blessed with the opportunity of going to the desert which is only 30 minutes away or traveling to the mountains which is only 30 minutes away … going Eastering each year with family … getting chill-bumps when you see the flag go by or hear the marching band or listen to a patriotic speaker … celebrating the 24th of July and remembering what our pioneer ancestors went through so that we could celebrate the 24th of July … giving humble service and enjoying the simple things … it means being able to walk at night or early in the morning and not being afraid … having fun at parades, county fairs, rodeos, picnics and pageants … It means this and much, much more.

It means that I love, honor and revere my wonderful state of Utah. It means that I am so very blessed to live here and enjoy life.

Living in Utah means that I can have fond and happy memories of my youth and the wonderful things that I enjoyed.

Thank you Heavenly Father. I am proud to be a Mormon and a Utahn.

Mary Frances Stegmann
Salt Lake County

Age 34; **Birthplace** New York; **Occupation** Housewife/Craft maker; **Religion** Catholic; **Race/Ethnicity** White

I am a Former New Yorker, now residing in Salt Lake City. Born in Staten Island, NY and raised in the Sullivan County Catskills of upstate NY most of my life, I moved out west April, 1991 initially to Portland, Oregon. I moved to Salt Lake with my husband who was transferred from Portland to Salt Lake for the company he is employed by.

When friends (from New York & Oregon) and family learned of my plans to move here, the comments, warnings and advice were plentiful. Such as, "You'll hate it because they control the people there," "They will try and force you to become a Mormon," "If you are not Mormon, they will shun you," "They have Polygamists there," "There's nothing to do there," etc. … I was rather amused by these comments considering the majority of these people have never even stepped foot in Utah! I'll admit, the *only* knowledge I had of Utah was learning the State Capitol in history class (in my school days), and yes, good old Donny Osmond, my idol of the 70's!

Needless to say, March 2, 1995 will be my 3rd year in Utah. I *do not* feel controlled by anyone, I'm *not* Mormon and do *not* feel shunned, I would not recognize a polygamist if they were standing right next to me, and I find there is *plenty* to do as far as activity is concerned.

It was amazing to me that people in public *look* at you, smile, say hello and do not show fear or violence toward one another. Although my "guard" will always be up (being a former New Yorker), I feel *extremely* safe here. When I watch KUTV news, I don't cry. It is no where near as depressing as the news in New York. Every state has crime, drugs, gangs etc. … but the violence here has *no* comparison to New York. I get extremely angry when I do see on the news a case where a Utahn gets scammed by someone who lives outside of Utah. I feel so protective of the people here because they are so nice and no offense, but gullible and innocent.

The mountains on the wasatch are the most beautiful sight to me. I'm sure my friends back East were tired of the pictures I sent of *every* season the first year I lived here! Again, that feeling of security with the mountains near me is overwhelming. (Although I do miss the Autumn colors of upstate New York!)

The golf courses in Utah are very beautiful, the ski areas are also gorgeous. (If you really love to *ice skate* "down hill," go to one of the New York ski areas!) I've played volleyball, and some darts here and love it!

The state "controlling" aspect, of Alcohol, is to me, positive. If this was done in every state nation wide there would be a lot more lives saved. It's also nice to be out in public and not see people doing drugs on a corner, or right in plain view. Or for that matter trying to sell me drugs.

To sum this up, I have been mugged, shot at, chased by a homeless man for a quarter, witnessed a woman on a subway platform in New York take out a machete and whirl it around her head like a samurai injuring everyone near her, witnessed corruption within the police force of "New York's finest" (ha), and on a daily basis witnessed the hatred and violence people showed for one another. Living in Utah to me, is as if I died and am in heaven. I'm happy, I'm safe and am proud to be a resident of this beautiful state. The Utahns here just do not know how good they have it!

Katherine Allred McConkie

Cache County

Age 39; **Birthplace** Farmington, New Mexico; **Occupation** Administrative Assistant; **Religion** Latter-day Saint (Mormon); **Race/Ethnicity** Caucasian

Utah means home to me. Although I was born in New Mexico and lived in Somalia, Malta, and Libya when I was growing up, Utah was always the place to which I was most strongly tied. It was where my extended family lived and where we spent our vacations. Even if I did not physically have a home here, I felt at home—it was always familiar ground. Utah was the place where I have established my own home and eventually where my parents and all my siblings have chosen to settle.

Just as Utah was a sanctuary for the Mormon pioneers over a hundred years ago, it has proven to be a haven for me and my family. Although we had a wonderful life during our years overseas and wouldn't trade our experiences for anything, we also saw oppression and revolution, beheld poverty and disease, encountered misunderstandings and hatred. Here we feel protected from the troubles of the world. That's not to say that we're unaware of the problems existing in our community, but they pale next to the magnitude of the discord and misery found elsewhere.

All of us still love to travel, but we return to Utah with renewed appreciation for this magnificent place we've chosen to call home.

Sabrena Larson

Millard County

Age 17; **Birthplace** Delta, UT; **Religion** L.D.S.; **Race/Ethnicity** White

"The water is coming!" The young girl yelled at the top of her lungs. Soon everyone was informed that the weekly irrigation water was on its way to the small town. The adults quickly got busy preparing for the event by raking, mowing, and picking up the toys from their lawns. The young kids came swarming out of their houses, by the hundreds, it seemed, running, as fast as they could to the favorite swimming hole. Some were wearing cut off jeans and others wore swim suits, but they all carried a towel. Jumping into the cold, dirty water they began to splash, yell, and dunk each other under the water. The banks of the deep watering hole were covered with small shoes, socks and many colored towels. We had finally found a way to escape from the hot summer sun.

Growing up in a little town has been almost like heaven, playing with the neighborhood kids all day and then well into the night. I never have to care about gangs, drugs, or getting kidnapped. Hinckley is a town that when you go to bed at night you don't have to lock your doors or windows. It's a place where everyone knows each other, and it's only a short distance to where ever it is you want to be, at the park, old school, rodeo grounds, or the famous willow tree. It's a wonderful little town where you can sleep out on your front lawn on a hot summers night and the only thing you have to worry about is getting mosquito bites.

People in Hinckley are always there for you when you have a problem. A while back a mans truck had broken down and a group of teenagers helped push it four blocks to the Hinckley service station. Another time two people needed directions to a certain house and they knocked on my front door. In larger cities you might be afraid to get out of your broken down truck, or even knock on a strangers door.

Does it sound too much like a fairy tale? Well it is real. I have lived in Hinckley Utah all my life and loved all of it, from walking out of my house and not being in my neighbors front lawn to being able to breath the fresh, clean Utah air every day of my life.

This town will always have sentimental value to me and probably to most of the people that live here.

So what does living in Utah mean to me? Fun, freedom, memories.

Jessie Fish Datwyler
Cache County

Age 42; **Birthplace** Brigham City; **Occupation** Book-keeper, Homemaker; **Religion** Latter Day Saint; **Race/Ethnicity** Caucasian

As a child I grew up looking at the mountains outside the kitchen window while I did the dishes. Now as I walk around the block in the morning nothing is more therapeutic than the pink glow that comes before the sun rises on snow capped peaks. Mountains come in many shapes and sizes in Utah and that is what makes Utah so unique.

Where else can you play in desert sand dune peaks; or hike in a high mountain meadow filled with wildflowers that border a sparkling stream; or find deep red-rocked canyons of smooth sandstone that form labyrinths of beauty for the explorer. All of this diversity is within a short drive. If one is too hot in one location, they can drive up in elevation and find snow the next night.

Living in Utah means river trips, wilderness experiences, and breathtaking views that help renew and restore ones inner self. Man needs places to go and Utah has had the foresight to keep parks and forest lands in good condition. Wilderness places takes us back to what we were, and they gives us the strength to carry on in our fast paced world.

Besides the mountains, and beautiful places to visit, Utah means home. It is where people I love and care about live. It means family and neighborhood parties, and not being afraid to let kids trick-or-treat. It's being a room-mother and helping at the annual school carnival. The high school musical is a big deal, and almost everyone likes to go to the homecoming football game. Its having cows in the pasture by your house, and occasionally cows in your garden, and getting milk from the neighbors tank. It's sledding, skating, and skiing in the winter, and biking, hiking and swimming in the summer. Living in Utah means lots of little towns with big amounts of community pride, best pie awards, cutest baby, most valuable citizen in the town, and best ball team in the county. It's the county fair, and the pictures made with seeds, fruits and vegetables, while passing by commenting, "Ours should have won first prize, it's much better than that other town's." It's riding the Ferris wheel at the carnival when it comes to town, and getting sick on cotton candy. It's marching in the fourth of July parade and being very hot, and wondering just how long the parade will last. Being near family means getting to make two cakes for a birthday party because so many relatives will be coming over.

It's walking to church to worship. It's pride in pioneer heritage. Living in Utah is a privilege I hope to share for many years to come.

Mindy Jones
Salt Lake County

Age 18; **Birthplace** LDS Hospital SLC.; **Occupation** N/A;
Religion LDS; **Race/Ethnicity** N/A

I'd been away for sometime, traveling. I loved to travel and I sprang upon every chance I got. But now I was coming home, home to Utah. How peaceful I felt. My travels had left me tired and weary. I was glad I was finally going home. My flight plan had fell through and I had the opportunity to drive. If you could call 10 hours of driving an opportunity. WELCOME TO UTAH, "Whew." I was home, or at least in my home state.

The dry, hot desert surrounded me. My vision was blurred because of the sun. The mirage of water dancing on my horizon kept me awake. It was always the same distance ahead of me. I could not catch it. But I felt secure knowing it was there.

Later, I found myself weaving in and out of rugged hills. Sage-brush poked out against the rich orange-red clay hills. The likeness of a red brick house was startling. The dark rust mansions surround me and I felt their quiet power. I continued on, thankful that because I was driving I couldn't get motion sickness.

I began to enter the Salt Lake Valley. I was home. I remembered what people had said when they found I lived in Utah. "Utah! How could that place have such a hold on you?" they would spit out. "What do you like about it?" "There is no other place on earth than Utah," I'd say. "I loved living on the west side where you could see the desert fields stretching. I loved the excitement of going downtown to the lights and glamour. I loved the peaceful, friendly people. I loved the crazy Utah drivers. I loved the stark, rugged and dominating Rocky Mountains. I loved looking at the mountains and knowing I was special to behold such a magnificent site. I loved the logical laid out streets and the four distinct seasons of Utah. I loved skiing, boating, hiking and exploring. I loved Utah! Utah is my home and here in Utah is where I would live and die.

As I rounded the point of the mountain I beheld my breathtaking city. The best sight of Salt Lake City was at night. Tonight I saw the glittering lights dense to the east and fading into the west. I saw the glimmering Great Lake peeking up to be noticed. And I saw the enormous mountains looming above me protecting their precious valley, their arms outstretched encircling the valley floor. I loved Utah.

David G. Shields
Salt Lake County

Age 32; **Birthplace** Murray; **Occupation** Loan Officer;
Religion N/A; **Race/Ethnicity** White

Utah is a study in poetic contradiction. Living in Utah means red hot desert rocks in the foreground and icy white mountain peaks in the background. It is a flaming red sunset followed by a silent black night. It can be mountain bikes gliding silently over pine needles or rush hour traffic moving noisily over asphalt. Utah is a placid glade covered with untracked powder and an arena full of screaming fans. Utah is a Deer Valley mansion and it is a West Valley trailer home. It is an arch sculpted by God and a viaduct erected by man. It is a road that is a river, and a river that is nothing but sand. Utah is a land defined by its season, so that each place is four. It is the falling golden leaf of an aspen and the green shoot of a germinating seed. It can be a snowflake landing on a child's tongue, then an old man looking for shade. Utah is a temple spire and a forest fire, an avalanche and a power plant. It is a red woman, a white man, a brown boy, and a yellow girl. It is a helping hand in a rugged land, and it is my home.

Anita Judd Messersmith
Utah County

Age 46; **Birthplace** Coalville, Utah; **Occupation** Graphic Designer; **Religion** LDS; **Race/Ethnicity** Caucasian

Living in Utah after being in Europe and the Middle East for a whole summer at age 17, began an appreciative awareness and new feeling within myself about patriotism and love of this country, and especially Utah.

Utah means Home—where I was born in a small mountain town hospital and have lived now for 45 years.

Most of all I think Utah means MOUNTAINS. God and I love the mountains. It was God's Prophets who climbed the tallest mountains to talk and get inspiration from Him, and on high mountains *anyone* can talk to God.

Utah means cold morning deer and elk hunts, it means maybe seeing a moose, a mountain lion or a bald eagle if you happen to be in that right place—in the mountains.

Utah means a large lake of salt water of which there are only two in the entire world, one in Utah and one where Jesus once lived. Utah has a Jordan River which looks a lot like the one—where Jesus once lived.

Utah also means deserts, small towns and cities. It means a weekend at Lake Powell which has more shoreline than the Atlantic or Pacific Ocean. It means a bar-b-que at your mountain cabin, having a horse of your own and a place for the dog to run.

Living in Utah means knowing your neighbors and loving and doing things for them. It means a family reunion with the whole family there because everyone in the family lives in Utah too.

Living in Utah means good hospital and medical care, a good environment to work and raise children in and good values. It means great colleges, theatres, a symphony, planetarium, ballet, art, skiing, golf and solitude. Utah is not having x-rated movie theatres on the streets or filthy magazines on the drugstore shelves, and it means still having a few good people to choose from for our government.

Utah means Lagoon, lights on Temple Square at Christmas, snowmobiling (in the mountains) with a full moon, sunsets behind Mount Timpanogas, rodeos, and the smell of a sweaty horse mixed with the smell of sagebrush. It means seeing the face of your son when he finally gets his first rabbit.

Utah means some still unpaved country roads, ruins of Ancient Indians—who were Utahns long before we were, clear country streams, arches and canyons. It means old mining towns and stories of my grandfather when he was a boy. Riding with his father to Park City with a wagon pulled by a team of horses, staying with the Chinese man at his restaurant for the day while his father sold milk and butter to the other restaurants in town.

Utah means old cemeteries with relatives buried there. It means having my grandma and mom members of the DUP (Daughters of the Utah Pioneers) as I will someday.

Utah is all of these feelings, smells, sights, heritage, family, a way of life, and home—and there's no place like home—in Utah in the Mountains!!

Jared Rauleigh Crowford
Salt Lake County

Age 15; **Birthplace** Cottonwood Hospital; **Occupation** Student; **Religion** Mormon; **Race/Ethnicity** Caucasian

I realize that what I am going to be writing is going to be seen by many different people in the future. I would just like to take this moment to say hello to all of the future people. Utah has beautiful mountains, lakes, etc. People can use the mountains for skiing or hiking, etc. The lakes can be used for boating, fishing, etc. I have done all of these things and more in Utah; Utah is just an all around beautiful state.

Utah has perfect seasons and beautiful sunsets. I love Utah because I've made so many memories here. I have played a lot of games outdoors in Utah. Utah has perfect weather in the summer to get active in sports. Utah has great sports activities such as the Utah Jazz which is my favorite basketball team. I'm also proud to be a Utahn. I recently took a trip to Washington, D.C. and proudly wore my Utah hat every day I was there.

I'm glad I was born where I was. Utah has all you could possibly want and more. Utah has wonderful animals and it is a pretty safe place to live. It's a special thing to be a Utahn, not just anybody can become a Utahn. You can't just live in Utah and call yourself a Utahn. You also can't just be born in Utah and call yourself a Utahn. You have to live in Utah and use and experience the land and the other things that Utah provides. I don't know what Utah is like in the future, but right now it's a wonderful place to live. I've lived here all of my life and have loved every minute of it. I've probably done everything you could possibly do in Utah. I've gone horseback riding, camping, watched the beautiful sunsets, driven through the beautiful winter scenes, gone to funerals, etc. I've done just about everything a real Utahn would do.

When you do everything a real Utahn would do you get this proud feeling inside of you every time the word Utah is spoken. If you don't get a proud feeling you're not a real Utahn. I'm proud to be a Utahn and I love it here and wouldn't change it for the world. The point I'm trying to make is that it doesn't matter if you like Utah or not; once you visit Utah and it gets into your soul, it will never leave.

Joshua Mark Thomas
Davis County

Age 14; **Birthplace** Oxford, England; **Occupation** Student; **Religion** Mormon; **Race/Ethnicity** Cocasion

What living in Utah means to me is … having a lovily, beautiful landscape that doesn't have alot of polution. A place where wild life is just around the corner. A place where I can sleep in peace and not fear danger. A place where my religion will not be persucuted, but cherished.

A place of kindness, a place of friendship, and most importent, a place of love.

Brent Anderson
Utah County

Age 16; **Birthplace** N/A; **Occupation** N/A; **Religion** N/A; **Race/Ethnicity** N/A

If I were to write a poem about Utah singing, I would write "The Sounds of Utah." It would include the sounds of children's voices, sounds of nature, music, and sports. Listen to Utah sing.

You could hear children's voices everywhere. Listen to them when they are all outside playing on a playground. Listen to them when they are at school trying to learn. Listen to them while they are at home.

Utah is also full of sounds of nature. Listen to the silent snow fall to the ground. Listen to the leaves that are falling off the trees. Listen to the wind blow through the trees.

Utah is full of musical sounds, too. Listen to the Tabernacle Choir sing with its world famous sounds. Listen to the Utah school choirs as they sing in competition. Listen to the church choir in thousands of churches in Utah.

Even sports have a sound of their own. Listen to Tom Moe ski as he swishes down the mountain for the U.S. skiing team. Listen to Karl Malone slam the ball down the basket for the Utah Jazz. Listen to the sound of Jamel Willis running through the Utah Utes defense for a B.Y.U. touchdown.

If you listen, you can here the different sounds of Utah. These are the sounds of children's voices, sounds of nature, music, and sports. I can hear Utah sing.

Joan Ray Harrow
Salt Lake County

Age 52; **Birthplace** San Francisco, California; **Occupation** Housewife; **Religion** LDS; **Race/Ethnicity** White

Brigham Young was right when he said, "This is the Place." At least this is the place for me. I love living in Utah. I feel that it is where I should be. Perhaps it is because my ancestors on both sides of my family came to Utah as pioneers, and many of them contributed a great deal to Utah. My great grandfather, Senator Joseph L. Rawlins, was, in fact, instrumental in gaining statehood for Utah in 1896 having introduced the Enabling Act in Congress. Several ancestors have been in the Utah Legislature. One grandfather was Heber J. Grant's personal secretary, the other was the head of a large Salt Lake law firm. My roots are here.

I love living in Utah because of its geographical diversity. I love being able to see the beautiful mountains from my windows. They look so majestic—especially after a snowstorm. And I love the lakes and streams and wildflowers in those mountains. On the other hand, there are vast expanses of desert and, to the south, Zions, Bryce, and the Grand Canyon.

I love the fact that within five minutes I can be at the mouth of one canyon (Big Cottonwood) and in ten minutes at the mouth of another (Little Cottonwood), sitting by a rushing stream far away from city life. And yet, within 25 minutes, I can be at a major university, downtown, at the world headquarters of the Mormon church, at a first-rate symphony, or at the top of those canyons for world class skiing—or a picnic!

Salt Lake is a perfect size—large enough to have fine ballets, symphonies, operas and plays, big-name entertainment, a top NBA team, yet small enough that you can sometimes find a parking space on the downtown street.

Living in Utah means I can still go out at night, alone, and not fear for my life. I can go to a ballet or see a friend and not worry about being out after dark. Unfortunately, this is not the case in so many of our cities.

Utah is a wonderful place to raise a family; it is a family oriented state. There are so many opportunities for our children: skiing, boating, fishing, hunting, hiking, biking, rock climbing, cultural events, the University of Utah and BYU and the advantages major educational institutions bring to a community.

As Utah approaches its 100th birthday, we can be very proud of our state and feel very fortunate to live in it. I am indeed grateful to my ancestors for making the long, difficult trek to this pretty and great state!

Linda A. Chisholm
Cache County

Age 56; **Birthplace** Greeneville, Tennessee; **Occupation** Education Diagnostician; Assistive Technology Cord.; **Religion** Catholic; **Race/Ethnicity** Caucasian

I came to Utah from Upstate New York in January of 1988. My husband had chosen USU which meant my giving up a lucrative job and a log cabin in the woods that my husband and friends had built and that my grown children loved and never wasted. My image of Utah was of a vast barren desert where platonuim was stored. Needless to say I was less than eager. In July of that year (1988) our 24 year old son was killed in a car accident in Tennessee where he was living at the time. Families experience few things in life as devastating as losing a child. In retrospect I truly feel that I was led to Utah for the healing process I would need to go through. In Paradise where we bought a home, I found the mountains and sunshine and fresh air to be magically healing. Neighbors were wonderful and filled our house with home baked food and flowers. In Utah people are kind and trusting in every kind of business and public office which make everyday living unusually pleasant. One day I went grocery shopping on a busy Friday afternoon. I left my purse open with $20 worth of bills exposed in a checkbook on the top rack of the shopping cart. By accident I took a different cart for over an hour when I realized the purse and the original cart had been abandoned by the bananas at the other end of the spacious store. Frantically I made my way back to see if by any chance I would find my purse. There it sat just where I had left it by the bananas, bills protruding as if to say "take me." Another day I left a grocery store without getting any change when I wrote a check ten dollars over the purchase amount. I went to a second store to make a small purchase and seeing that I had no cash in my purse, went back to the first store to the clerk who had failed to give me the ten dollars. I said to him, "If you are over $10.00 at the end of the day, remember me and I will come check with you." He said, "No problem, here is your $10.00."

Some of the best aspects of Utah are surprises for a new comer—a Cistereian Monastery not far from my house where Gregorian chants are sung throughout the day; a retreat house in the mountains of Ogden where retreats of every description are held including ones of silence for contemplative prayer; an exquisite historical landmark building, a Roman Catholic Cathedral designed by both American Indian Tribe members and those who could provide a European Rose window.

I liked Utah immediately. Over these few years I've grown to love it. I love the slow but meaningful pace of life, every season, the wondrous Bear Lake, the long hot dry summers, skiing out my front door in winter, the sun, seldom occluded in Paradise. I am grateful deep in my soul, for this state.

Amber Mathiesen
Salt Lake County

Age N/A; **Birthplace** N/A; **Occupation** N/A; **Religion** N/A; **Race/Ethnicity** N/A

Utah is many springs, blooming flowers
And April's rain showers.
Utah is an Easter day
to hunt for eggs and play.

In Utah you're always happy and never alone.
Utah is a place that I call home.

Utah is summers of having fun
Hiking, swimming and laying in the sun.
Utah is going to the beach with your family and friends,
Because they will be with you 'till the world ends.

In Utah you're always happy and never alone.
Utah is a place that I call home.

Utah is fall time playing in the leaves,
running falling down.
The leaves are so pretty many colors like
red, yellow and brown.
Utah is going trick-or-treating,
or Thanksgiving dinner and doing nothing but eating.

In Utah you're always happy and never alone.
Utah is a place that I call home.

Utah is winters of snowballs, sledding,
also Christmas songs and lots of weddings.
Utah is winters of dressing up
warmly in hats and mittens
and having a fire while snuggling, with my kitten.

In Utah you're always happy and never alone.
Utah is a place that I call home.

Utah is full of love and honesty and has no hate
Utah is my favorite state.

Pamela Pexton Speers
Salt Lake County

Age 37; **Birthplace** Salt Lake City, Utah; **Occupation** Bridal Seamstress; **Religion** LDS; **Race/Ethnicity** Caucasion

Perhaps you should really ask me, "What Living Means to Me," as all of my life has been in Utah and therefore being in the land called Utah and "being" are to me one and the same. Those of us lucky enough to be born here are sure to fall in one of two categories: those who cannot wait to grow up and get out and those of us who would never want to leave. I surely call myself one of the latter and have no understanding of the mindset of the former.

I live within fifteen miles of the home to which I was born. I have lived in such far off places as Holladay, the Foothill east bench and now in Central City, all contained by Salt Lake City. How limited, how unadventurous, how mundane! On the contrary, how really, really fortunate I am in that I need look no farther to have all I could ever want or need within easy reach. There simply is no other place on Earth where anything, anything, any form of living you could imagine is right here, just waiting for your attention.

There are days when I look out my window on snow as high as my tires, coming just from a quick storm overnight. Then I have spent a day making the two and one half mile loop hike around the plateau of Dead Horse Point on a July day that hit 107. I have been to a sandy desert and to a dead Lake that yet support complicated and interdependent systems of life. I have climbed in a canyon and become lost from the road, and suddenly found a trail to take me under a waterfall, crashing through a hole cut from solid rock onto my shivering neck in early September. I have been caught in traffic in an overheating car, stuck with a hundred others in a parking lot after watching fireworks on the 24th of July. I have stood on the top, the highest point of a mountains with an "H" painted on a rock, and I looked down to see faraway homes and even further-off headlights on the freeway: I stood there again last summer and looked directly into someone's backyard. I have gone for a run in my own neighbor hood and been overcome by exhaust; I have found that roses left on a grave in the City Cemetery were eaten overnight by deer mysteriously creeping down from the bordering mountains. I huffed and puffed my way up an inclined slickrock trail, muttering something to my spouse about sweat and blisters, and almost fell over a group of seated, sweaty and also absolutely silent people, people numbed by the beauty, the unbelievability found in their first sight of Delicate Arch. All this, both the good and the bad, creations of Nature and of Metropolis, all of them experienced no more than a few minutes walk or a few hours drive from my front door.

I know not of another place like Utah, and I love it with all my heart. I would wish to keep it always the way I remember, and I realize this cannot be so. It is a centennial of this "state" we celebrate, but this land named Utah is older and larger and more awe-inspiring than anywhere: to me a state and a state-of-mind.

Eva Westover Conover
Emery County

Age 86; **Birthplace** Huntington, Emery County; **Occupation** School Teaching, St. Legislator; **Religion** Latter Day Saint; **Race/Ethnicity** White

… I am a product of Utah. A product of Utah's lands. Why do I love Utah? I love it because we settled it and laid claim to it. I embrace its culture and its standards. I am a product of them, too. I am a reflection of Utah. Utah is me, born and bred in me. I was taught to become the best of what I could be, by its standards, its beliefs, its culture. And to give back the best of what I was, or am, to my family, to my pupils in school and Church, to my Church, to my community, my County, my State, and even in a small way, to my Country. I have endeavored to do just that. I realize that others have attained more and given more. I did the best I could.

I am eighty-six years of age. I'm getting old and I'm getting tired, but I am proud of my inheritance, my State, and my barren, rocky Castle Valley. I've traveled in Europe, Africa, the Middle East, Canada and Mexico, and to almost every State in the Union, and I always come home to my old ranch lying between rock-bound hills, and barren, blue mesas, to the desert lands of Castle Valley, content and happy. Why did I not settle or want to settle in more verdant valleys? Why? Because I belong to Utah, to its mountains, to its deserts. It is home. It belongs to me. It is mine. We settled it, worked its lands, built its Churches and its schools, its towns and its cities. I am Utah! and Utah is me, born and bred in me!

Zandria Merrill
Cache County

Age 43; **Birthplace** Salt Lake City; **Occupation** Training and Instructional Design; **Religion** None; **Race/Ethnicity** Caucasian

Several times I've tried to leave this state, this land of Zion. Oh, you've heard all the reasons—the reasons we Gentiles give. There are too many Mormons, there are no cultural events, it's too hard to buy liquor, there aren't any decent restaurants, people have such closed minds, there's that "carney" accent, it's so conservative. … The reasons are many.

Actually, I grew up in Utah. I come from hardy, Mormon pioneer stock. I found it much easier to leave "the church" than to leave this state that I love. Now that I've moved back a half dozen times from other beautiful western and southwestern locales, and travelled to many places around the world, I realize the reasons I left are the reasons I return. The healthy, family oriented values associated with this conservative culture make Utah an easy place to live. Yes, easy. We're approaching the second millennia and here in happy valley (Cache Valley), we still don't need to worry about always locking our homes, gang problems are nil, we have the oldest, healthiest geriatric population in the country, skies and water are clear (most of the time), pristine and varied recreation areas are as close as five minutes away. I could go on and on.

I've learned to live around the inconveniences and problems that earlier seemed insurmountable. It's pretty easy to get to the state liquor store before 7:00 p.m., and I can usually remember to buy beer before midnight on Saturday. Mormons make wonderful neighbors once they get used to the idea that you're not, and you're still OK. Cultural opportunities have blossomed since the restoration of our theater with opera, dance and plays. And there's one good restaurant in town.

Then there's the land. In my travels, I've only seen one other place that rivals the variety and beauty of Utah's geography, and you have to go to another continent and speak another language to enjoy it. But, the thought of living far from the Utah deserts leaves me with an empty feeling. The whispering canyons, the surprise and amazement of finding scratchings and scrapings from the ancient ones, the silent birds dancing and soaring on the wind, the shellacked red walls, the miracle of water in the bottom of a wash. All these draw me to the warmer country in the south of the state and keep me nearby.

I still whine about the "problems," about the love and hate of living in this state. It is something to do with friends, and a rite of passage with newcomers. But I'm here to say, to live and enjoy this state, my state, Utah.

Mary Jess Baker
Davis County

Age 60; **Birthplace** Boise, Idaho; **Occupation** Secretary/Free Lance Writer; **Religion** LDS; **Race/Ethnicity** Caucasian

My ancestral roots go deep into Utah's fertile soil, having been planted here in 1848 when Horace Roberts brought his family into the Salt Lake Valley by Conestoga Wagon; and again in 1849 when Great-Grandfather Cable stopped here enroute to California. Great Grandma looked around the thriving community and said to him, "I have traveled long enough, I'm staying here!"

What does living in Utah mean to me? It is standing on a hilltop and seeing the mountain ranges fading into the horizon. Like peeling the skin from an onion, you could peel away each mountain range to reveal the one behind it.

It is skiing through crisp powder in the back country where rubies, emeralds, topaz, and diamonds have been strewn by some unseen hand to garnish the surface. It is

mounds of fresh snow piled on the tangerine clustered berries of the Mountain Ash forming Christmas bells in the wilderness. It is hoar-frost clinging to each tiny branchlet of a small thistle, creating a flocked tree beautiful beyond anything Man could derive.

It is a moose, quietly munching the shrubbery, a ground squirrel scampering across the surface of the snow, enjoying the late winter sunshine. It is a coyote loping through the sagebrush, indifferent to my intrusion into his world.

Utah is the soft plop and gentle clink of ice melting from snow-laden trees. It is tiny green leaves and minute pink flowers emerging on the edge of a diminishing snowdrift. It is the ski slopes in June, their groomed snow now replaced by bluebells, daiseys, black-eyed susans, Indian paintbrush, wild geraniums, larkspur; the native wildflowers in their glory welcoming the warmth of the summer season.

It is camping along the South Fork of the Ogden River where every tree is filled with Juncos, Wrens, Bluebirds, Robins, and more humming birds than I ever imagine seeing in one place. Utah is dinner from a dutch oven, camaradarie around a campfire, and a quick wash-up alongside a long-legged grey bird in an icey mountain stream.

Utah is the view from the top of Mount Ogden after a gruelling five hour hike from the Snowbasin parking lot. This was an extra-ordinary feat for a 59 year old grandmother who 25 years ago couldn't walk to the corner mailbox without coughing and wheezing.

Living in Utah is driving down from Monte Cristo after a late fall rainstorm has washed the bright splotches of orange, yellow, and crimson of their summer dust. As we round a corner, the sun on the raindrops has turned the seedpods of the Ash trees into thousands of golden coins, sparkling in the sunlight. We drive into the golden haze of the setting sun and I am reminded this is one of those unique, one-in-a-lifetime experiences. I may drive this road hundreds of times, but never again will I see it just like this. Never again will I be here with the sun at this level, this soon after a rainstorm, this time of year. It is an experience to tuck into my memory forever.

That's the beauty of the Utah wilderness. Whether I'm hiking in the mountains, rock climbing in the canyons, or skiing in the back country, each day is a new, exciting experience. Around each trail is something I have never seen before, and will never see again. Each sunrise and sunset is unique; each cloud special in itself; each flower, shrub or tree has been fashioned by the ultimate creator.

Living in Utah means living in the deserts and mountains I love, savouring each day, each change of seasons, each bonus experience the Lord chooses to grant me.

Finally, living in Utah means being where my forebears carved the greatest nation in the world from the finest land God had to offer.

Joseph W. Spendlove
Salt Lake County

Age 52; **Birthplace** Provo, UT; **Occupation** Teacher; **Religion** L.D.S.; **Race/Ethnicity** Caucasian

Returning home following a short stint in the army, I peered out the window of the bus and "saw" for the first time what home really meant to me. Salt Lake Valley stretched wide and long below the mouth of Parley's Canyon. "This is the land I love" I thought. Then and there I knew I disagreed with Thomas Wolfe who penned the phrase "You can't go home."

My very roots are nourished from this place, and the fruit of my tree is sweet. The people who have shaped and molded me live in this valley. My wife and children,

extended family and friends are here, inextricably woven into the fabric of my life.

This cornered-rectangle, this desert beauty, this mountain wonderland, this value-laden people, this community of diversity, this Utah.

James Darren Stevens
Millard County

Age 10; **Birthplace** Fillmore Hospital; **Occupation** Student; **Religion** LDS; **Race/Ethnicity** White

I like Utah the best because it's one of the four states of the four corners. I went there about a year ago. It's lots of fun there. The states that make up the four corners are Utah, Arizona, Colorado and New Mexico.

Utah is the best state of the four because of the farms here. I live on one of them. Farms are great! There are lots of animals. I have lots of fun on our farm. There are lots of fields to run in. There is one thing in Utah that I don't like, INSECTS!!!

The great schools here in Utah are one of my favorite things. I like Fillmore Elementary School because I learned a lot from the teachers. It's the only school I have ever gone to, but next year I am going to MIDDLE SCHOOL. I am in 4th grade this year.

Many people hunt and fish in Utah. There are lots of things to hunt, like pheasants, ducks, and deer. You can catch many types of fish in our rivers, streams and lakes.

Utah is a great place to live. There are a lot of good people here. I hope it stays as good as it is now. I hope I will be able to live here all my life.

Mary Stacy Grosz
Kane County

Age 41; **Birthplace** Ohio (but traveled to Texas); **Occupation** Owner—Sound Room—Radio Shack; **Religion** Baptist; **Race/Ethnicity** White

To me, living in Utah is the secret to life. She gives us all the basics of what is missing to a good formula to live life by. So many of us in such a fast growing world can't see what's ahead of us, before it changes right in front of our eyes. Utah gives us more than we have asked for, and it's my goal to give back just a little by keeping spirits high as tourists come through our strategic location of the canyons in So. Utah. We found Utah moving west on our honeymoon 18 years ago. My husband wanted high desert, and mountains. We didn't know what we were driving into at night, and by morning we had quite a few surprises. There were red cliffs that felt as if they were protecting you, and colors in the rocks that seem to turn Vermillion purple at sunset. An hour away, and we're at 4 National Parks, and 4 State Parks, so we had access constantly to any terrain we care to take the kids on. The mountains of Utah make it seem as though you are the only one for miles, and it demands your attention like a child. You seem to be in an endless time warp, like it took to carve the spires of the canyons. We look forward to seeing the four seasons change. We probably wouldn't have had the "spices of life" as we have had in Utah. We have had a successful business for 12 years that keeps us busy. It's 5 businesses in one so we can get food on the table in a smaller town, but we like to work hard, so we can play hard too. My husband has been the President of the archaeology chapter in this area for 5 years. I have helped in a lot of community plays and charity functions, and it feels good to be part of a community whose moral fiber is important and family is first. I like that. My kids have grown up here and have never once come home feeling as if we were outsiders. Our *pride* is what makes us "high" instead of *material* "highs." We have spoiled ourselves to the outdoors. Utah has so much diversity in all four corners of the state, we have yet to travel the same road twice.

Our community has recently experienced a closure of a Sawmill, which has put over 200 families out of employment. This is just another change we have to go thru and learn from in the process. We will adapt and overcome. No one I talk to wants to leave because they know the quality of life we get from Utah cannot be surpassed. This keeps us going forward instead of looking back. We have been allowed to touch the grains of sand for but a little while. I thank her for allowing us to be part of just a little piece of her graciousness.

Tory Stirling
Cache County

Age 20; **Birthplace** SLC; **Occupation** Student; **Religion** LDS; **Race/Ethnicity** Caucasian

The summer after I graduated from high school I worked as a waitress on the north rim of the Grand Canyon, Az. While I worked there I had the chance to meet people from all parts of the world. After finding out I was from Salt Lake City, several of my customers were quick to ask me about my hometown, my religion and about the state of Utah in general. One gentleman from the eastern U.S. still does not, I believe, comprehend the fact that I am from Utah but was not raised in a polygamist family!

For the most part, people were very interested in the limited background I was able to tell them about our state. Some people immediately took offense at almost any positive mention about Utah because of the religious factor. But I was surprised by the several rare reviews I heard from tourists that had just passed through the state. I can remember several occasions when I would try to get a visitor from England or Australia, places I had always wanted to go to, and they instead insisted on talking about Utah!

Since that summer I have traveled to the eastern U.S. and to parts of Canada. The lush green and rolling hills of the central and eastern U.S. are wonderful. However, despite their beauty, I will always be biased toward southern Utah red rock or Uintah mountain autumns.

Near the end of my summer at the Grand Canyon I felt a certain pride when I told passerbys about Moab, Bryce, Angels Landing in Zion, and Temple Square in Salt Lake City. I no longer took for granted the rich cultures and beauty which I was blessed to grow up in.

Wendy Wright
Millard County

Age 17; **Birthplace** Delta, UT; **Occupation** N/A; **Religion** LDS; **Race/Ethnicity** White

I have lived in Utah all of my life, so I really couldn't compare living in Utah to living in any other state. And I was born and raised in Hinckley, so telling you about living elsewhere is out of the question. And, since my life is not exotic or exciting and full of adventure, I'll just bore you with a real-life account of what it's like to live in Hinckley, Utah.

Hinckley is a small town in central Utah. It is a tightly-knit community where everyone's lives are intertwined. Everyone knows everyone, and everyone cares. If a new family moves in, neighbors take food and welcome them to Hinckley. Many people are amazed at the friendliness, and some ask what we want in return. Of course, the only thing expected is a little kindness and friendship.

Hinckley is a small town, where the crime rate is practically zero. You can walk down the street and not worry about being mugged. You can park your car and be sure that it will still be in the parking lot when you leave. When your kids are outside playing, you worry about them falling out of trees and scuffing their knees, not getting kidnapped by a mad man. If you're out of town, you can bet that your neighbors will watch your house for you, even if you don't ask them to. That's just how the people are in Hinckley: caring and considerate.

And Hinckley isn't really close to any factories, so the air is usually clean and crisp. We don't have to worry about pollution filling our lungs every time we take a breath. And because we have so little pollution, we don't have to worry about acid rain or a lot of the other things that urban areas are faced with today.

Also, living in Utah we get four seasons. Some people take it for granted that the weather changes. But in some states, it's either winter or summer all year long. Here, we have cold winters, warm springs, hot summers, and cool falls. And, there aren't any natural disasters to worry about, either. The land is too mountainous for tornadoes, there aren't any active volcanoes near by, earthquakes are minimum, and, living in the desert, there is no chance of a hurricane.

Living in Utah, I benefit from a rich pioneer heritage, that began when my great-great-grandparents crossed the plains to come to the Salt Lake Valley many years ago. Learning about the sacrifices they made and the hard times they had has helped me overcome my own hardships and make sacrifices of my own.

Of course, living in a small town has its draw-backs too. For instance, if you do something wrong, within a few days the whole town knows about it. Slightly altered, a bit of back-yard gossip can be a real conversation piece.

And then there's the entertainment bit. There isn't a lot to do in a small town, so we must travel elsewhere to find something to amuse us. Of course, that isn't all bad. A 2–3 hour drive gives you a chance to improve your driving technique.

All in all, Utah is a pretty good place to live. Although I would like to try living somewhere else, right now I'll just stay in Hinckley.

Daniel Jon Hansen
Davis County

Age 14; **Birthplace** N/A; **Occupation** Student; **Religion** L.D.S. (Mormon); **Race/Ethnicity** N/A

Living in Utah means a lot to me. I was born and raised here so it is logical for me to like it. Utah's a great place with many things. I mean you wake up with the sun pouring over the mountains and with the Great Salt Lake behind you. Then you get houses that are built into the recesses of the mountains where natures animals pay little visits. It is almost like the garden of Eden even though it is a little barren.

A lot of people think that Utah is just some big, stupid desert with mountains and a huge Salt Lake that just sits there. I'm telling you now that it isn't.

A lot of people hate Utah for one reason or another. People outside the state only say negative things about us. Michael Jordan said the only good thing about Utah was that it is a hop, skip, and a jump from Vegas. What a crock! Utah has tons of things. We have Lake Powell which is fun for water sports. We also have the Wasatch and Uintah mountains for snow activities. We also got great hunting here too. We have tons of things but sorry the list is too long.

We might have the Olympics here soon and I hope we do so that we can show the world Utah is awesome and that we are proud to be a part of it.

Ruth C. Reyns
Weber County

Age 78; **Birthplace** Ogden, Utah; **Occupation** Housewife; **Religion** LDS; **Race/Ethnicity** Caucasian-English

We appreciated the fact that our children were safe to go anywhere. They were able to safely walk to school, to church, and their friends houses. We are able to drive anywhere in Ogden in 20 minutes, to visit friends, relatives, and for entertainment. Shopping is available with the least amount of traveling.

There are many cultural events close to home and many summer and winter sports.

Our children were able to get good educations in the Utah colleges and as a result were able to live and work in Utah. Clean air and four beautiful seasons are a definite plus.

NEW FACES

Utah has always been a haven for immigrants. Ever since native Americans moved throughout the area, the region has attracted outsiders with a desire to stay. From the Spanish priests to African American trapper Jim Beckwourth, ethnic minorities also determine the faces of Utah.

Contemporary Utahns come from a variety of locales and nationalities. Migration within the state has lead to a highly urbanized Wasatch front that reflects the values and ethnicity of rural Utah. However, new Utahns reflect a large Hispanic, Asian, and Polynesian immigration as well as others who have chosen the Beehive State for economic, environmental, and lifestyle reasons. Utah has become the place for those who seek opportunity in high mountain valleys.

The end result is that Utah maintains the unique position of having a predominant religion, yet ethnic diversity within The Church of Jesus Christ of Latter-day Saints, and the current rapid in-migration of numerous other individuals creates a state searching for contemporary definition. The feelings of those trying to move beyond the description of "outsider" forms a different face for the state.

—F. Ross Peterson

Joan Shaw
Cache County

Age 65; **Birthplace** Camden, NJ; **Occupation** Writer-editor;
Religion Episcopalian; **Race/Ethnicity** Caucasian

My husband brought me into this state—his state—through its southwest corner in December in 1965. We drove north on old State Highway 91, towing a Fiat van behind a Chevy station wagon, looking at the countryside. We drove past the Hurricane cliffs and Zion National Park, through sand dunes above Cove Fort, around fault scarps and quarries. Before reaching Salt Lake City, my husband pointed out the approximate position of the Bonneville Salt Flats, describing to me their blinding white vastness—miles upon miles of hard, flat, sodium chloride.

I'd been raised by the Delaware River on a spot where the channel measured over a mile across, where 30 inches of rain fell each year, where thick hardwood forests were commonplace, where vacant lots sprang up with weeds and grass and shrubs and trees without any help from anyone. I'd never seen, never imagined such desolate country as this we were driving through …

Our destination was Utah State University in Logan, so we kept on going north until, quite early one December morning, we entered a mountain valley that looked like the Alps in winter.

Well, it was winter. And the frozen beauty of Cache Valley that day was inescapable. But the mountains surrounding it looked bare, near treeless, and desperately, forbiddingly cold. It's wetter in Cache Valley, my husband told me. Seventeen inches of rain, he'd said—in a good year. Many months after this, we took possession of twenty Lewiston acres and the old house that went with it because I'd wanted to live on a farm. And I could stand on the back steps of this house and see miles of semi-arid valley with only one tree impeding my view.

I cried for years because I missed the rain. I missed the trees that came with rain and the green grass. I missed a normal growing season, too—I'd never lived anywhere in which winter lasted for over half a year. I missed dogwood trees and azaleas that grew wild under forest canopies. I missed tomato plants that started bearing in July. My youngest son piped up that I should plant trees. He said I should plant trees *all* over if I liked trees, and I *did* plant trees. I planted shrubs, too, and perennials and roses and bulbs and seeds of all kinds. A fair percentage of these plants actually survived. But I spent most of my gardening time during summer desperately feeding them water just to make *sure* they did survive.

That was all right. Here was something I could do, something over which I had some small measure of control—planting and watering things and beating off the mice that girdled trees in the winter and ate my bulbs, chasing the browsing deer, spraying for aphids and green worm and earwigs. But it wasn't only the rain—the effortless green of summer—that I missed while I was planting things here. It was the people.

No, that's wrong. It wasn't just people I missed, because there were many very nice, very good people here. What I missed was a *mix* of people. I'd been raised in a town in which I could count six different nationalities in two blocks—Italians, Poles, Jews, Irish, a Hungarian. The candy store was run by a woman who'd come to the United States from Manchester, England, in 1922. The town reflected the hodge-podge of nationalities of the eastern seaboard as a whole, and what's more, the people of this town were overwhelmingly members of the Democratic party.

So at election time in Utah, I despaired at the utter uselessness of my trip to the Lewiston Community Building where I cast my Democratic vote, standing in line with the good people of the town who all seemed to look and think alike—for what good did my few check marks do? My husband, whose family from the sagebrush hills of the northwest Utah were also Democrats, looked at the situation philosophically. This was his home territory and he knew the people here. The state's politics had inexplicably changed in the ten years of his absence from centrist to the right, but the political climate was bound to change back. I should just wait and see.

Well, the state didn't only not change back, it's moved even further to the right. But it wasn't the politics, either …

When I was young, I'd lived three blocks from a Jewish synagogue, and I'd walked every Sunday to my own Episcopal Church of the Ascension four blocks the other way. Across the street from this church was a Catholic seminary and the Baptists met in a big brick neoclassical building next to my high school. There were Methodists in that town and Lutherans, Presbyterians and Congregationalists, Seventh Day Adventists, and Pentacostals. A person could walk past ten houses and find that the families living in them were affiliated with ten different religions.

And in northernmost Utah of the sixties and seventies, what was it like? Many people have railed—and still do—against the religious monoculture in this state, but say little about the nuts and bolts of the real isolation that it meant to outsiders not attending their local wards, how they never seemed to know exactly what was going on in their towns, never learned the names of any but their closest neighbors, never felt the state was truly *theirs* but rather something loaned to them for a while, as visitors.

But all this for me was preliminary, a foundation that lay under my life in Utah like a layer of sand near a fault line.

I'd become involved in the women's movement at Utah State University in the seventies. The women there were fighting battles then that had been fought already and *won* almost a decade before in the East. An administrator told me—oh, years after the Office of Equal Opportunity and Affirmative Action was up and running—"You don't understand us here in Utah: we put our women up on pedestals."

This is ancient history, I know it is, but who was out of touch here? That's the question. Was it the power structure who'd lived all their lives in Utah or was it me, staggered by a cultural frame of mind in which pedestals that equaled thirty percent less pay were perfectly right and natural? The evidence shows only that this work was what triggered my own particular landslide, for I was never made for battle. And yet there I was, furious that I was trapped in this place, elbowing myself to the forefront of something that I knew then and know now was terribly important, but can't for the life of me, in this centennial year, see its worth in terms of its ultimate cost to myself. I was out of my depth, considered myself incompetent in my role even at the time, and often went to my office to hold my head, horrified at what new hell I'd got myself into. Nevertheless I kept on going because, you see, at that time there were so very few of us.

And then I got sick, good and sick, and I retired from the field, leaving the battle in the hands of the truly wonderful feminists in this state, strong women who were built to endure, women I love and admire without reservation. Instant mellowing followed; it had to follow. And with it my resignation to the facts of life.

So. What does living in Utah mean to me, a failed Wonder Woman, an introduced species—something like Dyer's Woad?

It means the home that I cherish and above all things—the small, 20 acre island of tranquility that my husband and I and our children have built for ourselves here in Lewiston. The old house we moved into so many years ago we've restored and expanded with our own hand into the comfortable Victorian it is today. I can no longer stand on its steps and see miles of semi-arid valley because the place is covered with trees—ash trees and maples, aspen and boxelder, elms and Russian olive, cottonwood and poplar and sumac. There are windbreaks of evergreens and evergreens on our hill. There are nearly two hundred roses in our garden and a dozen varieties of lilacs. An orchard of two hundred apple trees spreads south through what was once a ragged pasture, and there are flower beds everywhere and green grass and birds.

I still miss the rain, of course I do, and people who know how homesick I'd been in years past have suggested that we could leave, my husband and I, after he retires from Utah State University. We could leave and live in a place where it rains, and where trees and shrubs and grass and weeds grow up on vacant lots without anyone's help, where I could perhaps walk to an Episcopal church, perhaps hear again Yiddish spoken on doorsteps and an accordion played at some nearby Italian wedding.

But it's too late, you see. I'm too old now and, besides, I've grown fond of the place.

I've grown fond of the fact that I can deliver rain to my plants and trees when they need it and not have to depend on the whim of the heavens to keep them growing in a consistent way. I've grown fond of the crisp, clean air of spring, and the mist and cold of winter. I've grown fond of the mountains that surround this farm and the fields that change with the seasons, moving like seas of color down through the foothills and over the valley floor. I've grown fond of being a liberal curiosity in a conservative state and wearing my cross and chain and drinking my coffee among Mormon friends that I've found over the years to be extraordinarily tolerant and kind and funny and all completely different from each other.

Above all, since my children began to move from city to city throughout the United States and I've listened and laughed as they recounted their truly colorful experiences with various cultures in this wide country of ours, I've decided that on the whole I'm content to be living in Utah.

For there is no state, no region, that can honestly be called perfect. There are only places that can be called home.

Nicole Polson
Salt Lake County

Age 10; **Birthplace** LDS Hospital; **Occupation** N/A; **Religion** N/A; **Race/Ethnicity** N/A

When my mother and father lived in Cambodia they worked hard. They barely got to eat anything. Then they took a plane to Salt Lake City. When my mom went to get a job she was very smart. She already knew how to speak English! She now works at Litton Guidance Control Systems with my dad.

I was born at LDS Hospital. Utah is my home. It has the perfect climate and looks so beautiful. When I take trips to other places I feel sad to leave Utah. Utah just has so many interesting places to visit. A lot of people lived here and more came from all over the world. The mountains, flowers, and trees look so beautiful.

If I lived in a farm in Utah, I would always wander off and lay in fields. When I grow up I'll tell my kids all about Utah so they'll enjoy it as much as I do.

Alvin Olsen
Salt Lake County

Age N/A; **Birthplace** Denmark; **Occupation** N/A; **Religion** N/A; **Race/Ethnicity** N/A

I was born in Denmark, or as the Danes calls it Danmark, and they should know.

Denmark is the worlds oldest Kingdom, and probably the worlds oldest Democracy, and the Danes have always looked to the West for their friends, like Great Britain and United States, never have they sought friendship from the Soviet block.

When the war ended in 1945, which also meant the end of the German Occupation of Denmark, we were sick and tired of enemies and War, and many of us tried to get out of there, and made connections with our old friends in United States, which in my case meant friends in Utah.

In those days there was nothing called illegal entry of the United States, everybody had to come in on a quota, and I believe that a small country like Denmark probably was allowed something like 2,000 persons a year, and after that we had put in our application to the American Embassy in Copenhagen we just had to sit and wait until our turn came. Somebody had to wait up to 2–3 years, but I was lucky and received my visa for me and my family after only six months. …

Those who have not tried it, will never know how hard it is to give up your good job, the home you have build up over several years, and say goodby to family and friends, your father and mother, sister and brother, which you may never see again, and travel to an unknown place you have never seen, not knowing if you can find a place to live, and a place to work.

I for my own sake had made up my mind, never to look back to what could have been, but just to look forward to the future, after all it could never be any worse than what the first Utah Pioneers had to go through. I also decided that I would never start finding faults, but I wanted to love this place, and be a good citizen like I had always been in Denmark.

We arrived in New York on May 19, 1948 after a terrible stormy tour across the Atlantic Ocean which lasted 11 days.

After going through the Customs we boarded the train which should take us to Salt Lake City in three days and nights.

We arrived in Salt Lake City at 7:00 in the morning, and there they were all our old friends, about 50 of them, who had emigrated before us—oh happy day—we were not lost any more.

We stayed for about a week with old friends who had just got a small apartment on Gordon Place, and that same evening we walked from there and up to State Capitol. Standing up on the steps in front of that big building, I looked out over the big City and it was like a voice said to me "THIS IS YOUR INHERITED LAND."

May 22, 1948 was the happiest day of my life.

After a week search I was able to find an Apartment, and after looking for 3 weeks I got a job at $1.02 a hour and we could eat.

So what, if I didn't have money for the bus but had to walk to work. So, what, that there were cockroaches and stink bugs in our apartment. So what, that we had an old fashion coal stove for heat. So what, that there were no hot water heater. So what, that there wasn't any carpet on the floor, and that we had 3 different old chairs. We had a roof over our heads, and food on our table, and things could only be better.

And they did.

In Denmark I was a manager for an electric wholesale business, but over here I had to start completely from the bottom, and work my way up. Learning a new language, learning new ways to do everything, speaking with a heavy accent and many other disadvantages, but I knew one secret which many native born young people have not been able to find, and that secret is WORK, WORK, and more WORK. Believe it if you will, but America is still the Country of big opportunities, and everybody will have their chance if they will just work at it.

The sky is the limit.

Beside my day job at $1.02 a hr. I found a "part-time"

job as a janitor and watchman in a store. It paid me $5.00 a day for 10 hours work, it was hard work that many hours, but it enabled us to buy a much needed used Refrigerator, and a little later on an old Car, a 1934 Buick, which cost me $200.00.

I was burning my light at both ends, and when I got a chance for a part time janitor job in a bank which would only take me 3 hours a day at $5.00 a day, of course I switched over.

When I lived in Denmark I had never done any work beside sales and office work, but now suddenly I had learned a new trade, the trade of working as a janitor, no matter how much it could be looked down upon, it was a trade, and could help me if I took advantage of my new knowledge.

On my day job I worked with a bunch of nice guys, but most of them were the type, if they only had a good solid job where they could work every day from 8:00 to 5:00, that was all they expected out of life. I had been a manager once, and could not settle down with that. Every day in my own thoughts I was looking for an opening, and I prepared myself for the day when I felt that I could see the light at the end of the tunnel, and after about five years living in Utah I felt it was time.

I had to wait five years to become an American Citizen, and as soon as I could I took my Citizenship.

Now I was an American Citizen, not by chance, but by choice, and I was proud of it and have always been.

I started out as a Janitorial Contractor, talking to some companies who were moving in to new offices, and the day I got my first contract, was a proud and happy day. Of course I could not hire anybody to work for me, but had to do the work myself. I had 50 cents in my pocket, and had to borrow $5.00 so that I could buy my first dust mop, which I needed for the job ...

When I got my fourth contract I hired my first employee, and from that humble beginning I kept build-ing. I started specializing in Federal Contracts all over the Western States, and had up to 500 employees at the time ...

In 1972 I sold out my janitorial business, and switched over to Security Guard Contracts, also specializing in work for the Federal Government, and for the second time, I build a business with up to 500 employees ...

After that we retired fifteen years ago, we have traveled all over the world and been to five continents, and we have seen many interesting things and many beautiful things, but nothing can be compared with our own state, our Utah. ...

Kathleen Stevens
Grand County

Age 48; **Birthplace** Newport, RI; **Occupation** Retired college teacher; **Religion** Roman Catholic; **Race/Ethnicity** White

I only recently became a citizen of Utah (June 1994), but I've been coming here for the last 20 years. Formerly a resident of Chicago, I worked as a college teacher there. Always a traveller, I found myself spending all my non-working time in Utah. I would leave for Utah the day finals ended and come back two hours before my first class. Clearly, it was time to move to the state of Utah. Since it was the Moab area that attracted me, working as a college teacher was not an option. To accomplish our goal of moving to Moab, my husband and I simply saved all our earnings until we could "retire" to the Moab area and not have to work to support our moderate lifestyle.

Since moving to Utah was attained at some sacrifice, I believe that living in Utah means more to me than to some natives (who seem to take it for granted). The principal advantage of living in Utah is the availability of gorgeous public land. Vast stretches of the most amazing scenery on earth allow for copious outdoor recreation opportunities, as this land belongs to the public. Living in Utah provides unlimited outdoor recreation—and doubly so in Southern Utah. Utahns should treasure and safeguard their public lands. Many natives do not, sadly, realize the value of these lands—if they lived a while in Chicago, they might do so! The public lands cannot continue to be abused the way that some native Utahns have abused them.

Associated with all this public land are the special arid lands that are so unique to Utah—The Book Cliffs, the San Rafael Swell, the Escalante Country, Labyrinth Canyon, etc. Having the opportunity to explore such areas is what living in Utah means to me. Where else can one be treated to such magnificence?

While "blank spaces on the map" were my main reason for choosing Utah, the state holds other attractions, too. Utah is a cultured place, due no doubt to its historical settlement patterns. Other western states have public lands a plenty, but they also have a tradition of uncouth lawlessness. Utah is "civilized" and proud of its cultured past. This makes Utah somewhat unique among Western states. One hopes that an inane desire for complete homogenization does not lead Utah to completely eschew its traditions.

Living in Utah thus means unparalleled opportunities for quiet contemplative hiking in God's most magnificent handy work. This is combined with a cultured approach to community living. One hopes that Utah can continue this balance. This is what living in Utah means to me.

Christie Banks
Utah County

Age 24; **Birthplace** San Diego, CA; **Occupation** N/A; **Religion** The Church of Jesus Christ of Latter-Day Saints; **Race/Ethnicity** Caucasian

When I was very young, Utah meant vacation and family reunions to me. It was our destination for family vacations as we all would pile into the van to make the long drive from Virginia to Utah. It meant swinging on the rope swing in Oak City Canyon for Banks Family Reunions. Or visiting sites such as Hole in the Rock or Hell's Backbone, or fishing at Blue Spruce. It meant riding horses or four-wheeling in Escalante at Grandma and Grandpa's house.

When I was a teenager, my main connection with Utah was when people would move from Utah to the area I grew up—Falls Church, Virginia. It was young couples who had just graduated from BYU and had come to Washington D.C. for medical school or law school, and who had one or two small blonde-haired children. It was people who said things like "oh my heck" or "For cute."

When I graduated from high school and enrolled at Brigham Young University, it was culture shock. I had never been around so many caucasians before, and I missed the diversity. It meant quickly explaining to people that I only went to college in Utah, but I was actually from Virginia. Utah meant Provo to me, as the campus became my world. It meant BYU football games, shakes, and general college life stupidity.

When I graduated from BYU, I found myself accepting a job offer to work in Orem, Utah. I wouldn't change that for the world. Utah now means something completely different to me. It means living in a safe neighborhood and feeling a certain sense of community wherever I go. It means working with people who are generally good and feeling I can contribute somehow. It means visiting relatives, visiting friends, and visiting Salt Lake. Most of all, it now means home.

Marty Martin
Davis County

Age 72; **Birthplace** Hobbs, Indiana; **Occupation** N/A; **Religion** LDS; **Race/Ethnicity** White

In the fall of 1910 a train bound for the World's Fair in Portland, Oregon pulled in to the Ogden Union Station. A twenty-seven year old medical student from Indiana with his 19 year old bride stepped off the coach for a half hour break.

The groom had worked for the Nickel Plate Railroad since he was 18 years old. The job paid for his medical school and also provided the free transportation for this honeymoon trip to the Northwest. But other expenses encountered on their journey were far greater than anticipated. By the time the train reached Ogden their money had dwindled considerably. The Southern Pacific was hiring and their honeymoon trip ended abruptly when the boy secured a job to tide them over this rough spot. Forty-three years later he retired as a Southern Pacific conductor on the Salt Lake Division running from Ogden to Carlin, Nevada.

What did living in Utah in the early 1900's mean to this young girl? She was 1500 miles away from her home and family. Her husband worked away for days at a time, leaving her alone in a strange town. How fortunate for her that a motherly neighbor became her benefactor and provided a home environment within her own family. As they became better acquainted the girl questioned her friend about the irregularity of the father in the home. It was only then she learned her neighbor was a plural wife who shared her husband with another household. This was

a shock to the newcomer for she knew nothing about the Mormons except that they were suppose to have horns. But she was so intrigued by the unique lifestyle of this family she eagerly accepted the church books offered to her. In fact, she delved deeply into Mormonism in the next few years, becoming so knowledgeable on the subject that she was often asked to speak at club meetings and other gatherings when she visited her hometown in Indiana. It would be a perfect ending to this story to say she become a member and lived happily ever after. Although she lived happily among the LDS people for 55 years she never joined the church. What she became was an Ambassador of sorts. She loved the Mormon people, she adopted their standards as her own. She found the Saints to be sincere and truthful in their faith. She respected them for this and they respected her in return. She was not capable of being derogatory about the Mormon church.

There are many many non-Mormons who live in Utah who enjoy their association with their LDS neighbors. They are the silent majority. They are not the type to write letters to the editors. They are just truly grateful their children have LDS playmates.

This couple who made their home in Utah never regretted terminating their trip here. They bore five children, all of whom married members of the LDS church. Two of these five did join the church. …

Margaret Olivas
Salt Lake County

Age 47; **Birthplace** Bronx, New York; **Occupation** Housewife; **Religion** LDS; **Race/Ethnicity** White/Hispanic

Fortunate is an understatement, considering that I'm from New York and the many opportunities I've had to visit different states, territories, and countries, which allowed me to compare. I do not wish to be misunderstood, beauty and excitement lies within all places but, for me UTAH IS MORE. "This is the only place" where I can enjoy everything that has meaning to me. …

Only in this state I've seen people walking around with light jacket and IN SHORTS, while snow is falling like a feathered pillow fight. While in New York, as soon as two inches have fallen, I would start listening in the radio about schools shutting down and chaos racing loose. In Utah, it takes MUCH more than 3 inches to stop anybody—it is almost impossible for me to walk or drive while life here is as usual! When the temperature is around 48 degrees, in the dead winter, I leave my apartment only to find that Utahns are going around dressed feeling like it's summer. It is uplifting just to watch them. Once in Long Beach, New York I had an urge to walk on the beach. I looked for my heaviest coat and clothed myself like an Eskimo. To my amazement, at the beach, there was very nice lady, who just moved there from Utah, sitting on the sand, with NO coat, reading a book while her children were happily *PLAYING IN THE WATER!* I was in shock. We had a long conversation that afternoon, then, for the second and last time, the desire to move to the "Deseret" state possessed me. Only a few months later I WAS LIVING IN UTAH!

It's paradise when summer is here. Utah has so much to offer me that the day nor the season is long enough to do it all. Again the climate plays an important role in the way I feel in this gorgeous state. The temperature can be sizzling hot, the sun can be bright as to leave me blind but, the shade will always comfort me. It is wonderful to enjoy the coolness of the mountain areas or the adventure of the scorch dry desert!

There are so many outdoor activities for me such as walking the dirt trails in the mountains, exploring caves, racing in a 4 x 4 through the open desert, water paddling at Liberty Park, activities that suits almost any mood I might be in. If I can find so many things to do here that gives me that all time "high," then the possibilities for people which I consider "dare devils," such as water skiers or hot air balloon riders, are endless!

Utah is not a coastal state—no problem. I could practice most water sports and without the dangers of sharks. There is salt in the lake—no missing that either. I feel happy enough relaxing at shore with my towel, chair, radio, and beach ball. A dip in the lake will cool me down the same and bring me pleasure as well as any Hawaiian Island, but without the sticky sensation of the humid climate. Spring and autumn in Utah are my favorite seasons. Spring is full of excitement, planning what I wanted to do and where I would like to go once summer arrives.

I'm proud of living here. The friendliness and diversity of races, the way people live here in peace despite their great differences of ideas and creeds, the strength in numbers in times of need makes me feel one with humanity.

My travel experiences to the southern hemisphere and other places allows me to truly say that *UTAH IS A MILLIONAIRE STATE!* I will like to add that once I was homeless too.

Utah has given me plenty of both: miserable pain and extreme happiness still, I would get sick if I were to move from this majestic state.

I'm forever GRATEFUL to the state of UTAH for it is here where I now feel like THE RICHEST AND HAPPIEST WOMAN ON EARTH!

THANK YOU, UTAH!!!

Sangvane Insixiengmay
Utah County

Age 15; **Birthplace** Utah Valley Hospital; **Occupation** N/A; **Religion** Buddhism; **Race/Ethnicity** Laosian

I have been living in Utah my whole life. My parents and my older sister Olane lived in Laos for about a couple of years. Cause of the communist. They escape and came to Utah living with our sponsor Dan. Me and my younger sister Bouabane were born here.

Living in Utah is special. I am proud to live here. If my parents hadn't escape, I'd be in Laos. Laos is a cool place. I just don't like the communist for what they did to my people, living in Utah is safe. Cause you know that the communist can't come and hurt you. I am proud to live here. Cause I know I'm safe! Later on in life I'll go visit Laos. But I prefer to live in Orem, Utah. There is lots to do in Utah. And I am proud to be an American citizen.

Judith Grillo
Salt Lake County

Age 47; **Birthplace** Tokyo, Japan; **Occupation** CEO; **Religion** Presbyterian; **Race/Ethnicity** Caucasian

We love the low population, wide open spaces, the Utah Opera is respectable and Ballet West quite decent. (The personal taxes are a bit high for the return.) Everyone is really friendly. The Mormons are always ready to welcome someone as member or potential member and non-members are so greatful to have the pool diluted that one can't help but feel at home. Sincerely, I moved here six years ago, expecting to stay only about six months. Really find I like the people of Utah better as a whole than all the folks I have ever met anywhere.

It's not perfect—but it's a great place to live. We

stayed (My husband moved our furniture six months after I arrived.)

Sophana Anna Chanthasen
Utah County

Age N/A; **Birthplace** Thailand; **Occupation** N/A; **Religion** Buddhism; **Race/Ethnicity** Laos

Living in Utah means freedom. It also means happiness. When my family moved here we only wanted to be free from pressure around us. My dad was a prisoner in the airforce. The only way we can get out of Laos is by ascaping. So my Dad came to see us one day and we ran out the back door and went to Thailand and had me. After they had me we went to the United States. We went to New Mexico to have my sister. We lived there for a little time then we came to Utah to get away from all the gangs. This is where we stayed for the rest of my life. My mom died here and she wants us to take her to Laos this summer; we're not staying there because our home is in Utah.

Iwao Isobe
Weber County

Age 26; **Birthplace** Tokyo, Japan; **Occupation** Student; **Religion** L.D.S.; **Race/Ethnicity** Oriental

Utah is a wonderful, beautiful place. The Wasatch Mountains standing like the walls of a mighty fortress surrounding the Great Salt Lake overwhelmed me with their beauty and majesty. I feel that the land which speaks of greatness is like the people whose unique history is also full of wonder. I'm from another country, Japan, however

I have grown attached to both the land and people of Utah.

It was just six months ago that I came to Ogden to study at Weber State University. It was the end of a long air trip from San Francisco to Salt Lake City on my first day coming to Ogden. Looking at the terrain below as I flew across the Nevada desert, I realized that I was going to a place the map identified as part of the Great American Desert. Because we have only a very small desert on the west shore of Honshu island in Japan, I was amazed to see such an enormous region of desert land. Nevada looked dry and empty; then I saw the green which climbed up the sides of the Wasatch Range and filled the valleys. This green garden of Utah was a welcome sight after looking at the white lifeless salt flats extending for miles and miles across the desert. These signs were the proof that I was nearing my destination, Salt Lake City. From Salt Lake International Air Port I took a microbus to Ogden. On the way to Ogden I was quite amazed to see the light shades of springtime green on all sides. In contrast with the desert of Nevada which I had just seen, the Wasatch Front looked very beautiful. It didn't take me long to learn that this dramatic difference was not a natural phenomenon but that with much care the people living here had turned a desert into a garden.

On the second morning I was awakened not by my roommate but by the sound of sprinklers which kept everything living on the ground alive. Without them desert conditions would quickly return. In Japan I had never seen a sprinkling system except to settle the dust on an athletic playing field. I was very impressed by the industry of the people, past and present, in this dry country.

One very fine day, the beautiful weather invited me to walk from the campus up to the mountains. I went to the park which was on the north side of the WSU. On the way back to the dorm where I lived, I was passing through a residential area between the campus and the Dee Events Center. At that point, an elderly American lady with white hair spoke to me. She said, "Have you seen my little white dog around here? He has gone somewhere." I said, "Oh, I'm sorry but I haven't seen him. I have walked all the way from the park, but I haven't seen a white dog." I don't know whether she was able to find her dog or not, but that small experience warmed my heart because that old lady trusted me, a foreigner whose physical appearance was unlike that of her race. She spontaneously asked me to help her without hesitating to take note of the fact that I was an Asian. Unlike many people who stereotype others and avoid those who look physically different, she and many more people like here in Utah are open and friendly to newcomers from any places on earth. I know that racial differences cause divisions, here in America like everywhere else. However, I believe that people in Utah, compared to those in other states of America, are very tolerant and nice to the people from foreign countries. Even though there is a general tendency for the people in isolated mountain areas to be conservative in their lives, my statement about their friendliness is something I'm sure of. I am certain this Utah characteristic of friendliness comes from the religion which a majority belongs to. Over 60% of all Utah residents are "Mormons" and they believe that God is their father and Jesus Christ is the Savior of all mankind. Jesus said, "Love thy neighbor as thyself" and most of them practice what they believe in.

I am a Japanese Mormon. My father and mother joined the L.D.S. Church when they were young. They accepted the teachings of Christ which Utah people were first given and shared them with my parents. I, as a second generation Mormon, know that I can learn many great teaching by studying the history of Utah. One of them is to do what I believe is right and to exercise my faith in God even though I may have to experience bitter trials which I've never faced before. The people and the things which have given me so many blessings now in the church and community are the wonderful legacy of the old pioneers who dreamed of Zion in this dry but fertile valley.

Living in Utah is a wonderful experience for me. Utah is for a place of blessings, of beautiful scenery, of kind, progressive people, and of many kinds of well-organized church activities. However, the greatest thing Utah gives me is an example of courage to live with faith in God and in what I believe is right.

Esther Keyser
Grand County

Age 80; **Birthplace** Fredonia, NY; **Occupation** Retired; **Religion** Protestant; **Race/Ethnicity** White

When my husband and I moved to Moab, Utah from western New York twenty-six years ago, it was after we had spent five months traveling in our camper around the southwest looking for a small town where we could spend our retirement years.

We were attracted to Moab by the spectacular beauty of its natural surroundings and by the proximity of several state and National Parks and the nearness to a variety of

"January 23, 1952—Reschke, a German immigrant, arrived in New York aboard the S.S. Italia.*" Submitted by Horst A. Reschke, Salt Lake County.*

terrain to explore.

One morning soon after we moved here we were listening to the local radio when we heard an announcement that went something like this: "Anyone who has not paid their water taxes can work them off. Report to the ditch at 8:00 Saturday morning. Bring your own shovel." We knew we had come to the right place.

The most significant aspect of living in Utah is the friendliness and warmth of almost everyone here. The neighbor who brought us a hot meal right after the mover left the day we arrived, the driver of the pickup who waves when you meet on the back road, those who say "hello" when you meet them on the street.

While society has changed a lot since we moved here (and Utah with it) this is still a place to live among good people in a beautiful natural world.

Misaki Sato
Utah County

Age 28; **Birthplace** Tokyo, Japan; **Occupation** Student; **Religion** I don't know; **Race/Ethnicity** Asian

Utah has been bringing a lot of things to me. Academically, BYU gives me intellectual knowledge, and spiritually, the church (LDS) helps us progress and grow. And also, there are a lot of mountains and natural resources in Utah. I enjoy them a lot, such as camping, climbing, skiing, sledding and so on. People are very nice here in Utah. Especially people from Utah and who grow up here in Utah are something different from the others. They look very pure like children. If I get married and have a baby, I want him/her to be like them. But the climate is not so comfortable for me; It's very hot in summer and its very cold and there are a lot snow in winter. It's hard for me to keep healthy condition throughout

the year, because of such climate, though air is very clean and fresh (few people drink and smoke).

After all, living in Utah means to me is to grow and progress both in spiritually and academically. BYU is a very good college, I think and also the church affect people a lot in positive ways.

Janet SumYee Cheng
Millard County

Age 17; **Birthplace** Hong Kong; **Occupation** Student; **Religion** LDS; **Race/Ethnicity** Chinese

This is my second year living in Utah as an adopted child. Coming here means a lot to me. I have had unaccountable experiences, both good and bad ones. I have learned so much, life here has treated me better than I had expected.

People living in Utah are friendly. And for that, I am grateful, because I have made lots of friends. (They comfort me when I get homesick.) The socializing part is interesting. I did not know that being friendly to the opposite sex does not have any special meanings. From the life in my homeland, being friendly to the opposite sex would be interpreted as an absolutely different meaning.

School here is much easier than in Hong Kong and Uruguay, but I think I'm learning more here under the American Educational System. The teachers give me an abundant amount of opportunities to discover my talents and interests. I have realized that I love school, especially with all the activities I'm involved in.

Joining the L.D.S. Church has been something special. It helps a lot to know there is always someone caring and looking after me.

Life here is challenging, and I feel more confident, in myself than I ever have before. I'm able to be independent, I can do something that I want to do without worrying that I would fail and disappoint those that I love.

James Harding Gillespie
Weber County

Age 73; **Birthplace** Starkville, MS; **Occupation** Retired; **Religion** N/A; **Race/Ethnicity** African American

When I came to Utah in 1942, it was a place where almost all African Americans worked for the railroad industry; there were no black teachers. In Ogden, black residences, for the most part, were concentrated in a confined section of the city. Even though we were military personnel, we were not served in most white or Oriental restaurants, and were ushered to the balcony in movie theaters.

Now, Blacks can be found working in a variety of places; Salt Lake City has three African American school principals, and there are a number of Black teachers at all levels of education. Blacks are now living in more diverse areas of the State, and discrimination in public accommodations no longer exists.

Living in Utah has meant watching it change, and watching it grow.

Gloria Nohemi Nieto
Salt Lake County

Age 27; **Birthplace** Mexico; **Occupation** Housewife—student; **Religion** Adventist; **Race/Ethnicity** Hispanic

I have been living in Utah for 2-½ years, I came from Mexico to Los Angeles and, I lived in Los Angeles, California for 3 years before I came here.

I remember that when I came to Utah I didn't like it at all and I told my husband. I thought that this was a boring place to live, and that there were no opportunities for Jobs here. We almost went back to California because my husband didn't like it either, but then after the 3rd day of our arrival my husband found a job. It was a little difficult to find a house for rent but not as much as I thought.

Now after 2-½ years of living here, I think Utah has become as heaven to me compared to the place where I live before, because, when I was living in Los Angeles I always had fear to go out because of the gangs, the robbers, the killers, and the traffic accidents. Even when I was in my home, I was afraid of the earth quakes. Financially speaking, I think we were a lot poorer than we are now.

That is why we left Los Angeles and, because we were looking for an opportunity of economic and education success, not only for us but for our kids too. We are also looking for a peaceful place to live and I think we have found it here in Utah.

My only wish is that Utah won't become an unsafe and expensive place to live, like Los Angeles, California.

There are many beautiful things to say about Utah for example: Utah has beautiful lakes, wonderful mountains, big recreational parks, clean environment, life is not too expensive, and most of its people are warm and kind, and most of them are willing to help others.

Another good thing about Utah is that there are many religious people and maybe that is why I feel that Utah is the perfect and safest place to live with my family.

I thank Utah for giving us peace and tranquility. I thank Utah for giving my husband the opportunity of a better job: for giving a safe and good school to my kids and for giving me the opportunity to finish my education.

I thank Utah for all I said before and I thank God for giving us a beautiful place like Utah to live our lives.

In conclusion, I think Utah is the perfect place for

families who like to have a peaceful life, a clean place to live, and an opportunity to succeed in life.

Dorothy Martinez
Utah County

Age 65; **Birthplace** Nevada City, CA; **Occupation** Retired; **Religion** Catholic; **Race/Ethnicity** N/A

I want to tell you about what Utah means to me, but first I need to tell you a little about myself. I am a native Californian and I have always been proud of my state. I was born in California and lived my life within fifty miles of my birth city.

When my husband and I retired, I thought I would live my whole life there and die in the house where we raised our two children. Then my daughter and son-in-law moved to Utah. They wanted my husband and me to move with them. My husband was born in Colorado and yearned for the four seasons. He really wanted to move, and because we had always lived where I wanted to, I agreed we would try it.

When we made the move, I was quite honestly scared. We are not Mormons. We are Mexican Americans. Would the people accept us? Would we fit in? I was afraid not, but I would sure try. Soon after that, the people started coming to the house introducing themselves and asking what they could do to make us feel welcome. People called to invite us to things like luncheons and other fun get-togethers just to get to know each other better!

We went to a store in Sandy to look for a winter hat for my husband, Johnny. A man (who was another customer) started talking to us about hats. Johnny mentioned that he liked the particular hat the man was wearing. Immediately, he started helping us find one like it. The clerk in the store said they did not carry that kind any-more. This man (whom we did not know from Adam) took off his hat and offered to give it to Johnny!

Yesterday, it snowed about 18 inches. We got up this morning to clean the walks and driveway. When the dogs started barking, we looked up and there was a man on a snow plow clearing our driveway and the road. We did not know who the man was, and when we asked him he said he was just a neighbor helping out.

I just cannot believe the friendship the people in this community have shown to both my husband and me. When I think about the way people were in the "Good Ole' Days," I think people must have been talking about our neighbors in this little town of Alpine.

I hope nothing changes because I really like this place just as it is. This is definitely our new home.

Yuko Kawashima
Millard County

Age 17; **Birthplace** Hiroshima, Japan; **Occupation** Student; **Religion** Buddhism; **Race/Ethnicity** Japanese

It has been about five months since I came to Delta, Utah in the United States from Japan. I came here as an exchange student. I was very interested in English, so I wanted to come to America to learn English. Before I came here, I told my friends that I can go to America. Everyone was very surprised, because they think America is a very scary place. Sometimes, I heard scary news about America when I was in Japan. But I don't think Delta is scary place. I think Delta is safe place. My first impression of Utah is that you have a lot of beautiful places in Utah. I was very impressed. I've never seen such an beautiful natural place when I was in Japan. And also, people in Delta are really kind. When I came here for the first time, I felt uneasy, because I didn't know about America. But everyone was so nice to me. When I went to the bank, one woman said to me, "I have a kid around your age. I'll tell her to talk to you when she see you." One day, when I went to the city library, the librarian talked to me, "Are you from Japan? I was taking Japanese in college. Maybe we can be friend." Sometimes, I go to the library and study. She always talks to me when she see me. Every one is very friendly in Delta. Actually, I wanted to go New York or Los Angeles, because that sounded like fun to me. I think the big city is a fun place to play, but sometimes it can be a scary place, besides I think people in the big city aren't as friendly and open-hearted as people in Delta. I think Delta is a small town, so every one is friendly. And I'm also glad I could meet my host family. They are really nice. I learned a lot of things not just English since I came here. What living in Utah means to me is that I can learn a lot of things that I've never had in Japan. I want to learn more thing, and enjoy myself here while I am in Utah.

Wanda Heaton
Kane County

Age 51; **Birthplace** Atlanta, Georgia; **Occupation** research/evaluation—teacher; **Religion** LDS; **Race/Ethnicity** Native American

Living in Utah is my choice. I don't have to live here; I choose to live here. It is neither the place of my birth, nor is it the only state in which I have lived. However, it is the place where I have found security, beauty, love, and involvement.

I was born and raised in Atlanta, Georgia—a recognized city and state of beauty and history. It was a wonderful place to grow up and discover what I wanted to find in life. It gave me gentility, grace, and a great "drawl." I loved the trees, the beautiful flowers, and the thunder-

storms. As I grew older, I wanted to explore and try my wings a little more than the confines of this historic old city would permit. I had chosen a career—I wanted to be a doctor. My grades were superior, my college entrance score were high, and I received a scholarship to Northwestern University. I was on my way north to "Yankee" country!

Fate, however, stepped in and sideswiped my plans. I found that I "had" to go to Utah to school because of financial reasons. Utah—my mind reeled with visions of deserts, snakes, no trees, no green, no water! I had traveled to Utah at age 13, and all I remember were the barren mountains, the treeless hills, and my skin flaking off on my shorts. Of all the places to be dispatched, Utah would be my last choice—that is except for California!

At 16, I found myself encamped in a university dorm room with a view of those rocky, lifeless mountains. I knew I would never like—much less love—this ugly place. I was a Georgia girl through and through. Little did I know that this state would become the place I call home.

I lived in Utah for five years until I graduated from college. I hadn't found the husband I was "promised" when I paid my first tuition, so I left as soon as I could find my fortune. I had gotten used to the mountains, the snow, and the dryness; however, I could hardly wait until I got back east so I would be surrounded by green. As I drove down the streets of Georgetown, I was overwhelmed with trees, flowers, and GREEN! I knew I was home; I knew I would never miss the Rockies of Utah. I was wrong—oh so wrong!

Within days, I was claustrophobic with trees. I couldn't see the sky for trees; I couldn't see blue sky even if I could see through the trees! No blue sky exists in Georgetown—not like the blue sky in Utah. Not only was no blue sky available to me, the land is flat in Washington, D.C. and Virginia areas. If I got beyond the trees, the land stretched on forever flat—flat as a pancake. No majestic mountains hid the sun until it shyly peaked through the cracks. No multicolored sunsets dazzled me as I mellowed down from the days activities. No moonlit nights danced through the valley and shone like diamonds on the snow covered hills. I missed it all; I missed the beauty which is Utah. Nothing can rival it; nothing dares!

Today, I live in Southern Utah. As I look out my kitchen window, I see the red cliffs on the "back side" of Bryce Canyon National Park. The fog creeps over these cliffs like wispy ghosts trying to sneak up on the valley. I am surrounded by a valley which in the spring is dotted with newborn calves and lambs, various sprinkling systems spewing water into the wind, tractors plowing the newly thawed ground, and children playing barefoot in the gardens. Flowers push through the snow we still have in April and May, fruit trees let us know we will have fruit in the fall, stars appear close enough that you are tempted to reach up and pluck a few from the night sky, and the mountains surrounding the valley feel like your family as they close in to protect you from the world. The beauty is astounding; I choose the beauty.

As with beauty, I find that Utah offers me security which I have yet to find in other states. This is not to delude the reader into thinking that Utah is perfect or crime free; it is not. Utah, like any growing and maturing state, experiences problems. People without the "pioneer" spirit come here and try to change the state into that which they are trying to escape. Crime creeps into our lives one foot at a time, so slowly we hardly notice it is coming. We choose to accept and try to "fix" the bad rather than preserve the good.

I have lived in Chicago and Tampa—both in the top five crime areas in the United States. Compared to these places, my small Southern Utah town is heaven. We left our home ten years ago, and the keys were hanging on the inside of the front door. We came back, and they were still hanging on the same nail. Today we don't lock our cars when we go in the house for something we forgot—most of the time, we leave the car running. Our youth play basketball well into the night—every night but Sunday—during the summer and fall, and mothers don't worry about their sons and daughters. Our children get up early, work weekdays and Saturday, share their goodies, swim in the reservoirs, and take care of each other. Townspeople watch who comes into town; if a stranger ventures in, everyone in town will know almost immediately. We had "neighborhood watch" before it was "cool." I feel safe at night; I am safe. Should trouble ever visit any of my neighbors, we stand united. I choose security.

Christel Ruth Shaffer
Iron County

Age 63; **Birthplace** Poland (Klein Lunau); **Occupation** Retired; **Religion** LDS; **Race/Ethnicity** German

I moved to Cedar City only last August (1994) from Kirkland, WA (Suburb of Seattle) with my 89 yr old mother Linda Hahn, nee Krüger.

I had been to Cedar 5 times prior to my move; during the 2 yrs. before I came here. Given, that a move from Kirkland was eminent for a variety of reasons, my mind was open to other possibilities. The more often I came, the more the area grew on me.

I finally did some research on aspects that were important to me—so here we go:

1) Having lived in big—to very large—cities for most of the time since I migrated from Germany in 1956, I was definitely ready for a smaller town, though Cedar is growing. I expect it won't become a "Los Angeles." It still has vestiges of earlier times—which I like.

2) There is a sense of history in Utah; people are proud of their pioneer heritage. Being from Europe, where I grew up in a town that now is better than 750 yrs old—which is not unusual—I was used to a desire to preserve the

past. (However, my family became refugees in Jan. 1945 and we lost our house and all belongings.)

3) Though Cedar is a small town, its cultural offerings are not at all small town-like! See the Shakespearean Festivals, the Summer Games, and what the University has to offer. This helps to keep the town and area vibrant—Even the Senior Games in St. George!

4) Cedar is located near a Main North-South artery and even has an airport which makes travel easier.

5) Cedar is only a short hour from an LDS Temple.

6) Cedar's climate with its seasons—the cold winter and moderately hot "real" summers and its wonderful sunshine is very agreeable to me. I love the deciduous tree that, in Summer, offer shade, in the fall brightens the area, and in winter let the sun in. Sure makes sense!

7) The cost of living here in Southern Utah—esp. housing, is still much lower than the Seattle area; which is an important factor when you live on limited retirement income.

8) I love living among the wonderful, warm LDS neighbors.

9) Last but not least there are the wonderful mountains. They have done it to me! I think the stretch between Cedar and St. George is the most fabulous anywhere! My spirit gets touched anytime I drive to and from St. George. I turn the radio off so that the mountains can "talk" to me! This is wonderfull "gravy" that I had not anticipated! I love it!

J. R. Hankins
Davis County

Age 17; **Birthplace** Marietta, Georgia; **Occupation** N/A; **Religion** Methodist; **Race/Ethnicity** N/A

I have been in Utah for a little over a year now; perhaps it is not fair for me to make an evaluation of what Utah is. However, I will make a few personal observations that are "What Living in Utah Means to Me."

I suppose the first thing about Utah that I noticed was the mountains; how could one miss them. The large, graceful mountains put us at ease, and are always there, whenever we look to the sky. I also noticed how the mountains seemed to enclose the valley cutting it off from the outside world. Perhaps this reflects "what Utah means to me." The people within Utah sit secure behind the mountains, not wishing any other environment.

Another observation I made was the "laid back" attitude of the people in Utah. At first, I admit, I disliked this coming from the East Coast. I was used to a fast-pace style of living, but when I arrived here everyone seemed to be waving their SLOW signs at me. Perhaps this was for my own good. Utah has taught me to relax a little.

Among one of the main characteristics of Utah is conformity. Conformity, although some seem to think so, does not always have a negative connotation. The state seems to enjoy being alike; especially religiously. I share their joy in conformity, to a certain extent. I think we all need some kind of "identity." Sometimes, however, Utah seems to reflect the mountains; shutting the outside world away.

I think Utah is simple; a simplicity I enjoy. Once you have gotten used to its differences and accepted its (slightly less than) open-minded attitude, you can enjoy this simplicity, also.

Jessica Shirley Marie Alger
Weber County

Age 10; **Birthplace** California; **Occupation** Student; **Religion** Mormon; **Race/Ethnicity** Caucasian

What I like about Utah is mostly the people are all nice. and that they have nice churches and its fun in the summer time. But I dont understand why they don't have pools though.

Jason Mapes
Salt Lake County

Age 18; **Birthplace** Iowa; **Occupation** Student; **Religion** N/A; **Race/Ethnicity** White

I like Utah and its Mountains the most. The way they stick out against the city is almost breathtaking. After living in Iowa for 16 years and living in Oregon for 5 years, Utah has the friendliest people around. Unlike my other schools, at Brighton here in Utah I feel safe. Almost like it's a group effort that everyone succeeds.

Linda Henion Sappington
Washington County

Age 51; **Birthplace** Portland, Oregon; **Occupation** Public Relations; **Religion** LDS; **Race/Ethnicity** Caucasian

On a hot July day, my husband arrived at our California home and announced he had accepted employment in Salt Lake City, Utah. My roots ran deep into the southern California sand and I fought the move with every ounce of emotional strength I could muster, but pregnant with my fifth child, I accepted my fate and followed my husband to the very edge of civilization as I knew it … while hanging on to every freeway sign and palm tree within my grasp.

For the first two years we lived on the Wasatch Front, I saw very little to appreciate. My impression of Salt Lake City was "grey." I felt lonely and isolated. We had no neighbors on the barren hillside looking up into Little Cottonwood Canyon (off 9700 South in Sandy). Back in 1974, Sandy was considered the outskirts of Salt Lake City and those in our LDS Ward were aloof in their pride as direct descendants of the first settlers in Granite. But surprisingly, we bonded in a very peculiar way… I didn't want to be there—and, they didn't want me there. Our common attitude was also our common denominator.

We have now been residents of the Beehive State for nearly nineteen years. Four of our six children are Utah natives. We moved to St. George in 1978 and have watched this sleepy little community grow up around us. Our life in Utah is sweet—filled with many happy memories, good friends, a growing family, clean air, sunshine, security, luscious scenery, wide open spaces and many interesting employment opportunities.

Move back to California? Never! I hope to spend the rest of my life right here in Dixie's red sand.

Thomas L. Allen
Cache County

Age 48; **Birthplace** St. Louis County, Missouri; **Occupation** Professional Fundraiser; **Religion** United Methodist; **Race/Ethnicity** White

I moved to Utah in 1986 with my wife and two children after having lived almost all my life in St. Louis, Missouri. I came here to work and study at Utah State University and this was supposed to be a temporary stop along the way. We had not lived here very long until we knew we wanted to make a life for ourselves in Utah.

This is a fascinating place to live. The scenic beauty of the entire state is breathtaking. We still have clean air and water. The crime rate is low and there are simply different assumptions about life here compared to other places in the world.

Persons who are Utah natives and who have never lived elsewhere may not fully understand that Utah is unique. My wife Sharon and I were Peace Corps volunteers in the Ivory Coast, West Africa from 1969–71. That was my first experience in learning how to live and work in a culture other than the one I grew up in.

I am a first generation city dweller. My mother and father moved to St. Louis from rural Wayne County, Missouri during World War II. When my father returned to Missouri from duty as a machine gunner with the infantry in Italy, my parents decided to remain in the big city. I grew up a city boy with frequent visits and summer vacations in the country on a farm. This gave me a perspective on life in the Midwest. I still love Missouri and most of my relatives are there, but when our family talks about going home, we mean going to Cache Valley, Utah.

Utah's Mormon heritage, and the fact that such a large majority of its residents are members of the LDS Church, both exert influence on virtually every facet of life here. Our children returned from their first day of Utah elementary school with a twinkle in their eyes. My son said, "you'll never guess what they say here. They say 'My Heck' and 'Dang Good'!" My daughter said she used the phrase "Oh God!" in talking to a schoolmate and she was cautioned that she should not take the Lord's name in vain. Several days later our neighbor children asked Nathaniel and Rebekah if their parents drank coffee. They nodded solemnly when they were assured that yes, indeed, mommy and daddy began every day with a cup. "We thought we could smell it," they were told. We found out that we were one of only three non-LDS families in our town. We learned very soon to describe our home as being in the Third Ward. This was *not* a change because, as Methodists in Catholic south St. Louis we were used to describing our neighborhood by its Catholic parish. Shortly after moving in, our immediate neighbors brought us a *Book of Mormon,* inscribed with heartfelt testimonies about the importance of this book in their lives. It is one of our prized possessions.

In St. Louis we had several good friends among our neighbors but most were strangers. There were relatively few children in our neighborhood and many of our neighbors were elderly retired couples, widows or widowers. None of our neighbors attended our church. Our neighborhood was declining and the houses there were mostly built around 1900. Our home was burglarized twice, our car was vandalized while parked out front, and I slept with a loaded handgun between the mattress and box springs. Our neighborhood was a melting pot of native South Siders of German, Irish, Italian and Syrian origin, newcomers from the Ozarks, and immigrants from Southeast Asia. Children passing on the street ignored you, if they didn't sass you. Drivers cut each other off and gave each other the finger in traffic. When you walked down the street, you paid attention to who was behind you, ahead of you and across the street.

Utah is different. We are listed in the Ward directory and we know what house to report to if there is an earthquake so we can join our neighbors to help each other. Sharon sometimes attends Relief Society and learns new crafts and makes new friends. Our son has helped harvest crops for needy people and our daughter attended Mia Maid camp for several years. I have performed programs on the western fur trade dressed in my frontier garb for the Scouts, the grade school and the Ward. We have been recognized as being different, our differences have been respected, and we have been integrated into this community.

Utah is different. On Sunday a deathly quiet descends as ALL our neighbors go to the same church. Most of our houses have been built since 1960. Our neighbors don't lock their front door and they leave their car keys in the ignition. Virtually all of our neighbors were born in Utah, many in Millville, but enough from other areas to make the cliquishness attributed to other local communities (rightly or wrongly) not a factor. Most of our neighbors are of Western European descent, and particularly of Scandinavian origin. Our Rebekah was once the only girl in her classroom with dark hair. I know that you can spell one family name Christensen, Christenson, Christiansen, Christianson, and probably several other ways to boot.

Utah is different. Children passing on the street wave and smile. For several months I thought they were mistaking me for someone they knew. Then I decided that these kids wave and smile at everyone! People in traffic allow other drivers to enter traffic ahead of them. People walking on those lines painted on the street cause traffic to stop and let them get across. I almost flattened several pedestrians until a native passenger gently explained this to me. (The mere concept of traffic stopping in mid-block for a pedestrian would be both inconceivable and hilarious to a St. Louis driver. Pedestrians were the enemies of our blood.) I have never seen anybody give anybody else the finger in traffic. You don't dare. Last summer some teenagers gave somebody the finger on Main Street in Logan and it made the letters-to-the-editor column in the "Herald Journal" for days. Everybody knows everybody else, or is related, or goes to church together, or is an in-law. We never knew we came from "back East" until we came here. We thought Missouri was the Gateway to the West. We will never be natives, but we are welcome here.

Utah is different. A rubber band is an elastic. The ditch along the road is a borrow pit. There are dugways to drive on. Women become P G (pregnant). There are great bargains and old books at D I (Deseret Industries Thrift Stores). A classic Utah menu would be corn dogs, Kool-Aid, tater tots, scones with honey butter and lime jello. At a Scottish Burns Society dinner the haggis is toasted with pink punch (and there is no Scotch Whiskey in the place, honest!). At McDonald's you may have to wait while somebody brews you some coffee. Mormon coffee is either the strongest or weakest coffee you have ever drunk.

Utah is different. Many people have never engaged in a conversation with a black person. This is not through prejudice, but rather through a lack of opportunity. In St. Louis our children went through most of their elementary school classes with black teachers and as white minority group members in the classroom. In Logan black persons in the grocery store are likely to be looking for plantains and to speak to each other in French or Wolof.

Utah is different. If The Church has a position on horse racing you don't have to ask which one. A girl in my teacher wife's high school classroom asked if Methodists had ever heard of Jesus Christ. In finest Utah tradition my son and his buddies set up a table with a candelabra and violinist in a high school classmate's front yard so he could ask her to the prom in style. Her father wouldn't let her go with a Non-Member. A neighbor couple are assigned to visit us at least once a month just to make sure we're ok. Non-Members come to feel their Otherness—sometimes overtly, but usually completely unconsciously. Religious faith comes up in conversations in school classrooms, stores, and gas stations. It is important to people.

Utah is different. If your car breaks down and you already have a wrecker coming you may have to wave off ten carloads of people offering to help you. If you stop in a strange neighborhood to ask for directions the five-year-old who answers the door will probably invite you inside. There is a presumption of honestly, an expectation of good will.

I wish many things for my adopted state for the next 100 years. I would wish more of our citizens were more concerned for our environment. I believe many people in Utah sincerely believe this world is about to end, and that we should take advantage of the chance to put as much of our natural resources to good use as we can. I would prefer not to take this chance, and to be a good steward of this world.

I would wish some of my neighbors could have a little greater sense of humor about life, love, religion and the human condition. It should be mandatory to attend at least one performance of James Arrington's one-person play, "The Farley Family Reunion." When the little girl asks Heavenly Father to bless that country music star Willie Nelson should join The Church so he can sing in the Mormon Tabernacle Choir, every Utahn has reason to smile.

I would wish that Mormon women could receive the priesthood and be more fully integrated into the leadership of their church. I say this knowing that the current interpretation of LDS religious belief makes this unlikely.

I would wish that Utahns could feel comfortable in limiting the size of their families. I understand the religious belief that encourages providing earthly bodies for waiting spirits, but I worry about the young couples I see beginning their families at 17 and 18 and trying to balance the dream of completing their education with their dreams of an ideal Eternal Family.

I would wish that the LDS Church could find another Prophet in his 40's like Joseph Smith to give the church leadership this perspective of age from a viewpoint nearer the cradle than the grave.

I would wish that native and adopted Utahns who are not Mormon would treat their neighbors and their beliefs with the respect they sometimes demand most vociferously for themselves.

Finally I would wish that the whole world could emulate the good in Utah. There is much good here.

I believe "Utah is Different" would be a more meaningful motto for our license plates than "Greatest Snow on Earth." It would not be as boastful as "Utah is Better" although it is at least arguable that this last is true. What Living in Utah Means to Me is the chance to live in beauty, among loving, caring people, in greater security and with less stress than most other places on Earth. If I ever stop looking in wonder on the mountains as I drive to work, it will be time to move on.

Happy 100th Birthday, Utah.

Ryan Conner Daley

Age 12; **Birthplace** California; **Occupation** Student; **Religion** LDS; **Race/Ethnicity** White

Utah
Utah has a lot of cities
and a few lakes.
I didn't move here for the Lakes, Religion.
I moved here, because we
had a dream that me and my
brother wouldn't have to
grow up in a city where
all anybody cared about was

Money,

Beer,

Guns,

Drugs.

I may not be happy with Utah now,

But it's better than L.A.

Utah is growing too fast too much.

We don't have time to stop and smell the flowers.

Julia E. Barrett
Cache County

Age 64; **Birthplace** Lubbock, Texas; **Occupation** Homemaker; **Religion** LDS; **Race/Ethnicity** Caucasian

Until now I have resisted flying into the pigeonhole labeled "A Utahn" because of the stereotypical implication of one-way narrowness the word, Utah, calls up. But I have lived here for 18 years now and I confess I find myself fitting more and more into that snug holy place. I still haven't got used to reading the paper and seeing "Missionary Suits on Sale," nor do I carry my scriptures under my arm whenever I leave the house, but as my California wings have begun to lose feathers and my beady eyes capable of only seeing that which is close by, Utah seem to be more and more a place I can comfortably call home.

I wasn't born here, but my ancestors participated in the trek West via handcart and covered wagon. The pioneer stories were a part of family folklore from my earliest memory. My mother has kept the arts of soap-making, food-preservation, quilting and simple, wholesome cooking alive to this day. She is in her 90th year. My father taught us to work, to cultivate our gardens and minds and to be honest and upright. Both parents influenced their seven children with their light-heartedness, laughter, sternness, expectancies and optimism.

Our decision to move to Utah (my husband was born in Logan) was made hastily, but with that faith in self and God that we both inherited from our families that all would turn out well. And it has. A majority of our married children live within a two hour drive. We see our 21 grandchildren frequently. Now that our first great-grandchild has been born, we move one more notch down the ladder to oblivion, but are reassured that living in Utah is probably the best place families can live. Not only is the atmosphere unusually supportive of full-time moms and unworldly children, but the very ambience and geography of the State seems to echo this philosophy. Utah is still relatively wide, free, clean, open and pure. There are places to hike, places to bike, swim, fish, camp, hunt, boat. Every family-loving activity from marathon-running to little theatre is available.

Now as I look at this picture of five generations, all but my parents living in Utah, and look out at the picture I see from my window of blue sky and white mountain peaks, I have to say, "Yes, I'm a Utahn and I've got it all right here!"

Frank Alan Coombs
Salt Lake County

Age 57; **Birthplace** Billeville, Kansas; **Occupation** University Professor; **Religion** Unitarian Universalist; **Race/Ethnicity** Caucasian

This is written from the perspective of one who is not a native Utahn. I was born and raised in Kansas where my father worked as an educator and I am sure many of my instinctive attitudes are still conditioned by having grown up in the Middle West/Great Plains. But when my father attended U.S. Government Indian Service Summer Schools at Intermountain School in Brigham City, Utah, in 1951 and 1953, the family accompanied him and I received my first exposure to Utah, its physical attractions, and its culture. Indeed, I learned to swim in the swimming pool on the Intermountain campus, loved hiking up the hills above town, and my first paying job was scooping ice cream in the Intermountain cafeteria.

So many years later, when I was finishing my doctoral work at the University of Illinois and seeking a position teaching history at the college level, I was delighted to discover that such a position was open at the University of Utah. Although other jobs were offered to me in Texas and North Carolina, I opted for Salt Lake City and have never regretted the decision. The analogy with adopting a child may be apt: If Utah was not the place of my birth, it is a place I have *chosen* to live for the past quarter century. The attractions that impressed my wife and me immediately were the ready access to scenic wonders (an incredible number within an easy day's drive from Salt Lake), all manner of outdoor activities, along with the generally friendly demeanor of the local citizenry (not unlike Kansas, I might add) and the congenial and stimulating atmosphere of the University of Utah. As one who has frequently been involved in recruiting new faculty, I have found myself repeatedly telling candidates of the advantages of living in a major urban area along the Wasatch Front (a first-rate symphony, ballet, great health care facilities, an excellent NBA basketball franchise, and a host of cultural opportunities) without having to worry about the truly severe problems that afflict most big cities in our time. Perhaps because I grew up on the Kansas plains I have never learned to ski, but I have developed an affinity for mountains and often note the large number of transplanted Midwesterners who, at one time or another, discover Utah and have never found any reason to leave.

What people *really* want to know from a "Gentile" when they ask for an opinion of life in Utah, of course, is what it is like to live in Zion if one is not a member of the L.D.S. church. Non-Mormon friends from other parts of the country sometimes express amazement that we should have remained so long in what they are sure must be an oppressive environment. I understand their concern; anyone who supposes that Mormon attitudes do not have a substantial impact on Utah's politics and society is kidding himself. But I have never personally found that oppressive and I have trouble comprehending why some people who come to the state from other parts of the country or the world torture themselves for decades with resentment. The state is what it is in a cultural sense and it seems to me you either accept it "warts and all" or drive yourself crazy. We have never personally experienced any "hard sell" efforts at conversion and have rather been the subjects of both tolerance and thoughtful inclusion in our heavily Mormon neighborhood. It seems to me in retrospect that our children may have been effectively limited in the kinds of things they could hope to achieve in their public school careers (class presidents and head cheerleaders often seemed to be chosen in L.D.S. seminary), but both compiled superior academic records, excelled in selected activities, and maintained good friendships across religious lines. They continue to regard Salt Lake City as "home" and a place to which they love to return.

So for me I suppose the judgment finally becomes comparative. Every locale has its idiosyncrasies and Utah is no exception. Sometimes, as a college teacher, I wish this society encouraged more introspection and critical thinking, but that can be said of many places. Meanwhile, I continue to reap the benefits of a generally well-ordered, hard-working, family-centered, and friendly community at a time in the history of the United States and the world in which those qualities are increasingly rare. Utahns can take pride in their achievements in the century since statehood and I am happy to have been able to play a small part in that story.

Anja Dinter
Utah County

Age 17; **Birthplace** Berlin, Germany; **Occupation** Student;
Religion None; **Race/Ethnicity** White

In five months I'm going back to a country where even the capital has 3 times more inhabitants then whole Utah. Will I miss it? I'm sure about that! It's very different but I enjoy it. A big crowded city and the width of state is probably the biggest difference.

When you are here just minutes away from cities you can be alone for hours, barely meet people.

Especially in Berlin it is hard to enjoy the beauty of nature without hundreds of people around you.

These thoughts and feelings became very strong a few days ago when I went hiking with my friend Daniel. We drove Payson Canyon and tried to find the best and most interesting looking mountain around us. Finally we started to hike up through the snow. We talked about everything that came in mind. We didn't meet one person and the silence was only interrupted by a driving car down on the road through the canyon.

The higher we came the better sight was. We found petrified bones shells and other little animals in rocks that probably lived thousands or even millions of years ago. We started to imagine what Utah used to look like by the time these animals used to live.

We came higher and higher and the snow was more and more steep. We already used hands and legs to get up there. Finally we reached the top. The sight was breathtaking. I knew what I love Utah mostly for—the landscapes. All around us snowcovered mountains, the big valley with the lakes and no people of any sort around us except the rush of the water. We felt like Kings of the Mountains.

Utah offers me more what I like to do than Berlin does. I'm a nature person. I enjoy doing things like climbing, hiking, mountain biking, and skiing. Utah's landscape offers me all of that whenever I want to do it. And thats probably what I will miss most with my new found friends. The only things that brings little difficulties sometimes is the religion. Because of it I don't have a certain kind of freedom I used to have at home. It is not hard to accept and adapt to it but still I've to be careful what I say, wear and do.

But also the religion has an impression positive influence here. The church is one part why I think Utah is unique almost like a own country.

I'm really thinking about coming back and go to college or work here. I think job chances are good here, because the state is relatively young and still developing. So it offers many things to do.

Except life problems I really enjoy living here. Maybe I even put it over my own country.

Melissa M. Materazzi
Salt Lake County

Age 18; **Birthplace** Wilmington, Delaware; **Occupation** Not yet; **Religion** Catholic; **Race/Ethnicity** who cares

I moved to Utah 3 years ago, and it was quite a culture shock at first, but I quickly jumped into the groove of things. Despite the political and religious aspects of this state, Utah was probably the best thing that happened in my life. I've met some of the most incredible and influential people I will ever meet. I am thankful beyond words for living in such a safe environment that is healthy and beautiful.

Utah is a sheer geographical goddess. From mountains to lakes to rivers to deserts, I have seen breathtaking and celestial sights. Not only have I seen them, but I've experienced them too. If you are a hiker, a skier or a rock climber, Utah is your Graceland. The same goes for camping, fishing and waterskiing.

Valerie Morita
Salt Lake County

Age 18; **Birthplace** Willingboro, New Jersey; **Occupation** N/A; **Religion** Presbyterian; **Race/Ethnicity** Japanese/Caucasian

Living in Utah has made me deal with almost always being the minority. Being half Japanese and attending a Presbyterian Church has, more often than not, put me in a minority stance.

I have lived in Utah ten years. Two years prior to that, I lived in Utah five years. I remember moving to Utah the second time and being absolutely shocked at the way I was treated. Some children in the neighborhood were not allowed to play with me, justified with the fact that I didn't attend the predominant church. Many, many times when I was younger I yearned to become Mormon so I would (per say) "fit in." Now ten years later, I'm proud I stuck to my religion, but I suppose something inside still hurts to remember things people said or did. The accusing looks I will always deal with for the crucifix I bare upon my chest.

In conclusion, Utah is an original. I just had to feel what it was like to be the minority, not only physically but socially.

Kameka Pasborg
Cache County

Age 18; **Birthplace** Arizona; **Occupation** None; **Religion** Catholic; **Race/Ethnicity** Mexican-American

Utah is …
Heavenly blue skies in the warm evenings of August.
Utah is …
Beautiful colorful rainbows in the lovely month of
    April
Utah is …
Truly, wonderful mountains painted with orange,
    yellow, and brown in those cool days
    of Autumn.
Utah is …
Bright colors of green around the homes of residents,
    in the warming month of June.
Utah is …
Fluffy white snow falling gently to the ground in
    those chilly days of winter.
Utah is …
Pure clear water running smoothly along the river
    bottoms, with steam rising above the coolness
    of the water.
Utah is …
in Big bushy clouds accumulating the warmth of the
    summer sun.
But most of all
Utah is …
My home … and home is where the heart is.

FACING THE FUTURE TOGETHER

Utah is growing and Utahns are nervous. Almost all of these writers who "look to the future," worry about what they see.

They disagree on what poses the greatest danger. A few fear "… liberals with their insidious intrusions and assaults on morals and fundamental decency." In contrast, others say Utah remains too "conservative" and intolerant of diversity, especially of non-Mormons. More prevalent is the fear of rising gang violence, crime, and drug use. And most fearsome of all is the burgeoning number of people who bring traffic jams, building booms, and pollution. More than anything else, these writers urge preservation of nature in Utah.

Surprisingly, none of these writers looks forward to the increased money they or their children might earn from a growing economy. None cheers because more culture may come with more people. These writers believe Utah is different from other places, and that difference should be preserved. The prospect of change makes old things look better.

—Rod Decker

Craig W. Fuller
Salt Lake County

Age 50; **Birthplace** Salt Lake City; **Occupation** Historian; **Religion** LDS; **Race/Ethnicity** White

Growing up and living in the unique place of Utah presents some interesting personal societal challenges and changes. I have witnessed dramatic changes in the attitudes of Utahns as well as in my own towards Utah's fragile environment. Increasingly, with an ever growing number of Utahns (and the nation as a whole) demanding more of the state's natural and recreational resources, these resources are rapidly and unalterably being changed and consumed, to the detriment to the environment itself as well as the quality of life in Utah. I am much more aware of the fragile and limited nature of the state's environment and now have joined many Utahns in recycling all that can be recycled. I am trying to use the environment in a caring and sensitive way. Utah's society and culture are changing, becoming more cosmopolitan, and yet, it is increasingly becoming more hostile and self-centered. In some ways, my attitude about living in Utah is schizophrenic. I like and enjoy many of the changes occurring in Utah's society. But, on the other hand, many of the peoples' behavior and attitudes grates on my own attitudes toward the state and the people living here. Even as the state is becoming more cosmopolitan it is selling its uniqueness, even with many of its negatives, to the world. We in the state are willing to make available open space for the refuse of the rest of the nation, all in the name of jobs and economic growth. The state is prostrating itself to the world's Olympic movement, not for winter competition but for the glory, recognition, and maybe a few million dollars. But this glory, recognition, and maybe the dollars is at a sacrifice to the environment and to the society generally. This Olympic bid as well as other political and economic developments are forever changing the lifestyle found in the state.

Fay Staples Starr
Sevier County

Age 74; **Birthplace** Kanosh, Utah; **Occupation** Retired Secretary; **Religion** LDS; **Race/Ethnicity** White

To me living here in Sevier County in the Great Salt Lake of Utah means I can see beauty for miles in every direction. I can gaze into the blue, unpolluted sky and watch the ever-changing cloud diorama.

The fertile soil in my garden generously yields an abundance of vegetables and fruits, plus myriads of flowers, trees and shrubs. Richfield is only a short drive from many fantastic natural wonders such as Capitol Reef, Goblin Valley and Bryce's Canyon; as well as historic points of interest like Cove Fort.

My neighbors are friendly and caring. People take pride in their neighborhood. Late at night I can go to the grocery store without fear or being mugged in the parking lot … at least for now it's safe.

On the other hand I see our quality of life being undermined by the ACLU and other liberals with their insidious intrusions and assaults on morals and fundamental decency.

I am disappointed to hear our young people communicating by using vulgar and profane language.

It concerns me that Utah is under siege by the great influx of people from other states who come to Utah to escape the deteriorating conditions in their area, then bring the decadence with them. Dwellings are popping up in fields and creeping up the mountainsides like a plague of measles. After all, Utah is a desert, and while we are still blessed with some wide open spaces, WATER is the limiting factor. Most towns in Utah are experiencing unprecedented growth. It isn't likely that any town has had a knowledgeable hydrologist make an accurate assessment to see how large a population a given town can sustain.

In less than twenty years it is doubtful that any of us

will recognize Utah as the state it once was.

Oh well, Utah currently is still the best place on the planet. I mustn't let my concern for the future rob me of enjoying its present virtues.

Carol D. Starr
Salt Lake County

Age 43; **Birthplace** Salina, Sevier County, Utah; **Occupation** Multi-language Word Processor for LDS Church; **Religion** Church of Jesus Christ of LDS; **Race/Ethnicity** Caucasian

Utah has been my residence since birth, by choice, all of my life. I've lived through the economic busts as well as booms. I've seen more drought years than flood times, more population outflows than inflows (until the past 2–5 years). Because the US Government controls a high percent of Utah, I've watched conservationists and cattlemen battle each other, and the government all of my life. Because Utah's average salaries don't match cost of living, rent raises, taxes (especially property taxes), and the large child population—it seems to me that Utah schools are always advocating more and more educational expenditure.

Born and raised in the Mormon Church, I learned the value and necessity of hard work, courtesy, honesty in all dealings, service to church, community, others in need, and how to be self sufficient. As I grew to maturity, I learned from example and observation that racism, bigotry, intolerance and hatred were enemies to peace and prosperity. Friends of all different races, cultures and creeds have immeasurably enriched my life.

I've vacationed in other U.S. states, but could spend the rest of my life vacationing in Utah. From the magnificent mountains towering over the Wasatch front, the austere challenge of the West Desert, the sparkling beauty of Fish Lake, the awesome wonder of Utah's National Parks, the rugged grandeur of the San Rafael Swell, the wild beauty of Southern Utah's red rocks, the lovely mountain streams and meadows, the fascinating Native American pictographs, the proud pioneer structures; all of it continually fascinates me and rejuvenates my soul.

I thoroughly appreciate and enjoy the various fine arts, cultural, multi-cultural, and sports events offered in Utah. The diversity is such, that I feel anyone who is perpetually bored in Utah must have very shallow interests!

My concerns for Utah's future are that the safe streets and neighborhoods I have lived in all my life are losing that safety by degrees, and I see barred doors and windows in quantities I've never seen before. I'm concerned that our civic and state leaders lack or won't practice the knowledge, foresight and selflessness to wisely utilize and conserve our natural resources of water, land, air and minerals; not to mention wildlife. I'm concerned whether or not they'll manage monetary and human resources wisely and with common sense.

I love Utah very much, and want the quality of life that I was raised with to continue for all Utahns for years to come.

Susan Crosby
Davis County

Age 53; **Birthplace** San Antonio, Texas; **Occupation** Ballet Teacher; **Religion** LDS; **Race/Ethnicity** Caucasian

She is twelve years old, my daughter; she lives in Bountiful, Utah. Forty years ago when I was that age, I too lived in Bountiful—so changed a town it is, that when I wander back in memory to my youth, I feel a loss—deep and lacerating. Forty years ago I was a sixth grader at Stoker School—Bountiful's only grade school. I walked there from my nearby home on Center Street. A year later I attended Bountiful Junior High—the only junior high school in Bountiful. There was no high school at that time, but by the time I was high school age, one had been constructed. My classmates and I were the first students to travel its halls. Only three LDS churches served our small town's religious needs—the 1st, 2nd, and 3rd Wards. I spent many endless and stupefyingly boring Sunday mornings in the 3rd Ward's chapel. Summers were hot with no air-conditioning, and fans were distributed at the entrance. The drowsy flutter of those fans in the still and stuffy meeting hall only intensified the monotony of the services.

The First Ward was and is located on Main Street, which in those days consisted of a few buildings ranged along 2nd South to 4th North—Lee's Barber Shop, Bountiful Lumber, the Clipper Office, library, police station, Bountiful Drug, Servus Drug, DeMont's, the Co-Op, MiLadys, Carr's Stationary, Penny's, Haywood's Market, The Bountiful Theater (where many of us spent our nervous first dates), the Dairy Queen, a doctor's office, the inevitable mortuary, and various residences. I walked Main Street five days a week on my way to junior high, a moody teenager, alone, or with my equally moody girl friends.

When my family moved into a new home on 650 East, my years of exploration began. It was as a high school student that I became infatuated with my surroundings. The new house had been constructed on subdivided orchard acreage. It was also at this time that I began to feel the inexorable onslaught of development: orchards became residential districts with startling rapidity, new houses, new churches, new schools, seemed to sprout from the very soil. One of my favorite spots is now a school ground and parking lot. In the days of my discovery, it was a place of almost mystic allure, an easy walk from my home, up to a stream gently elbowing its way through scrub and foliage. There to my wonder I discovered the heart-rending exqui-

siteness of nature in the glint of a dragonfly wing, a bird cry, a leaf sheen. The stream bank, sequined with sun and shadow, was the playground of a family of skunks, a fearless group which I would often observe tumbling over each other in mock ferocity. Deer followed the stream bed down from the hills. I would glimpse their fleet forms bounding from my approach. How they sprang in a sure-footed, deer-ballet, grand jete. A line from Walter de al Mere, "—lissom, and, jimp, and slim—," describes them perfectly.

I found that same stream on other walks, just a few blocks North from my house and through an unkempt orchard (now a completely developed residential area). Summer evenings it beckoned to me irresistibly...

My dog and I often pass it now, for I am an indefatigable walker to this day, but it is much maligned, much reduced from its former more untrammeled days. Its colorful bed is in many places cemented for flood control as are its sides, its banks fenced for safety, its surroundings encroached upon by human expansion.

My wanderings took me ever further. I discovered other streams, gullies, rises, clearings, paths. Where the Bountiful Golf Course is now located, I found magpie country, deer country, grasshopper, squirrel, and jay country, my special never, never country. One summer day, from a ridge shaped like a jello mold, I traveled east toward a narrow canyon mouth (I later learned its name—North Canyon) which was to become a place, the charm of which would draw me back again and again. The peacefulness of that small canyon and its attending stream has been ravaged by development. The entire area is now the sight of the golf course, houses, condos … I have watched my adored childhood retreats dwindle one by one, and I have felt as though they have been torn from my body in an agonizing amputation. I grieve for the severed limbs and uprooted bodies of so many trees.

Living in Bountiful, living in Utah, means change and growth. My daughter loves present-day Bountiful, as

I did when I was her age—as I still do in a past-nostalgic sort of way. What changes will she witness and remember forty years from now? Will the Utah of the future be a place she will be proud to call home? I hope fervently, yes.

Jane E. Townsend
Salt Lake County

Age 43; **Birthplace** Evanston, Illinois; **Occupation** Director of Admissions (college); **Religion** no formal religious affiliation; **Race/Ethnicity** White

I've chosen to live in Utah because of its natural beauty, but I also feel that I've made a trade-off in exchange for it: the political and social climate of the state is much more conservative and reactionary than I prefer. I've lived here now for 20 years, having moved here in 1974 when I was 22 years old, and during the most of that time I have been able to ignore, laugh off, or shake my head in disbelief at the more blatant manifestations of this extreme conservatism; it never really "got to me" because I have always been able to find friends and colleagues (of all religious backgrounds including LDS) who are open-minded and genuinely appreciate the difference as well as the similarities among people.

Now that I have a 3-year-old daughter, living in Utah means something a little different: I will need to become vigilant and careful to be sure that she also has the chance to be with other children who are different from herself and who are tolerant and accepting of her. Small children do not really "choose" their circle of acquaintances, and I am told by many people that the public schools, particularly in my section of the valley, can be very difficult for children who do not belong to the LDS church because they are excluded from many of the church activities which their classmates participate in and which tend to cement friend-ships outside the schoolroom.

I have even experienced, with her, outright rejection already by the mother of one potential playmate who, after learning that I was not LDS, would no longer return my calls or let our children play together. As painful as that kind of rejection is for me, it is much worse for a small child who cannot possibly comprehend why her friend can't play with her anymore.

Still, the trade-off seems to be worthwhile—at least for now. The desert canyons of southern Utah provide a peace-giving experience which I don't think my husband could live without! And we both love winter sports and are teaching our daughter to ski. The crime rate, while rising, is still lower than in many other urban areas, recreation areas are nearby, and the climate is perfect.

The gang violence bothers us a lot; in fact, we sold our home in Central City three years ago and moved to Holladay after several drive-by shootings occurred in our neighborhood and we began finding used needles in the street gutter in front of our home. We hated to leave, because we believe that middle-income families like ours need to stay in the cities to help keep them economically and socially strong. But with a brand-new baby, the prospect of raising a child in that environment became unacceptable. If gang problems continue to escalate, we may consider moving to a smaller town, but that would require total career changes for both my husband and me.

So—living in Utah is a mixed bag! But after 20 years, I guess it's really my home, and it's still a place where people feel that they have some control over their lives and their futures. That's not possible everywhere, and I am grateful that my daughter will grow up in a place where people believe that their dreams can come true. While it may be tough for her not to belong to the dominant religion, she's a strong and independent girl already and her "differentness" may help her develop those traits even more fully. She'll certainly need them, *wherever* she chooses to live!

Iris A. Rowland
Salt Lake County

Age 87; **Birthplace** Skane, Sweden; **Occupation** Steno-grapher—Housewife; **Religion** Mormon; **Race/Ethnicity** Swedish—Female

Many years ago, when my parents (with my sister and me) came to Utah from Sweden. They believed they were coming to the "Promised Land"—and I still believe it.

Mountains girdled, it became a sanctuary.

The mountains to me are like good friends—always wanting to be together when I was young, in the summer, I hiked to the top of Mt. Olympus, Lone Peak, Twin Peaks, Mt. Timpanogos, etc. In the winter, skiing became an activity beyond compare. This was before there were ski lifts. The sparkling snow and skiing was mine to enjoy—free of charge. There was "Balsom Inn" in Brighton and "Welcome Inn" beyond Parley's "Summits." The mountains call to me. I yearn to be there; happiest when I am.

Utah is still "country" enough to be able to surround our homes with lawn, flowers, brushes, trees, evergreens.

We have beautiful sunrises and sunsets like rainbows; as I watch the sky, a feeling of peace permeates my soul.

To have all four seasons—spring, summer, fall, winter is desirable to me. The climate, too, suits me. Because Utah is partly desert, even when summers are hot, very little humidity exists.

A Christian atmosphere prevails. Here, there are not so many crimes committed; less drunkenness; fewer homeless people. By sending checks to places like the Salvation Army; St Vincent de Paul Center; Rescue Mission, etc. You are able to help families survive hardships and give their uphill struggle toward a good life a boost.

Politically, I wish we were not the most Republican state in the U.S.A. To me, Republican and "Rich" are synonyms. Too, I don't like that Utah has become the major "dumping" place for hazardous radioactive, nuclear waste. But our Republican Governor Mike Leavitt is strongly opposed to it. That, I like.

I'm convinced that there are truly more *good* people in Utah than elsewhere; who, through prayer, let God and Jesus be the guiding influence in their lives.

It's Home!

Tiffany Nichole Rants
Uintah County

Age 14; **Birthplace** Vernal, Utah; **Occupation** Student; **Religion** N/A; **Race/Ethnicity** Caucasian

I personally think living in Utah is a great honor. Utah has many different things that attract people from everywhere. We have cities, and towns, and small countries. I love Utah mostly for the people that live in it. I live in Vernal, Utah; its a small town with alot of people. I very like living here. I don't think we have very good schools in Utah, but I think they're working on their problems. Utah has many problems with teenagers; like violence, truancy, gang activity, and drugs. If they could cut part of the violence they could also get rid of so many problems. Hunger is also a very dramatic problem. Vernal isn't bad for the problems of hunger, but in the larger towns and cities of, like Salt Lake City. They have some horrid hunger problems. Utah also has very high pregnancy rates. They also have high drop out rates. But they have much lower death rates, such as compared to California. Utah is getting much better at its problems, maybe in the future everything will work. Vernal is great but we have nothing to do for teenagers. We could always go to Salt Lake but no one could really afford it, and they don't want to have to go all the way there. I personally think the reason people get into so much trouble is because they don't have anything else to do. I also think the laws need to be enforced or changed so people are doing what they are supposed to do.

Dwight and Sylvia Huntsman
Millard County

Age N/A; **Birthplace** Dwight—Fillmore, Ut; Sylvia—Kansas; **Occupation** Retired USAF; **Religion** Protestant; **Race/Ethnicity** Caucasian

We love living in rural Utah! It is incredibly beautiful; the air is crystal clear, and the quiet and solitude give life a dimension of value often lost in cities. There is a sense of healthiness and a pace slow enough to appreciate small joys. There is ample access and opportunity for fishing, hunting and communing with nature. Having lived in numerous different states, and having traveled the world over, we picked Utah as "the place."

But Utah is not without problems. Some are a wake-up call that we must heed or lose our precious way of life. We seek growth and development and yet these very elements threaten all that we love about this state. Continuous increases in population, in industry, in building, will push into our back country and contaminate our gorgeous mountains and the beauty of our parks. If, indeed, the Olympics come to Park City in 2002 we will pay a horrendous price. Utahns, who are so unique and so wholesome seem willing to sell their souls for the sake of money, growth and "progress." It is a pity. We fear our grandchildren will miss out on all that we hold dear about Utah.

Because of our "wholesomeness" we Utahns often ignore real problems around us. Drugs, alcohol, abuse, gangs, prejudice and narrow-mindedness abound—and yet we smile and say it can't happen here, everything is wonderful. Small towns especially must get beyond denial of such problems and start to assess and deal with them. Our greatest enemy is not from the outside, but from within our own communities. The real progress we should be seeking is a willingness to be honest and open, to admit our faults and work on improving ourselves …

Dwight is the fifth generation of a non-LDS family in Utah. It can be lonely for those of a faith other than LDS. Though the "dominant church" tries to be generous in its attitude toward others, it still ignores us, belittles our beliefs, give favors to its own, and constantly tries to convert us. This attitude creeps into politics and government on both the local and state level. Our children suffer the most. Schools allow LDS missionaries to visit, have LDS seminaries on or next to the campus and give release time for seminary classes. Such privileges are not granted to other religions. Our children are often ridiculed and criticized for their beliefs. They feel minimized and devalued. But it does give us the chance to identify with the feelings and needs of other minority groups. Many of us have become more devout in our faith because of the challenge.

After a career in the United States Air Force which took him all over the world, Dwight came back to Fillmore, the small town in which he was born and raised. The mountains and scenery in Europe, South America, Canada could not compare to the beauty in Utah. And it is not only the physical beauty surrounding us, but also the beauty of the people living here whom he had known from his youth.

And so we love living in rural Utah. Though our fellow Utahns are a bit provincial and sometimes naive, we are proud and happy to be two of them!

Louise Hartvigsen
Salt Lake County

Age 37; **Birthplace** Provo, Utah; **Occupation** Homemaker;
Religion LDS; **Race/Ethnicity** White

When it's possible, on Memorial Day I visit the Peona cemetery, the town where I grew up. Abraham and Lydia Marchant, my Great-great Grandparents, are buried there, some of the first settlers of Peoa, sent by Brigham Young. Generations of both sides of my family are also buried there, including my father. Most of my childhood was spent in the home that my Great-Grandfather and Grandfather built at the beginning of this century. My father was born in that house; he died there. When I take the time to reflect, I realize how those who went before cleared the land for farming, worked hard to build their homes, raise their families. Living in Utah means being connected with the past, my heritage.

The mountains of Utah give me a sense of orientation. Whether in the town of my youth in Summit County or Salt Lake City, my home for more than the past decade, with the mountains visible, I feel grounded with a sense of direction. When in other places, the sprawling run-on cities of Southern California, the green, wooded cities and suburbs of the East or the flat areas of the Midwest, I miss the orientation of the mountains. Living in Utah means knowing both where I've come from and where I am.

I've hiked to the top of Timpanogas. I've cross-country skied in the canyons east of Salt Lake Valley, the Uinta mountains and in the spectacular red rock of Bryce Canyon. I've watered skied in the cold, yet glass-like water of Bear Lake as well as in the magnificent setting of Lake Powell. I've picnicked in alpine mountains and on the shores of an island in the Great Salt Lake. I even commuted to a job in Utah's west desert and watched the change of seasons in what many assume to be a lifeless place. Living in Utah means being able to appreciate the beautiful variety of spectacular scenery.

I was raised by faithful LDS parents and still embrace that faith. I love seeing Mormon temples throughout the state, whether it's the Salt Lake Temple where I was married, other pioneer temples in Manti or Logan, or the newer, modern temples in Bountiful or Jordan River. I have felt at home in LDS wards in a small town and in downtown Salt Lake City. But my life has also been enriched by other Utahns, native or recent "transplants," who do not share my religion. Living in Utah means living with and learning from people from many cultures, religions and backgrounds.

I am thirty-six years old. I remember making a detour through Emigration Canyon when I-80 was first constructed through Parley's Canyon. Shopping in downtown Salt Lake used to mean wearing a dress and walking between ZCMI and Auerbachs on Main Street. My father taught school in Park City before it was a famous resort destination. Now the interstates are full to overflowing, with projected growth only adding to the traffic problems. I worked in several malls during my ten year career in retail. My first job after college was in Crossroads Mall in downtown Salt Lake, the mall which helped bring an end to the old way of shopping. I've watched the growth along the Wasatch Front spill over into adjoining counties and drastically change lives for those rural areas. Living in Utah means enjoying an excellent quality of life, but being concerned about how that life will change with more growth.

Keri Nigbur
Salt Lake County

Age 16; **Birthplace** Salt Lake; **Occupation** Student; **Religion** Mormon; **Race/Ethnicity** Caucasion

UTAH, UTAH

I've lived here since I was born
but that was back when
there were fields and fields of corn.

I woke up every morning and
helped mom milk the cow.
We wake up early daily
I really don't know now.

Everything is different
Now in 1995.
I'm amazed by the way things are today,
and that I'm still alive.

Instead of peace,
people want war.
Instead of less,
people want more.

It used to be that
people would work together.
Now these days they kill
the bird only for a feather.

I really hope that
what I say is wrong.
Or the Utah I remember
will soon, all be gone.

Tosha Koyle
Davis County

Age 14; **Birthplace** N/A; **Occupation** N/A; **Religion** LDS; **Race/Ethnicity** White

While I really didn't ever think about that before. I guess one thing I enjoy about Utah is the four seasons. The weather is just right for each season. I like how the spring is warm not to hot. I like how the summers are nice and hot. I like how the falls are nice and cool and the winters are snowy and cold. I love that it is so peaceful here. There aren't any gangs here like in California and I hope we can keep it that way. I love how Utah gives you a bit of both country and city. Since I come from Idaho this is really important to me.

I think we need to do something though. We need to stop and clean up graffiti and gangs. There is a lot of bad going on around us teens. Most of us don't help clean it up, only make it worse. People also need to learn to find a different way to get around besides cars. The pollution in Utah is so bad. In the factory area is so bad I can't stand it. If we could take care of these few things Utah can and will almost be "Heaven on Earth."

Karen L. Garrett
Salt Lake County

Age 61; **Birthplace** San Francisco, California; **Occupation** Teacher/Media Coordinator; **Religion** None; **Race/Ethnicity** Caucasian

Having lived in Utah for most of my 60 years it means something different to me than to younger people and/or those who have recently moved here.

To me, living in Utah means crowded highways, too

many people, uncontrolled building on every open field and back lot, destruction of the canyons by developers and the ski industry, over-crowded schools with constant tax increases to pay for them (and those with the most number of kids paying the least!) a once unique "down-town" that now looks like all other down-towns, large impersonal grocery stores taking the place of small corner stores where you felt your business was appreciated … the Olympic bid being shoved down our throats, buildings, such as the Salt Palace, paid for with tax dollars, torn down because some government official decided it should be torn down, etc and etc. The list could go on and on! Seldom does a day go by that you can't see some kind of destruction of what was once a pleasant place to live!

For the first time ever, my husband and I are considering moving out of state upon retirement.

Whitney Esther Barrus
Salt Lake County

Age 15; **Birthplace** St. Marks Hospital, Salt Lake City; **Occupation** N/A; **Religion** L.D.S.; **Race/Ethnicity** Caucasian

For the most part I like Utah. It's pretty and has a lot of nice scenery. One of the things I like most about Utah is Lake Powell. My family goes there a lot. Another thing I like is the snow. It's great for skiing! One thing I *really* hate is the pollution. From our school, we can see the valley and on days it's polluted it looks *really* gross! I am glad I live here though because it is a lot nicer then a lot of other places I've been. I think one thing that needs to stop is the crime. Another thing that bugs me is how people keep building houses on the mountain. It's kind of dangerous and it ruins the view but the worst thing is it is kicking animals out of their homes. I think we need to put an end to these things. Especially the pollution because no one will even be here

in one hundred years if it doesn't stop.

I think there should be more women professional sports in Utah. There should also be more soccer (mens and women). I like how most of my family lives here because it is nice to see them whenever I want to. I like the weather here. It's perfect in the summer and even though it's cold in the winter, I like the snow. A lot of people hate it, but I'm glad we have it. I really like the scenery and parks. There are a lot of National Parks here and I enjoy them a lot. We have a lot more than other states and I think it really adds to life here.

John Snarr Hummel
Davis County

Age 73; **Birthplace** Salt Lake City, Utah; **Occupation** Retired; **Religion** L.D.S.; **Race/Ethnicity** Caucasian

I have lived in Utah for over 70 years. I have been deeply saddened by the changes that have taken place in that time: the hideous growth that has occurred (especially that due to immigration), the influx of gangs, the gridlock on the freeways, the pollution (air AND people). I bitterly resent The Department of Economic Development, the Department of Tourism, the Olympics Committee, the Chamber of Commerce, and anyone else who is trying to entice people to come here and take up room we no longer have. When a wise fisherman has found a good fishing hole, he NEVER advertises it—he knows that other fishermen will quickly overrun it and there goes the fishing hole. Thus it is with Utah.

Back in the days when I was very young I thought I lived in the Garden of Eden. But I have seen that Garden of Eden change into a trash heap. I'm sure there are good places to live in Utah, but they are DEFINITELY not along the Wasatch Front. A 95 year old friend told me, "I would rather be in the city cemetery than be a witness to what is going on in Centerville." He was referring to the growth taking place here.

What does living in Utah mean to me? It means looking forward with dread to a vastly accelerated decrease in the quality of life here. It means looking back with deep sorrow for the Utah that used to be.

Marcus Boyer
Utah County

Age N/A; **Birthplace** N/A; **Occupation** N/A; **Religion** N/A; **Race/Ethnicity** N/A

I've been told there were times, not long ago, when my father used to drink from a brook in the mountains. He used to gulp clear, cold water from a spring near Squaw Lake. In my time the water was still crisp and cold, but I did not drink it as it broke the rocks. When I visited the wild and untamed land, I pumped my water through a purifier. My father drank, I pumped, and my children will do what?

Every "Labor Day," my father took his two oldest sons to the Uinta mountains to hike, camp and fish. This wonderful and renewing activity was anxiously anticipated all year. With eager preparations our little convoy would organize our backpacks to fit the most amount of useable material in the least amount of space, while at the same time never compromising for weight. We each included our favorite camping supplies and our most useful gadgets. Dad brought his small baking unit to accompany each of our tiny camp stoves. We would don our cotton denim, our plaid wool shirts, and our sturdy leather hiking boots. All was loaded into the car and we sped toward our rugged destination. Our convoy reached the Henry's Fork Trail Head early Sunday morning after a lengthy car ride. A common silence rose as we strapped on our burdens and

began our trek into the wilderness. Hours and miles of hiking behind us, we looked for the perfect camping site. Inevitably we found the ideal spot every trip. For the next few days, our homes were based in a tent, and our activities rotated around the "cooking rock." Days in the mountains were spent summiting a mountain, fishing, or busily doing nothing in general. These trips are some of the most cherished memories I own. My fellow campers and I not only felt recharged after days of blissful peace, but our family came closer together as our surrounding spread out. It was not necessary to prod our souls and reveal our feelings in group sessions, we needed only to enjoy the same peace together.

Years from now, as I suppose, years will pass, I wonder how I will spend my Labor Days. I wonder if my children and I will enjoy relative seclusion next to cold, snow capped mountains away from the stress of society. It worries me that they will not be able to draw their water from a natural spring. They may need not find the perfect camp site with fire wood to spare. Perhaps they will not meet a cow moose with her calf as they cross over summer feeding grounds. Maybe wild flowers and lush undergrowth will not tickle their bare legs in the morning. If these things do come about, as it seems now may be irreversible, a beautiful part of our state will have been lost. It is my hope that beauty will remain.

Stephan M. Borton
Uintah County

Age 42; **Birthplace** Michigan; **Occupation** Teacher; **Religion** Free thinker; **Race/Ethnicity** White/German

Life in Utah is a true menagerie of experiences. There are people who will hate you and even harm you, just because you look different or think differently from them.

There are folks who will do anything in their power to help you. On my first visit to Utah in 1976, I well remember the kindly, elderly Latino gentleman who helped me. My car had broken down in Wyoming and had to go to Salt Lake for a new rear axle. After three days of living in a campground, I got lost trying to walk across the City to the repair shop. This man was working in his yard and I asked him for directions. Rather than having me walk, he insisted upon driving me and refused to take a penny for his gas or time. Since that time I've met many people in various parts of the State, who are filled with the same feelings of kindness and compassion for their fellow person.

On the other hand, I have also met many people full of hate and bitterness towards anyone whose parents were not born in Utah, whose skin color is not as white as theirs, whose hair is longer or politics more liberal. When I moved to Vernal 12 years ago, some folks loved telling me, over and over, how Vernal is the town where the "Cowboys" beat up Robert Redford right on main street! I was told I'd better watch out where I went or what I did or I would get beat up, too, because of my long hair and liberal thinking. Just last year one of our County Commissioners told me it was their job to protect the "custom and culture" of the Uintah Basin. When I asked what he meant by "custom and culture," he informed me the only "custom and culture" that counted was that brought by the pioneers over those mountains in the wagons when the Mormons arrived. Many people, like this man, are very good at making non-Mormons feel like second class citizens. All too often being a non-Mormon in Utah is similar to being black in Mississippi in the 1950's. Even as I write this, I wonder if I could lose my job for daring to say such a thing. Many freedoms which other Americans enjoy without thinking about are not so easily enjoyed here.

For all their expressed love of children and admiration of learning, traditional Utahns seem to love money even more. It hurts me to see we have the most over-crowded and underfunded schools of anywhere in the nation. Child abuse and neglect rates are much too high for a people who love children so. Even Vernal has a growing gang problem. However living in Utah is much like living in Japan, in that it is considered rude to publicly discuss our problems.

Utah has some of the best features of any state. Our National Parks and Forests are a wonderland. Most people are truly nice people. Still there is a nasty side to things as well. I've lived here 12 years and still wonder if I will ever be truly accepted as an equal member of Utah society? I work hard, pay my taxes, do volunteer work, live a clean life, yet still I do not feel a complete part of my community.

I've made some of the best friends of my life in Utah, but it is sad to say most of them were not born here.

On balance I've found more things to love about Utah than to hate, so I hope to stay here. A lot of things are changing, whether the "old timers" like it or not. I just hope the changes are for the better.

Thomas Glen Alexander
Utah County

Age 60; **Birthplace** Logan, UT; **Occupation** Professor of History; **Religion** LDS; **Race/Ethnicity** Celtic

For me, Utah means home. I grew up in Ogden during World War II. The junction city provided an exciting location for a young boy largely because of the new defense installations that the federal government constructed there. The city experienced a flux and change never again achieved until the recent rapid growth.

After studying at the University of Utah, Weber State, and Utah State, I went to Berkeley for a Ph.D. in history. In the meantime I had married—to a Utah woman, Marilyn Johns—and I returned as a professor of history at

BYU. We have lived in Utah again almost continuously since 1964. I have always believed that we made the right decision to return to Utah after graduate school. I have associated with colleagues who share the same research interests that I do, and the interaction has stimulated my work and, I am sure, theirs as well.

Utah has been a great place for Marilyn and me to raise our children. In general they have met and associated with good friends who have helped them become better people and more caring human beings.

My only regret is that so many Utahns seem so much more conservative than I am. I would like to see in more of our people a sense of compassion for the poor rather than calculating first how measures will impact on the wealthy. I would also like to see Utahns become more concerned about the damage we are doing to the environment rather than calculating first how much the necessary environmental protection will hurt business.

Nevertheless, even with its problem I prefer to live here because of the general quality of life and because of the generally good people who have chosen to live here as well.

"Mt. Ben Lomond, Ogden." Submitted by Robert T. Beckstead, Weber County.

Elisabeth Kealohilani Rossean

Utah County

Age 18; **Birthplace** Monterey Park, Calif; **Occupation** N/A;
Religion Latter Day Saint; **Race/Ethnicity** Hawaiian American

As the great founder of Utah, Brigham Young, entered the Salt Lake Valley he said, "This is the place." The pioneers believed that Utah was "the place," the place where they could govern themselves and raise their families well, in happiness. I'm not sure that Utah today is what they would have envisioned.

Utah may not be what they hoped. Various factors contribute to a difficult and unstable society today. Some possess extravagant amounts while others are struggling just to live. Utah means so much to so many people, it is a place where they have contributed their lives and work. But Utah is changing. Things need to be done to bring it back up to the level that it has been in years past. Crime and misfortune have changed some people's views of our wonderful state. Something needs to happen.

We need to start with the children, the leaders of tomorrow. Many of the social "elite" believe that the well being of the people follows the economy in level of importance. Children are growing up in schools and communities all over the world not knowing what a difference they can make. They believe that they don't matter to anyone and are then accepted into groups you would call juvenile delinquents.

I have seen many good programs start in the last few years which can really make a difference to the future. Activities have been organized to keep teenage kids safe, off of the streets, out of the gangs, and off of drugs. They have tried to give kids something productive and fun to do to occupy their time.

Still others have seen the need to start at the bottom with the young children. AIDS and drug awareness programs have been implemented into many elementary school programs. Kids have been introduced early on to the choices that they will be faced with, and they have been taught to make an educated decision. I have worked somewhat with the D.A.R.E. program in schools (Drug Abuse Resistance Education). The sixth graders I have seen in the program have loved it and have learned so much about how to be strong, have self-esteem, and stand up for themselves.

Recently, measures have been taken to take this program from the schools. They believe that it needs to be taken to the colleges. If a person is going to be introduced to drugs or alcohol, the real life fact of the matter is that it will happen in the teenage years. Taking beneficial programs such as D.A.R.E. out of the schools will only harm. Kids will be uninformed and in turn, won't know how to make the right decisions. These kids need guidance, and real help if they are going to make Utah a better place for future generations.

Are the leaders of Utah seeing the whole picture? Utah is a wonderful state, beautiful and prosperous. But it is going downhill. The fact is, children are the key. Being a high school student myself, I know what the world is like for kids like me. I know what goes on when parents and teachers aren't looking. I also know that you can't teach an old dog new tricks. Nothing will change the way that we have formed ourselves in these crucial years of our lives. You can't change us when we're already adults. Think about the future now. Together we can change tomorrow. This is the place. The place where all of our dreams *can* come true.

Winagene Church Eyre

Juab County

Age 68; **Birthplace** Panguitch, Utah; **Occupation** Retired;
Religion L.D.S.; **Race/Ethnicity** White

… This year has contained events that I had not anticipated participating in at this age. This period of time has been called "the aging of America." People over eighty are the fastest growing segment of our population.

My husband is seventy four and I am sixty eight and both of our Mothers are still living. My mother-in-law, who is one hundred and one years is living with us now. Her mind is as sharp as it ever was, but she is extremely frail, weighing only eighty pounds. She eats but has frequent anxiety attacks, sometimes brought on by fear of death. We feel good when she is with us because we know she is receiving loving care.

There is a feeling of guilt always with you when you are senior citizens whose parents need special care. My Mother is eighty nine and I would love to have her with me all the time, but she hates to be in Nephi and while she is here all she talks about is getting back to Panguitch.

We have a hospital and clinic in Nephi. As a senior citizen with supplementary health insurance, I have access without much charge to fairly good health care. This year brought a gall bladder procedure, called in the language of 1994, a lapraroscopic cholecystectomy … a very simple procedure, they said. Two days in the hospital and I would be a new woman. Well, I had heard from Hillary Rodham Clinton that health care was expensive, now I have personal knowledge of that fact. This procedure, with a follow up procedure called an Endoscopy of the bile duct and the pancreas, at Utah Valley Hospital seven months later, cost over $10,000. I am recording this because the high cost of health care is really a major problem for Utah and the nation at the end of Utah's first one hundred years of statehood.

Living in Utah has been stressful, interesting, fun and rewarding. The years pass swiftly and when we pause to record what has happened, we wonder why we haven't tried harder and done more but we are fortunate to have a good library in our town, so while I wish I would accomplish more, too often, I find myself in my recliner reading yet another novel and looking forward to bedtime and my "adjustamatic" bed with an old fashioned feather tick on top of the orthopedic mattress.

Sarah (Tad) Loutensock

Salt Lake County

Age 81; **Birthplace** Magna, Utah; **Occupation** School Teacher; **Religion** Latter Day-Saint; **Race/Ethnicity** N/A

… Many years ago one of my good friends with a heart of gold opened her home to welfare children. She kept in close touch with her case-worker and tried to conform to the rules one of which was not to ask the whereabouts of a child once it was taken away by the case-worker. My friend opened her home to dozens of children knowing that no matter how much she loved them they belonged to the birth parents.

The welfare children came and went with his own special problem—fear of the dark, fear of people, and fear of being left alone. One little girl was very special. She was a pretty child with blond curly hair, blue eyes and a sweet disposition. When the case-worker took her away my friend had an unshakable desire to know what had become of her. She broke the rules and visited the child in her real home. The little girl was sitting on a cement floor—cold, wet and dirty, crying, holding a nursing bottle half-filled with clabbered milk. My friend never again had the desire to break the rules.

When I was much younger my niece invited me to visit the homeless shelter in the heart of Salt Lake City. Her ward was taking dinner to the people living there.

As our car pulled up in front of the shelter I noticed a group of men standing on the south side of the building. Later, my niece explained to me that no men are allowed inside the building only women and children. I remember thinking, Where do these men sleep? What do they eat?

Inside the building the homeless women and children were waiting for us. When the dinner was served I lined up and took a tray filled with delicious food. Not until later did I learn that there was not enough food for the ward members to join with the women and children in a spirit of comraderie which only eating together can bring. In taking a tray of food I was completely out of order but I wanted to visit with these people, to know something of their plans, hopes and dreams. The women and children sitting close to me, although polite, did not seem inclined to talk much beyond yes and no.

After the women and children had finished eating, the ward members presented a short musical program. When they were finished the audience applauded. As soon as the applauding ceased the audience cleared out of the hall like magic. They just faded away into thin air. I had lost my last opportunity to talk with someone, to know something of their hopes and dreams.

Before we left I asked my niece if we could look around for a few minutes. We passed down a deserted hall but we didn't see anyone we didn't hear anyone—not the voice of a scolding mother or the sound of a crying child. A door did not open; a door did not close. The eerie silence was broken only by the sound of our own footsteps echoing through the empty halls and our own subdued voices which seemed out of place.

Were these homeless people sending us a message? Were they saying, "We have eaten your food, we have clapped for your singing, we have laughed at your jokes, now go away and leave us alone." On the way home my very attractive niece who is my namesake seemed very pleased with her performance of her young men and women. They had helped prepare the food, they had presented the program and they had helped to clean up. All six of the "full of the old Nick" young people would be one step closer either to their Duty to God or their Community Service awards.

In Salt Lake City some of the homeless are unrepented drug addicts and alcoholics. They receive no welfare. They live in as out-of-the-way places as possible—under the viaduct or in Pioneer Park. Some of these people have lost all respect for themselves and others. They urinate and defecate wherever and whenever they feel like it. They are beyond caring either for man or for God. They are without hope.

A few of the rich people feel that these poor people are the "dregs of society." A small minority of the rich people go about with high heads and stiff necks mincing as they go asking only one favor—that these "dregs of society" stay out of their sight. These homeless people who receive no welfare have two aims in life—to stay out of sight of the rich and to stay out of sight of the police. When their numbers become too great the police are called out to "clean up the place." The police break up the camp of the viaduct people destroying their makeshift garbage-can firebox, their tin-can dishes, and their dirty, ragged blankets. The police also periodically drive the drug addicts and prostitutes from Pioneer Park. Where do they go? Who knows? Who cares? And yet, in a religious sense, they are our brothers and sisters. …

The state of Utah is called Zion. Moses, many thousands of years ago, defined Zion as a place where there are no poor. The following quote is taken from "A Compendium of the Gospel" written by Apostle Franklin D. Richards and Elder James A. Little in 1916 p. 247: "To the Elder or Saint who has studied the revelations of our Lord

Jesus Christ, as given in the Doctrine and Covenants, by the light of the Holy Spirit, it is most abundantly manifest that the human family has departed, degenerated or apostatized from original methods in their secular or business concerns, as truly, and as extensively, as they have in their spiritual interests, or the matters of their religious faith."…

Zion is a place where there are no poor. The saints as the keepers of God's storehouse have a wide, wide river to cross.

Kylie Fagan
Utah County

Age 16; **Birthplace** American Fork Hospital; **Occupation** N/A; **Religion** Latter Day Saint; **Race/Ethnicity** N/A

To me it means my family and religion. For awhile in my life it meant safety. I felt safe tucked away in my nice quiet community. As I have gotten older my feeling of safety is taken by fears. Gang violence was never a big problem when I was little, now to me and many others it is a threat. Utah is my state, I would never want to leave. My expectations of having my children grow up here are changing rapidly. I want my kids to be exposed to the life I grew up with but with gangs and violence I can't. I know Utah will never become California, and as long as my family and I are safe Utah will mean living in safety. Lets try to keep it safe.

Carl J. Chindgren
Salt Lake County

Age 79; **Birthplace** Salt Lake City, Utah; **Occupation** Retired Chemical Engineer; **Religion** N/A; **Race/Ethnicity** White

As a native born in Salt Lake City nearly 79 years ago, I have lived during a period of the greatest technological discovery and change in human history, and have observed and seen the effects of the change on city life and the natural world in which we live. In each of the periods of my life from childhood thru' the educational, career, the scenic natural lands and areas abundant in this state are available for everyone to view and enjoy…

In looking back in time it now seems strange that the main route out of Salt Lake Valley to the east into Parley's Canyon was up 21st South to above Wasatch Blvd and then south to the entrance. Twenty-first South also was for quite a long time considered to be a test hill used by many people to determine how far their car could go up the hill in high gear. My first memories of traveling up Parley's Canyon to the summit recalls traveling on a gravel road along a tree and shrubby lined meandering stream. A railroad track detracted somewhat from the serenity and attractiveness of the lower canyon. Further up the canyon the train track circled and turned many times to gain elevation and at considerable distance from the road. There was a combination service station and restaurant at the summit at about 7,000 feet elevation. After several visits to Parley's summit we were taken by surprise to find quarter slot machines available for patrons of the establishment. A year or two later the slot machines were no longer available.

The early visits to the summit of Parley's Canyon were particularly memorable for the view of the hills to the East and the higher mountains appearing in the distance. This was like seeing for the first time an area still untouched by man. This feeling for the distant country (The High

Uintas) was exhilarating and exciting. A neighbor friend invited me to their mountain cabin situated in the above area on the upper Provo River at the Soapstone Bridge turnoff about 16 miles above Kamas. The road from Kamas was a single lane twisting dirt road cut through tall evergreen forest. The cabin was virtually the only cabin between Kamas and Trail Lake another 16 miles further up the canyon. The cabin was located about 50 feet from the river next to huge tall pine greenery and wild flowers. Along the road the vegetation became even better as the high lake country of the High Uintas was approaching. The high Uinta Mountain area became my favorite close by country for fishing and back packing.

Parley's Canyon will also be remembered as the route to the Ecker Hill ski jump in the late 1920's and early 30's. The hill was located on the mountain above the old Rasmussen Ranch golf course and beyond the right curve of Interstate 80. World record jumps of up to 300 feet were made on the steep hill by Alf Engen and other professional world class jumpers. Thousands of people gathered at Ecker Hill to watch the jumps. My contribution at the time was to help in tramping and grooming of the hill. My skill in jumping extended to jumps of a little over 100 feet and winning a meet in the Class C division. During this period of exciting jumping, there was no one in the Salt Lake area experienced and capable of downhill and slalom skiing. Skiers obtained better skiing after the construction of a gondola transporting skiers to the top of the mountain. Small privately owned rope tows flourished for a short time until ski areas were taken over by commercial operators of rope tows. The design and perfection of chair lifts stimulated the sport and promoted the development of ski resorts at Park City, Brighton, and Alta in the Big and Little Cottonwood Canyons and other areas after gaining proficiency in the sport of downhill and slalom skiing many enjoyable winters were spent on the slopes of Brighton and Alta. I participated in races but never excelled. The best I

did was 3rd place in a cross-country race. Alta was skied prior to any ski resort development. The ski resorts have become big business catering mostly to well-to-do skiers.

Mill Creek Canyon offers excellent scenery and hikes to areas overlooking Salt Lake Valley. Hiking trails lead to Lamb's Canyon (up from Parley's Canyon) and two different trails lead to upper and lower sections of Big Cottonwood Canyon. Both Big and Little Cottonwood Canyons are rich in early history, Brighton for timber harvesting and early pioneer celebrations, and Alta for its mining. Big Cottonwood Canyon particularly in the lower section because of the exposed colorful massive slanting rock layers is the most picturesque canyon. This canyon has also provided the best stream fishing and fishing in lakes above Brighton. In early years horse riding was permitted in the canyons but now both dogs and horses are not permitted in order to avoid contamination of the culinary water supplied to the valley. The glaciers formed in Little Cottonwood Canyon during the ice age traveled all the way down the canyon and dipped into old Lake Bonneville. During the passage the entire canyon was gouged out to a V shape. There are many hiking trails in both canyons leading to lakes, high passes and impressive peaks.

There have been big changes in the canyons over time, primarily for construction of roads to accommodate the increased traffic for both summer and winter recreationists and those visiting the canyons for their still great scenery. Parley's Canyon has been completely changed and buried in the lower section to allow for the high volume of traffic on Interstate 80 passing thru the canyon. Dry Creek canyon is a narrow roadless canyon of interest to hikers, however the entrance to the canyon has been marred by dumping. The old trail going directly up the U on the mountain has been lost to new home subdivisions.

After having graduated from Stewart school, and East High School in 1933, the outlook on life became more serious. There seemed to be no answers to what I should do with my life. Since jobs for young teenagers were very scarce, joining the CCC's seemed the only thing to do. At Mount Pleasant where I was stationed, the daily passage of a train, blowing its whistle, made me so homesick that at the first opportunity, after a few months of work, I returned to Salt Lake City. Through luck and help from friends I obtained a job as a janitorial assistant employed by the University of Utah enabling me to start working my way through college. The work paid 33 cents per hour, and the cost per quarter exclusive of books was about $45.00. After 5 long years of hard work and study, I graduated in 1940 with a B.S. degree in engineering. I was very disillusioned to find that jobs along the entire Wasatch front were practically non-existent, even ditch digging jobs. With persistence and exceptionally good luck I obtained a career job in my chosen vocation, and of all things, returned to the University campus where I was employed in metallurgical research for 32 years. Yes, I was very lucky and thankful to be able to stay in Salt Lake City. As time and work permitted I continued over the years to enjoy winter skiing and hiking and back-packing trips in the primitive high mountain areas of Utah, Wyoming, Montana, and as well to camp in the beautiful areas of central and southern Utah, and desert areas of Arizona.

During the period just before the start of World War II and during the years shortly after the War, there was considerable expansion and growth in Salt Lake in war related industries. The University of Utah more than quadrupled in size expanding on to the area of Fort Douglas reservation.

In 1946, the building of homes in the southeast part of the valley had not reached 39th South. The area above 25th East was wide open fields with an occasional farm house in sight. This was a period of slow to moderate growth and ideas were expressed that this was a favorable time to consider land use planning for sensible guidance in construction and location of homes and small businesses.

The electorate were also presented with a bonding proposal to obtain money for purchasing areas needed for parks and recreation. The bond proposal was rejected and land use planning was cast aside in favor of allowing continued freedom for builders and developers. During this period of moderate city growth statements were made that we in Salt Lake Valley were smart enough to not make the mistakes that had plagued California with exploding population growth, massive traffic, housing, and other related problems. Steady moderate growth continued through the 1950's and increased fairly rapidly into the 1970's and 1980's. The entire section of Southeast Valley was filling up to the mouth of Big Cottonwood Canyon and beyond. From the years 1985 to the present time of 1995 there was explosive building growth that extended to Draper, the last open section in the Southeast end of the valley. The development and building activity was even greater in the Western valleys since the remaining sites in the southeast became prohibitively expensive. The building in the West was beginning to approach the Oquirrh mountain ranges so that in a few more years the valley would be essentially completely occupied.

Utah officials have been too successful and anxious to stimulate industrial development and population growth. We in the valley are now suffering the consequences. The great pinch from people migrating into the valley became apparent as early as 1987 to 1990. The effect of this influx of tens of thousands of new residents was virtually catastrophic. Streets and highways are overloaded so that traffic congestion and gridlock, along with daily occurring accidents, have strained drivers patience and taken the joy out of driving. There is little if any possibility of improving traffic conditions on the freeways. The traffic at all of the main city street intersections is mostly stop and go, and is backed up for blocks at peak traffic times. This explosive growth caught city and state officials unprepared and confronted with virtually unsolvable problems. The quality of life in the valley has been adversely affected for years to come with unpredictable consequences.

The beautiful mountains surround Salt Lake City, the attractive natural landscape, and the near by canyons have all been major attractions for visitors and tourists alike. However, there is now hardly a single noteworthy natural surface landscape feature that remains preserved and unaltered by man. Many picturesque mountain slope springs have been capped or covered, ponds and wet lands have been dried-up for homes and apartments. A few small areas set aside as wildlife sanctuaries have been neglected and abused. One of the more beautiful meadow-like riparian areas along Cottonwood Creek (Spring Run) has disappeared. Incredulous changing zoning laws have allowed developers to build homes higher and higher up the mountains. Hiking trails to many side canyons have been restricted or blocked. The best agricultural lands cultivated in the past have been sold to developers. A geological mark of historical significance in the valley is the old Lake Bonneville ledge at the base of Mount Olympus. The ledge is an excellent site for a nature walk and park for viewing the valley. A home built on the ledge now blocks use of an existing trail and development of a park.

This apparent neglect or lack of effort to preserve the natural beauty of the Salt Lake Valley is difficult to understand. Hopefully the oversight has not been intentional. However, since our congressional representatives over the years have also shown great aversion to preservation of the beautiful natural areas in Southern Utah, the so called wilderness areas, there is a feeling that perhaps governing authorities have had an unrevealed agenda to develop and populate the state as completely as possible as resources would allow with little or no regard for the natural values. The world is changing rapidly and hopefully the people of Utah will change course after realizing the potential seriousness of excessive population growth, more than what has so recently happened to life in the Salt Lake Valley.

The following was gathered from the Local daily news, and should not be dismissed as of little importance. Population growth is the cause of worsening World conditions rather than the solution for world's ills!!! An unfortunate paradox is that our present economic system requires a continual, expanding growth in population to maintain prosperity. Another unsettling thought has recently been postulated. According to scientists 300 species of animal and plant life are lost per day in the world with 5 to 10 of these as large species. This rate of biodiversity loss per day in the world with past mass extinctions, and from fossil record we are in an early and highly accelerated stage of biodiversity crisis that could possibly bring mass extinction of all species within the next 50 to 100 years.

Population growth is the main cause of rain forest destruction and loss of animal and plant habitat. Not to heed forewarning signs to slow population growth and begin actions to preserve and protect all animals and plant habit, including our Utah scenic lands, would be irresponsible and uncaring behavior. We should at least do as much as possible to insure a better life and a more natural life for future generations.

Kathy L. Archibald
Weber County

Age 53; **Birthplace** Virginia, Idaho; **Occupation** Teacher; **Religion** L.D.S. (Mormon); **Race/Ethnicity** Caucasian

Before I share what living in Utah means to me, let me write a little about my life. I was born in Idaho but moved to Utah when I was nine years old so the majority of my life has been spent in Utah. I am married, have five children and five grandchildren. I live in an upper middle class neighborhood and both my husband and myself hold masters degrees. I have been teaching school for the past ten years. This year has not been the easiest year I have taught. There are 22 boys and 10 girls in my class. Although this had not been an easy year for me I do have many students who are eager to learn and who come from supportive parents.

School is very socially oriented. Most children come to school to have a good time first and to learn second. Many children that I teach come from dysfunctional families—families where there is only one parent, families who use drugs, and families who have a lot of crime experiences.

The students wear the latest style of clothing—very expensive jeans (about $50.00), expensive shoes ($150.00), and have pierced ears (even many boys have pierced ears).

I'm concerned at this time with the increasing number of children involved in gangs and gang-related activity (graffiti, violence, drugs, etc.).

Utah has had an increase in people migrating to the state because they desire the conservative way of life here and the emphasis that "Mormons" place on the family. However, once here the "migrants" proceed to try to change the very way of life that attracted them to Utah in the first place. I find this very interesting!

I love living in Utah! I've lived in Calif. for a few of my married years and love living beneath the clear, blue skies and the majestic mountains. I love the big, fluffy, white clouds that drift over us in the summer. I love the stability of the Church influence in Utah and the underlying standard of living that comes with its presence.

Even though I sometimes worry about my posterity as society continues to change I am so thankful to be living in Utah. I hope that 100 years from now will see my worries to be for nothing and my posterity enjoying life in Utah even more than I have.

Jordan Elise Smith
Salt Lake County

Age 10; **Birthplace** Salt Lake City; **Occupation** Student; **Religion** N/A; **Race/Ethnicity** American

I think UTAH is a clean place to live. It only takes me four minutes to walk to school. I've lived in UTAH my whole life time. UTAH has tall mountains. Something I don't like in UTAH is it's getting crowded. We used to have a field by my house but the house builders are building houses in the field. In a wide open place they built an Albertsons and Ernst. I think UTAH has changed alot since it was a big desert.

Chelsea Lynne White
Salt Lake County

Age 9; **Birthplace** N/A; **Occupation** N/A; **Religion** N/A; **Race/Ethnicity** N/A

I don't like my neighborhood because there's to many ganges, robber's, bombthreats and murder's. I like my neighborhood because there's nice flowers, nice grass. It's just that it's not peaceful and to much CHILD ABUSE!

I like to visit Mirror Lake. I also like to visit Downtown. I like to visit Mirror Lake because every time I catch a fish.

I hope that in *one year* that there is not as much pollution. I also hope that there won't be many homeless. And that there will be more schools.

"Facing north towards the Ogden welcome sign." Submitted by Robert T. Beckstead, Weber County.

Georgia Moore Loutensack

Salt Lake County

Age 58; **Birthplace** Salt Lake City, S.L. Co; **Occupation** Teacher/Librarian; **Religion** L.D.S.; **Race/Ethnicity** White English/Swedish

Having been born, raised and spent most of my life in Utah, specifically Salt Lake Valley, it has always meant home. I have always had a sense of security here. As a child when my family would return from our annual vacation, I always felt we were "home" as we came around the Point-of-the-Mountain and entered the valley even though we still had miles to go and were almost an hour from our house. Coming from the west I had the same sensation rounding the Oquirrhs and seeing the valley open before us with those beautiful mountains on the far side.

That ring of mountains around the valley have always given me a safe feeling as though nothing could harm me or mine. They were and still are loving arms embracing the valley and everything in it. I once heard a woman from the east say she couldn't stand being so close to the mountains because she was afraid they would fall on her. I was stunned to realize that not everyone loved mountains and there were people who were actually afraid of them.

The mountains have always had special meaning to me. Growing up here in the late 1940's we spent many wonderful hours in the canyons. I remember my father coming home from work and many times saying. "Let's take our dinner up the canyon and eat." This happened so often my mother had a box handy all ready packed with dishes, silverware, a tablecloth, etc. She had another sturdy wooden box that could easily hold the pans containing our dinner. Within five minutes of Dad's arrival home we would all be in the car headed for the canyon. We usually went up Millcreek Canyon which was only minutes away. We never had to have a reservation and I don't ever remember not being able to find a table on which to spread our dinner. Many weekend mornings we would go up the canyon and cook our breakfast. Those meals always tasted better than any around the kitchen table even though the food and the people were the same.

My own children have not had those kinds of experiences because the canyons today have been discovered by a new and larger population. Planning ahead, having to make reservations, etc. takes away the spontaneous fun we knew those many years ago.

The valley and for that matter the entire state has changed. The open space we played in, the snowed packed streets we sledded on, the corner grocery store where everyone called each other by name, the soda fountain in the drug store where they made real "fresh Limeades," the neighborhood movie theater where there was a matinee with our favorite serials every Saturday, that close feeling of community that held us together, all are gone. But the mountains remain.

But even they are not exactly the same, the houses have crept up the side and hide the high-water mark in places, but the peaks are still the same. As I drive east on 4500 South on my way home from work the peaks of Mt. Olympus look just the same as they did when we came home from those long ago vacations. They welcome me home still.

Michael W. Small
Washington County

Age 46; **Birthplace** Chicago, Ill; **Occupation** Wildlife Biologist; **Religion** Protestant/Pres.; **Race/Ethnicity** White

As a 45 year old non-Mormon white male who has lived in Utah, specifically in southern Utah, for the past nine years, I am grateful that I wound up in Utah and think Utah is one of the best places left in this day and age in which to raise a family. I am married, have three children, and family concerns are of prime importance to me.

I never really planned to live in Utah, I had no relatives here, I came to Utah for one reason—my job. I think I have stayed for three reasons; my family is here, I am content, and there have been no outstanding opportunities elsewhere.

Recently I heard pollsters find people in Utah, when asked a question, rarely say they have no opinion. Apparently I have lived in Utah long enough to acquire this characteristic. What follows are my straight forward, and honest, impressions of Utah and its people. Any bluntness should not be mistaken for anything more than an attempt at clarity. I mean no offense to anyone by these observations and hope all those who read this are able to show a great deal of tolerance for either my insight, or lack thereof.

Objectively, Utah is one of only a few states which have such a unique history that they are set apart, with their people, from other states. The people of Utah enshrine their unique history and identify quite closely with it. Tied to their history, the Utah people regard themselves as different and somewhat superior to those of other states. In my experience, only the states and people of Texas and Alaska are similar in this regard. Furthermore, because as an adult I have lived mostly in Texas, Alaska, and Utah, I find that in writing this document in my impressions of Utah and its people, my impressions are comparisons to other states, especially Texas and Alaska.

Obviously, the Mormon Church is a major influence on life styles in Utah. On a personal level, I find that I am somehow able to separate the cultural values from the theological beliefs of the Mormon Church and am usually in agreement with most of the cultural values, such as the emphasis on family values, self-sufficiency, moderation, clean-cut activities, and even emergency preparedness.

I have known some non-Mormons who came to Utah just knowing they wouldn't like it and wouldn't fit in. Sure enough, they didn't. Some people simply do not fit in with the values here. Fortunately for them, Las Vegas is just down the road.

However, from at least one standpoint I do worry that Utah is too lily-white and squeaky clean, with too little diversity. Will my children growing up in southern Utah be too naive and not know how to cope with urban society in most of post-industrial America? Then again, with what I see in the media about big city life in Phoenix, Dallas, L.A., and everywhere else, I find it is comforting to raise my kids in safe, little old St. George.

I believe a great many people from other places will move to Utah in the next couple of decades. Most will move to the small and mid-sized cities and towns, but not to Salt Lake City. Many will actually be fleeing the continued collapse and crime of the big cities. They will come to Utah seeking a quality of life which they have lost. We have friends from Texas, people who have lived all their life in Texas and whose family all lives in Texas, visit us for a few days, and then tell us that Dallas is not the same as when we lived there, that the crime problem is now so bad that we do not know how lucky we are to live in St. George, etc.

We did have one communication problem when we first moved to Utah. As soon as we found a house, my wife and I tried to register to vote. At the place where we went to sign up, an elderly lady election official asked us where we lived. I proudly told her my new address and was dumbfounded when she didn't understand where it was. I repeated it in a louder voice. She still did not comprehend what part of town we lived in. Then she asked, "What ward do you live in?" I had no idea; I couldn't do wards and she couldn't do street addresses. We had to register with a different lady.

Seventy years ago it was illegal to gamble in any state. Now, only Hawaii and Utah have no legal gambling. I also have read that people in Hawaii and Utah have the highest longevity of all states. Coincidence?

I do not drink or smoke and am actually a little uncomfortable around those activities. Living in Utah means I am usually not around people who drink and smoke a great deal, and I like this. In Alaska, the problems caused by alcohol, especially among the Natives but also among others, were absolutely overwhelming. Frequently in downtown Anchorage, one would have to step around unconscious drunks sprawled on sidewalks. At times it was scary and threatening; fully 50% of the drivers on weekend nights had been drinking to the point of impairment. I was a captain on the local volunteer fire department in Alaska and we had a lot of fire calls. I think the cause of every fire I went to in the first year or two was attributed to either drinking, smoking, arson, or a combination of these factors.

Drinking alcohol, like gambling, is a funny thing: among those who drink, some can handle it, and some cannot. This is true of people in any state; it is just that in Utah, problem drinkers are usually more out of sight. I understand Utah actually has about the same percentage of heavy drinkers as do other states, what it lacks are the moderate drinkers. Then again, Utah also has a fairly high percentage of people who abuse illegal and prescription drugs. I believe the lack of moderate drinkers may be related to the drug problem in a round about way.

Utah is perceived as having the most restrictive and confusing drinking laws in the nation and that the Mormon Church gets a bad rap for the drinking laws in this state. But I can remember living in Oklahoma—prior to 1959—when the entire state was officially dry, and also going to college in Lubbock, Texas, where the liquor laws were by precinct, and one had to drive out of town to even buy a beer. I will never understand why the Baptist Church in Texas and Oklahoma, which had strong influence in those two states' legislatures, was able to escape similar condemnation.

Hunting in Utah is interesting to analyze, as well. I moved to southern Utah from Alaska and I was surprised how focused upon trophy hunting many in Utah seemed to be. In Alaska, people hunt for meat; trophy hunting is something for tourists.

Focusing too much upon trophy hunting may destroy the future of hunting, I believe. Utah hunters, in their quest for trophy animals, presently seemed poised to demand permit only type hunts and even closures to hunting in some areas. I think this will result in more trophy animals, but also in a significant decline in public support for hunting.

To illustrate, Utah's neighbor to the south, Arizona, has utilized a different strategy for managing hunting. For years, every big game hunt in Arizona has had only a limited number of permits and drawing a permit to hunt in Arizona can be very difficult. Arizona has conservatively regulated the number of hunters and this has now resulted in most all of their hunting areas having healthy populations and trophy size big game animals. In my view, biologically their program has worked very well, but politi-

cal support for hunting in Arizona has declined significantly. When hunters do not get drawn for hunting permits, their guns stay in the closet and gather dust. The hunters lose interest.

In Utah, all the people live in the modern world; some especially like to hunt and hunting is an important part of their life. In remote parts of Alaska it can be different; for those who live very close to the land, like some Eskimos, hunting is not an integral part of their lives, it is their life.

Hunting is an activity which traditionally is passed down from one generation to the next, and current hunters usually first went hunting with their fathers. Until recent, and unfortunate, political and bureaucratic involvement, in Utah the deer hunt in particular was a family affair and even a school holiday. Everyone was assured of being able to get a license and permit and could go to their favorite area year after year. Admittedly, there were too many hunters, few bucks and even fewer big bucks, the ratio of bucks to does was poor, etc., but everyone who wanted to could go hunting every year. Hunting licenses were sold by private vendors and the opening of the general deer hunt was a big day for many local businesses, especially in small towns. All this has served to create strong popular support for hunting in Utah, at least up to now.

Related to the hunting is the observation that in Utah people perceive snowmobiles, the three and four wheeled off-road vehicles, and boats as being for fun and recreation. In Alaska, they were more often thought of as work vehicles.

With the notable exception of Utah farms, Utah is a very clean-cut place. Perception is important. Most people keep their cars clean. Appearance of houses from the street are important. Some people may not have any furniture in the rooms, and have all their credit cards maxed out, but their "curb appeal" is preserved. While not unique to Utah, it is characteristic of it. When one drives from St. George to Texas, one notices as soon as the state line into Arizona is crossed, the houses are not quite as well kept up, generally speaking. Curb appeal continues to go down across the Navajo Reservation and thru New Mexico, but then a funny thing happens, as soon as one crosses into Texas, it is immediately apparent that curb appeal, maybe it is pride, is back. And in Texas, even the farm implements are parked in neat rows.

One thing that I think is unfortunate about Utah is that people are sometimes judged by their name. Perhaps it comes from the Mormon emphasis upon genealogy. Individuals are known and judged, not as individuals, but by their family relationships. Sometimes how they are viewed is more determined by to whom they are related rather than by their actions and deeds. Maybe I am fortunate I have no family here by which to be judged.

Most Utah people generally seem to be very patriotic, as well. This is surprising to me given the historic persecution and the more recent atomic testing experiences. I am not sure that I am as forgiving and tolerant.

One problem with excessive tolerance (for which I have no tolerance) is that people are allowed to be weird. Utah has more than its share of strange groups, cults, and individuals. Just today, a man was arrested in Utah for threatening President Clinton, and it seems too often when these things happen, there is a Utah connection. Incidentally, the vast majority of Utahns are boringly normal and breathe a loud sigh of relief whenever a strange group or cult has a shoot-out with the "feds" and the cult is from Idaho or Texas.

Finally, when it comes to violent crime. I think I have noticed an interesting thing. Murderers in Utah seem to like to use bombs. Why this would be, I am not sure, but bombs are somewhat of a non-confrontational tool. In contrast, I think violence in Texas or Alaska typically is more straight-forward and in your face. In Texas and Alaska, if someone wants to kill you, they will likely use a knife or a gun. But in both Texas and Alaska, independ-ence is prized and confrontation is more acceptable. While in Utah, conformance is more important: direct confrontation is rare, perhaps this carries over even into crime.

It might be wise for me to quit at this point with my impressions of Utah and its people. Please remember when I started this piece I stated that I meant no harm. I want to especially stress this point to any readers who might be mad bombers or from other states. Thank you.

George Emert
Cache County

Age 57; **Birthplace** Sevier Co., TN; **Occupation** Biochemist; **Religion** Methodist; **Race/Ethnicity** Caucasian

What will Utah be like 20, 50 or 100 years from now? No one can say with certainty. But if the past is prologue, future generations of Utahns will continue to enjoy a quality of life that is the envy of the rest of the nation.

In recent years the world has come to realize what we in Utah have long known: This is a uniquely blessed state which is thriving rather than shrinking from dizzying change. The plaudits come so fast they barely make news anymore: Utah in 1995 was named America's "most livable" state; Utah's economy ranks in the top two or three in the U.S.; more new jobs are created here than almost anywhere else.

Our citizens as a whole are remarkably healthy, with rates of crippling disease far below national norms. Typical males in Cache Valley, home to USU, live 14 years longer than average American males; females live 12 years longer than their counterparts.

None of this results from happenstance. It is a natural outgrowth of traits crucial to successful societies. Utahns have a remarkable work ethic that is a magnet for businesses seeking to relocate. And Utahns are quick to share their good fortune with others. This sense of community sets our state apart from many areas where the prevalent attitude is every man for himself. Utah also prospers because of a deeply rooted commitment to education. Largely because of Utah's uniquely large families, our state's public spending per pupil ranks near the lowest in the nation. But that has not stopped dedicated teachers and families from producing students whose academic achievements routinely rank higher than most of their peers across the nation.

While many state systems of higher education face dire financial straits because of shrinking enrollments, Utah's system has grown like topsy in recent years—and will continue to do so into the foreseeable future. Utah's nine public colleges and universities had about 56,000 students in 1984. A decade later that figure had ballooned to 83,000, and in the year 2000 it is projected to hit 105,000.

Pressed by a myriad of other needs, Utah almost certainly cannot build enough traditional facilities to accommodate such growth. Instead our schools must aggressively adopt and enhance the most promising of the new communication technologies, and create a learning environment that balances the traditional with the innovative. As we do so, we will continue to show the world that, in education as well as in numerous other ways, Utah is still the right place.

Norma W. Matheson
Salt Lake County

Age 66; **Birthplace** SLC, UT; **Occupation** Community activist; **Religion** LDS; **Race/Ethnicity** Polish/English

It means living near family and friends—people I love and respect. There is a stability to Utah life that is unique.

It means having neighbors who care about each other and the neighborhood. There is a genuine effort to keep it friendly, attractive and safe.

It means being part of greater community that has a sense of responsibility to each other. I suspect that Utah has more volunteer activity going on than almost anywhere in the world.

It means being surrounded by the most spectacular scenery where-ever you are in the state. Whenever I leave Utah, one of the things I missed the most is the mountains with that wonderful western-blue sky overhead.

It means having the opportunity to enjoy a multitude of cultural events. The commitment to the arts in Utah is remarkable.

It means worrying about the next hundred years and beyond. The scenery is threatened by people and pollution. The family and community ties we value are being strained as social problems escalate. If anything is going to affect these issues, it will be how the total community responds. I hope the future generations perform as well as their forbearers.

EPILOGUE

Faces of Utah: A Portrait introduced you to the people of Utah. Through their essays, you explored their feelings, values, attitudes, becoming acquainted with the actual texture of their lives. These portraits provide us a glimpse of Utahns, fixed in time and place.

The essays sensitize most readers, and developed in them a personal attachment to many of the writers, making them desire more information. For that reason we decided to print the demographic material collected on the form for each essay. It will become a valuable source of information for future researchers.

At the top of each official essay form, a uniform block was printed as seen below. You will notice the request for voluntary basic information from the individual writing the essay: name, location, gender, birth date, birthplace, occupation, religion, ethnicity, and schools attended. We discovered during research on the Ithaca project that, from a human interest point of view, knowing the name, age, and occupation of the writer made what was said more interesting. To historians, sociologists, and other future researchers the information supplied will be invaluable. Historians may wonder why some questions were asked and others were neglected and may question the impor-

tance of those we did ask. Brevity was of primary importance. It was imperative to leave most of the form blank for the written essay.

The collection is still too new to have yielded to analysis, but some data have been collected. We can supply answers to questions of who responded, which sections of the state are represented, and what they wrote about their state.

The first week in January it appeared that about half of the citizens of Utah were critical of their state, with 50% of the essays containing a negative tone. However, the second week the tide turned, with the collective voice predominately positive. By the end of the month, positive essays out-numbered negative by the thousands. At this tabulation point, three percent are written in a negative voice, and ninety-six percent are positive. Our readers determined less than one percent of a 100,000 essayist wrote neutrally about their state.

Tabulations indicate that people of all ages participated—the oldest Utahn was 101, and the youngest was less than one year, aided by her mother in her production of a drawing contribution. The age group most represented to date was the 11- to 14-year-old group, followed

FACES OF UTAH: A CENTENNIAL PORTRAIT
"What Living in Utah Means to Me"
Thank you for helping to create a Utah social history document which researchers expect to use for 100 years.
Submission implies that you are willing to have your writing and any attached art quoted and available for public use.

Name_____Address_____
      Last   First   Middle
City_____County_____State_____ZIP_____

This voluntary information is helpful for future research.
Gender_____Birth date_____Birthplace_____
Occupation_____Religion_____
Race/Ethnicity_____Schools Attended_____

by school children 5 to 10 years old. The adult group least likely to write were the 20-something group, with adults 35 to 55 the most likely to participate. However, we must be cautious while drawing conclusions about this information, because the age tabulations may change when the entire collection is read.

Despite the fact each essay recounted a unique experience, there are remarkable linquistic and thematic similarities in the collection as a whole. The themes mentioned most often were chosen for chapter segments: roots and heritage, memories, religion, environmental concerns and love of the four seasons, of people and families, and of values identified as both personal and collective. Utahns mentioned the environment more often than any topic, and had a special attachment to the beauty of the physical surroundings. Many mentioned their special mountain or canyon, which they viewed as a sanctuary or heavenly gift. In each geographic area the mountain (or mountain range), streams, canyons and colors changed, in accordance with the essayist's locality. Lastly, concern was expressed about the state's ability and willingness to keep our vistas free of pollution and undamaged by the increasing numbers of people visiting and moving to the state.

A distant second, but common, theme was heritage/roots and religion. The role of religion in the lives of Utahn's looms large and is intertwined with personal and family heritage. Religious heritage is seen as a source of pride for many, a source of strength for others, and as a source of Utah's communal value system. While most viewed the religious pioneer heritage of Utah as an asset, some wrote that it was oppressive and that it precipitated discrimination. Still others not of the dominant faith felt the strong presence of The Church of Jesus Christ of Latter-day Saints was responsible for a strengthening of their own religious beliefs. But, positive or not, the religious influence was felt.

New arrivals viewed the state through somewhat less emotional eyes. Although many commented on the friendly people and the warmth of their welcome to the state, their ties were more tenuous. Some newcomers liked Utah for the variety of the seasons, the strength of its people, and their feelings of relative security. These people have stayed and adopted the state as their own. Others are less receptive to the social, religious, or physical climate and in some cases are in a hurry to leave.

Themes are present in the collection that were not chosen for this centennial portrait but appear to a lesser degree in individual essays. These include personal physical safety, the number and variety of our national parks, the opportunities present in Utah, the quality of life, the availability of various sports and activities, the educational benefits, and Utah's political climate. Safety is mentioned by young and old, and everyone in between. Most Utahns claim with the same voice "We don't have a gang problem, at least not like California or New York." In the words of Mary LaVerda Saderup: "I feel safer in Utah than states like New York, California and others." Robert Christensen of Lehi said simply "you can sleep in your back yard; without fear." But there are identifiable areas in the state where children like Lindsay Carol Griffith express their concern for "some bad things like ganges and robbers."

National Parks, quality of life, and sports activities are also frequent topics. Utahns write with pride and enjoyment of the National Parks in Utah. Berneice Nash Neeley, Salt Lake City, said "… Then of course there are the National Parks and Monuments. I wish we could go more often and I wish I could go to all of them. I think Utah is unique in having more National Parks than any other state in the Union!"

While the quality of life here is heralded in many cases the state is given credit for regulations and conditions dependent upon the federal government: "freedom," clean drinking water, and the pure food and drug act ("no bacteria in the food to kill you"). Angie Carnell and a number of others credit the state of Utah with insuring "freedom in speech" and other personal liberties guaranteed by the Bill of Rights.

Finally, Utahns are active energetic people who enjoy spectator sports, individual sporting activies, group and team sports, and a variety of recreational activities. Every team in Utah is praised as being "number one," and our enjoyment doesn't stop with local teams: professional in-state and national teams are followed by hosts of fans. On a personal-involvement level, water skiing, four-wheeling, cycling, hiking, skiing, and swimming are all enjoyed and recognized as being connected to the environment and Utah's four seasons.

The pleasures of the collection are many. One of them is that the essays will be read and understood in many ways, speaking to us on different levels. It is certain that the call for essays allowed the participants to preserve something of their individual lives for the future. They sensed this, and many openly acknowledge it. This collection of essays is truly a gift of Utahns to all of us.

APPENDIX
Schools Participating in "Faces of Utah: A Portrait"

School	District
HIGH SCHOOLS	
Alta High School	Jordan
American Fork High School	Alpine
Bountiful High School	Davis
Box Elder High School	Box Elder
Brighton High School	Jordan
Carbon High School	Carbon
Cedar City High School	Iron
Cedar Ridge High School	Sevier
Clearfield High School	Davis
Cyprus High School	Granite
Davis High School	Davis
Delta High School	Millard
Dixie High School	Washington
East Carbon High School	Carbon
Emery High School	Emery
Fremont High School	Weber
Granite High School	Granite
Grantsville High School	Tooele
Highland High School	Salt Lake
Hillcrest High School	Jordan
Hunter High School	Granite
Jordan High School	Jordan
Juab High School	Juab
Kearns High School	Granite
Layton High School	Davis
Lehi High School	Alpine
Manti High School	South Sanpete
Millard High School	Millard

School	District
Mountain Crest High School	Cache
Mountain Valley High School	San Juan
Mountain View High School	Alpine
Northridge High School	Davis
Ogden High School	Ogden
Olympus High School	Granite
Orem High School	Alpine
Parowan High School	Iron
Pine View High School	Washington
Richfield High School	Sevier
San Juan High School	San Juan
Skyline High School	Granite
Skyview High School	Cache
Snow Canyon High School	Washington
South Sevier High School	Sevier
Spanish Fork High School	Nebo
Springville High School	Nebo
Tintic High School	Tintic
Tooele High School	Tooele
Uintah High School	Uintah
Valley High School	Kane
Viewmont High School	Davis
Wayne High School	Wayne
West Jordan High School	Jordan
Woods Cross High School	Davis
JUNIOR HIGH SCHOOLS AND MIDDLE SCHOOLS	
Albion Middle School	Jordan
Bear River Middle School	Granite

School	District	School	District
T.H. Bell Junior High School	Granite	Helen M. Knight Intermediate	Grand
Bennion Junior High School	Granite	Layton Junior High School	Davis
Bonneville Junior High School	Granite	Lehi Junior High School	Alpine
Bountiful Junior High School	Davis	Midvale Middle School	Jordan
Brockbank Junior High School	Granite	Millcreek Junior High School	Davis
Butler Middle School	Jordan	Mont Harmon Junior High School	Carbon
Cedar City Middle School	Iron	Morgan Middle School	Morgan
Centerville Junior High School	Davis	Mound Fort Middle School	Ogden
Central Davis Junior High School	Davis	Mount Logan Middle School	Cache
Churchill Junior High School	Granite	Mueller Park Junior High School	Davis
Crescent View Middle School	Jordan	North Cache Middle School	Cache
Delta Middle School	Millard	North Layton Junior High School	Davis
Dixie Middle School	Washington	North Sanpete Middle School	North Sanpete
Eastmont Middle School	Jordan	North Sevier Middle School	Sevier
Eisenhower Junior High School	Granite	Northwest Middle School	Salt Lake
Elk Ridge Middle School	Jordan	Olympus Junior High School	Granite
Ephraim Middle School	South Sanpete	Oquirrh Hills Middle School	Jordan
Fairfield Junior High School	Davis	Orem Junior High School	Alpine
Farmington Junior High School	Davis	Payson Junior High School	Nebo
Fillmore Middle School	Millard	Pleasant Grove Junior High School	Alpine
Glendale Middle School	Salt Lake	Redrock Intermediate School	Iron
Grand County Middle School	Grand	Riverview Junior High School	Murray
Granite Park Junior High School	Granite	Rocky Mt. Junior High School	Weber
Helper Junior High School	Carbon	Roosevelt Middle School	Duchesne
Highland Middle School	Ogden	Roy Junior High School	Weber
Hillside Middle School	Salt Lake	San Rafael Junior High School	Emery
Hunter Junior High School	Granite	Sand Ridge Junior High School	Weber
Indian Hills Middle School	Jordan	Snow Canyon Middle School	Washington
Jefferson Junior High School	Granite	South Jordan Middle School	Jordan
Joel P. Jensen Middle School	Jordan	South Sevier Middle School	Sevier
Juab Middle School	Juab	South Davis Junior High School	Davis
Kanab Middle School	Kane	South Ogden Junior High School	Weber
Kaysville Junior High School	Davis	Spanish Fork Intermediate	Nebo
Kearns Junior High School	Granite	Spring Creek Middle School	Cache

School	District	School	District
Springville Junior High School	Nebo	Beehive Elementary School	Granite
Sunset Junior High School	Davis	Belknap Elementary School	Beaver
Tooele Junior High School	Tooele	Bella Vista Elementary School	Jordan
Treasure Mountain Middle School	Park City	Bell View Elementary School	Jordan
Union Middle School	Jordan	Bennion Elementary School	Granite
Valley Junior High School	Granite	Blanding Elementary School	San Juan
Vernal Middle School	Uintah	Bluff Elementary School	San Juan
Wahlquist Junior High School	Weber	Bonneville Elementary School	Salt Lake
Wasatch Junior High School	Granite	Bonneville Elementary School	Ogden
Wayne Middle School	Wayne	Boulton Elementary School	Davis
West Jordan Middle School	Jordan	Bountiful Elementary School	Davis
West Lake Junior High School	Granite	Edith Bowen Elementary School	Logan
Westridge Middle School	Carbon	Brookside Elementary School	Nebo
		Brookwood Elementary School	Jordan

ELEMENTARY SCHOOLS

School	District	School	District
Academy Park Elementary School	Granite	Bryce Valley Elementary School	Garfield
Adelaide Elementary School	Davis	Bunderson Elementary School	Box Elder
Adams Elementary School	Davis	H.C. Burton Elementary School	Davis
Adams Elementary School	Logan	Butler Elementary School	Jordan
Alpine Elementary School	Alpine	Canyon Rim Elementary School	Granite
Alta View Elementary School	Jordan	Canyon View Elementary School	Jordan
Altamont Elementary School	Duchesne	Castle Heights Elementary School	Carbon
Altara Elementary School	Jordan	Castle Dale Elementary School	Emery
Antelope Elementary School	Davis	Cedar North Elementary School	Iron
Arcadia Elementary School	Granite	Centerville Elementary School	Davis
Art City Elementary School	Nebo	Central Elementary School	Box Elder
Ashley Elementary School	Uintah	Central Elementary School	Wasatch
Ashman Elementary School	Sevier	Central Elementary School	Uintah
Aspen Elementary School	Alpine	H. Guy Child Elementary School	Weber
Thomas W. Bacchus Elementary School	Granite	Clearfield Elementary School	Davis
Barnett Elementary School	Nebo	Cleveland Elementary School	Emery
Barratt Elementary School	Alpine	Clinton Elementary School	Davis
Bates Elementary School	Weber	Columbia Elementary School	Jordan
Beacon Heights Elementary School	Salt Lake	Columbia Elementary School	Davis
		Corinne Elementary School	Box Elder

School	District	School	District
Cook Elementary School	Davis	Ensign Elementary School	Salt Lake
Copper Hills Elementary School	Granite	Ephraim Elementary School	South Sanpete
Copper View Elementary School	Jordan	Escalante Valley Elementary School	Iron
Cottonwood Heights Elementary School	Jordan	Fairview Elementary School	North Sanpete
Cottonwood Elementary School	Granite	Farmington Elementary School	Davis
Creekview Elementary School	Carbon	Philo T. Farnsworth Elementary School	Granite
Crestview Elementary School	Granite	Farr West Elementary School	Weber
Crescent Elementary School	Jordan	Fox Hills Elementary School	Granite
Davis Elementary School	Uintah	Ferron Elementary School	Emery
Dee Elementary School	Ogden	Fiddler's Canyon Elementary School	Iron
Delta North Elementary School	Millard	Fillmore Elementary School	Millard
Delta South Elementary School	Millard	Foothill Elementary School	Box Elder
Dilworth Elementary School	Salt Lake	Forbes Elementary School	Alpine
Discovery Elementary School	Box Elder	Franklin Elementary School	Salt Lake
Discovery Elementary School	Uintah	Fremont Elementary School	Davis
Dixie Downs Elementary School	Washington	John C. Fremont Elementary School	Granite
Doxey Elementary School	Davis	Robert Frost Elementary School	Granite
Draper Elementary School	Jordan	Garland Elementary School	Box Elder
Howard R. Driggs Elementary School	Granite	Geneva Elementary School	Alpine
East Midvale Elementary School	Jordan	Goshen Elementary School	Nebo
East Elementary School	Duchesne	David Gourley Elementary School	Granite
East Elementary School	Iron	Gramercy Elementary School	Ogden
East Elementary School	Tooele	Grandview Elementary School	Ogden
East Elementary School	Washington	Granger Elementary School	Granite
East Layton Elementary School	Davis	Grant Elementary School	Murray
East Midvale Elementary School	Jordan	Grantsville Elementary School	Tooele
East Sandy Elementary School	Jordan	Green Acres Elementary School	Weber
Eastwood Elementary School	Granite	Greenville Elementary School	Tooele
Edgemont Elementary School	Provo	Greenwood Elementary School	Alpine
Edgemont Elementary School	Jordan	Grovecrest Elementary School	Alpine
Libbie Edward Elementary School	Granite	Hanksville Elementary School	Wayne
Ellis Elementary School	Logan	Harris Elementary School	Tooele
Emerson Elementary School	Salt Lake	Hawthorne Elementary School	Salt Lake
Enoch Elementary School	Iron	Harris Elementary School	Tooele

School	District	School	District
Highland Elementary School	Alpine	Lincoln Elementary School	Ogden
Highland Park Elementary School	Salt Lake	Lincoln Elementary School	Salt Lake
Hillcrest Elementary School	Alpine	Loa Elementary School	Wayne
Hillcrest Elementary School	Logan	Lomond View Elementary School	Weber
Hillcrest Elementary School	Ogden	Lone Peak Elementary School	Jordan
Hill Field Elementary School	Davis	Longview Elementary School	Murray
Hillsdale Elementary School	Granite	Lowell Elementary School	Salt Lake
Hillside Elementary School	Granite	Lynn Elementary School	Ogden
Holbrook Elementary School	Davis	Maeser Elementary School	Uintah
Holladay Elementary School	Granite	Majestic Elementary School	Jordan
Holt Elementary School	Davis	Horace Mann Elementary School	Ogden
Honeyville Elementary School	Box Elder	Sally Mauro Elementary School	Carbon
Hooper Elementary School	Weber	Manila Elementary School	Alpine
Horizon Elementary School	Murray	Manila Elementary School	Daggett
Hunter Elementary School	Granite	Manti Elementary School	Nebo
Huntington Elementary School	Emery	Mapleton Elementary School	Nebo
Hurricane Elementary School	Washington	Marlon Hills Elementary School	Weber
Indian Hills Elementary School	Salt Lake	McKinley Elementary School	Box Elder
Jackling Elementary School	Granite	McMillan Elementary School	Murray
Jackson Elementary School	Salt Lake	Meadowbrook Elementary School	Davis
Jeremy Ranch Elementary School	Park City	Meadowlark Elementary School	Salt Lake
Jordan Ridge Elementary School	Jordan	Midland Elementary School	Weber
Kanesville Elementary School	Weber	Midvale Elementary School	Jordan
Kaysville Elementary School	Davis	Midvalley Elementary School	Jordan
Knowlton Elementary School	Davis	Mill Creek Elementary School	Granite
LaPoint Elementary School	Uintah	Millville Elementary School	Cache
Lakeview Elementary School	Weber	Mona Elementary School	Juab
Lake View Elementary School	Box Elder	Monroe Elementary School	Granite
Larsen Elementary School	Nebo	Monroe Elementary School	Sevier
Layton Elementary School	Davis	Monte Vista Elementary School	Davis
Liberty Elementary School	Murray	Monticello Elementary School	San Juan
Lincoln Elementary School	Cache	James E. Moss Elementary School	Granite
Lincoln Elementary School	Davis	Morgan Elementary School	Morgan
Lincoln Elementary School	Granite	Morgan Elementary School	Davis

School	District	School	District
Morningside Elementary School	Granite	Peterson Elementary School	Carbon
Mount Pleasant Elementary School	North Sanpete	Phelps Elementary School	Washington
Mountain View Elementary School	Box Elder	Pioneer Elementary School	Granite
Monroe Elementary School	Salt Lake	Plain City Elementary School	Weber
Mountain View Elementary School	Ogden	Pleasant Green Elementary School	Granite
Mountain Shadows Elementary School	Jordan	Plymouth Elementary School	Granite
Municipal Elementary School	Weber	Providence Elementary School	Cache
Naples Elementary School	Uintah	Quail Hollow Elementary School	Jordan
Nephi Elementary School	Juab	Reading Elementary School	Davis
Newman Elementary School	Salt Lake	Red Rock Elementary School	Grand
Nibley Park Elementary School	Salt Lake	Redwood Elementary School	Granite
North Summit Elementary School	North Summit	Rees Elementary School	Nebo
Northlake Elementary School	Tooele	Ridgecrest Elementary School	Jordan
North Ogden Elementary School	Weber	River Heights Elementary School	Cache
North Park Elementary School	Box Elder	Riverdale Elementary School	Weber
Northridge Elementary School	Alpine	Riverside Elementary School	Jordan
Oak Hills Elementary School	Davis	Riverside Elementary School	Logan
Oakridge Elementary School	Granite	Riverton Elementary School	Jordan
Oakwood Elementary School	Granite	Rolling Meadows Elementary School	Granite
Oquirrh Elementary School	Jordan	Roosevelt Elementary School	Granite
Orchard Elementary School	Alpine	Roosevelt Elementary School	Weber
Orchard Elementary School	Davis	Rosamond Elementary School	Jordan
Douglas T. Orchard Elementary School	Granite	Rose Park Elementary School	Salt Lake
Orem Elementary School	Alpine	Rosecrest Elementary School	Granite
Pahvant Elementary School	Sevier	Rosslyn Heights Elementary School	Salt Lake
Panorama Elementary School	Washington	Roy Elementary School	Weber
Park Lane Elementary School	Jordan	Sage Creek Elementary School	Nebo
Park Elementary School	Nebo	Salem Elementary School	Nebo
Parkside Elementary School	Murray	Salina Elementary School	Sevier
Parkview Elementary School	Nebo	Carl Sandburg Elementary School	Granite
Parowan Elementary School	Iron	Santa Clara Elementary School	Washington
William Penn Elementary School	Granite	Sego Lily Elementary School	Alpine
Perry Elementary School	Box Elder	Sharon Elementary School	Alpine
Peruvian Park Elementary School	Jordan	Shelley Elementary School	Alpine

School	District	School	District
Silver Hills Elementary School	Granite	Valley View Elementary School	Davis
Calvin S. Smith Elementary School	Granite	Valley View Elementary School	Weber
Thomas O. Smith Elementary School	Ogden	Vernon Elementary School	Tooele
Snowville Elementary School	Box Elder	Viewmont Elementary School	Murray
South Clearfield Elementary School	Davis	Wasatch Elementary School	Davis
South Jordan Elementary School	Jordan	Wasatch Elementary School	Ogden
South Summit Elementary School	South Summit	Wasatch Elementary School	Provo
South Weber Elementary School	Davis	Washington Elementary School	Davis
Southland Elementary School	Jordan	Washington Elementary School	Washington
Spring City Elementary School	North Sanpete	Washington Elementary School	Salt Lake
Sprucewood Elementary School	Jordan	Washington Terrace Elementary School	Weber
Stansbury Elementary School	Granite	Webster Elementary School	Granite
Stansbury Elementary School	Tooele	Wellington Elementary School	Carbon
Stansbury Park Elementary School	Tooele	West Elementary School	Tooele
J.P. Stewart Elementary School	Davis	Westbrook Elementary School	Granite
Sunrise Elementary School	Jordan	Westland Elementary School	Jordan
Sunset Elementary School	Davis	Westside Elementary School	Nebo
Sunset Elementary School	Washington	West Bountiful Elementary School	Davis
Syracuse Elementary School	Davis	West Clinton Elementary School	Davis
J.A. Taylor Elementary School	Davis	West Kearns Elementary School	Granite
Taylor Elementary School	Nebo	West Jordan Elementary School	Jordan
Taylorsville Elementary School	Granite	West Point Elementary School	Davis
Terra Linda Elementary School	Jordan	Westmore Elementary School	Alpine
W. Russell Todd Elementary School	Uintah	Westvale Elementary School	Jordan
Tolman Elementary School	Davis	Whitesides Elementary School	Davis
Harry S. Truman Elementary School	Granite	Whittler Elementary School	Salt Lake
Twin Peaks Elementary School	Granite	Willow Canyon Elementary School	Jordan
Uintah Elementary School	Salt Lake	Wilson Elementary School	Logan
Upland Terrace Elementary School	Granite	Wilson Elementary School	Nebo
Vae View Elementary School	Davis	Windsor Elementary School	Alpine
Valley Elementary School	Kane	Woodruff Elementary School	Logan
Valley Elementary School	Weber	Woodscross Elementary School	Davis
Valley Crest Elementary School	Granite		
Valley View Elementary School	Alpine		